Human Resource Development
in Twentieth-Century Japan

JAPAN LIBRARY

Human Resource Development in Twentieth-Century Japan

Inoki Takenori

Translated by
Tony Gonzalez

Japan Publishing Industry Foundation for Culture

Translation Note

Hepburn system of Romanization is used for Japanese terms, including the name of persons and places. Except in familiar place names, long vowels are indicated by macrons. The local custom of placing the family name first has been followed for the names of Japanese persons.

Human Resource Development in Twentieth-Century Japan
Inoki Takenori. Translated by Tony Gonzalez.

Published by
Japan Publishing Industry Foundation for Culture (JPIC)
3-12-3 Kanda-Jinbocho, Chiyoda-ku, Tokyo 101-0051, Japan

First edition: March 2017

This book is a complete translation of *Zōho gakkō to kōjō: Nijū-seiki nihon no jinteki shigen* (Chikumashobo Ltd., 2016), which is a retitled and revised edition of a book first published in 1996 under the title *Gakkō to kōjō: Nihon no jinteki shigen*, volume seven of the series, *Nijū-seiki no nihon* published by Yomiuri Shimbun.

English publishing rights arranged with Chikumashobo Ltd.

Jacket and cover design: Lapisworks

As this book is published primarily to be donated to overseas universities, research institutions, public libraries and other organizations, commercial publication rights are available. For all enquiries regarding those rights, please contact the publisher of the English edition at the following address: japanlibrary@jpic.or.jp.

Printed in Japan
ISBN 978-4-916055-78-1
http://www.jpic.or.jp/japanlibrary/

CONTENTS

FOREWORD TO THE ENGLISH EDITION

This book was originally published in 1996, as one volume in the Yomiuri Shimbun newspaper's *Nijū-seiki no nihon* (Japan in the Twentieth Century), a series of which I was on the editorial committee. My goal in writing this book was to provide a broadly historical depiction of how human resources development and selection took shape in post-Meiji Japan, not only through schooling, but also within companies, government, and the military. That edition was titled *Gakkō to kōjō: Nihon no jinteki shigen* (Human Resource Development in Japan). I was fortunate enough for this book to have been selected as a textbook or supplementary reading for labor economics at several Japanese universities, providing a certain reader base.

In June 2016, through Chikumashobo I released a revised edition that incorporated results from my research conducted over the two decades since the book's initial release, and this is a translation of that revision. I am overjoyed to have had this book selected for inclusion as part of the Japan Library series of works translated with the support of the Japanese Prime Minister's office.

It is no simple task to describe a country's social institutions and customs in another language to persons in other countries. The words and concepts of a given country or society are formed over the course of its history, complete with its own sense of universality and uniqueness, making perfect correspondence with another language difficult. Such a translation is all the more arduous for a text not originally written with a foreign readership in mind, no matter the skill of the translator. I thus express my sincerest thanks to Tony Gonzalez for his hard work at overcoming such difficulties, and similarly to Tamura Taichi of Ryutsu Keizai University for his proofing of the translation with a specialist's eye.

It is my sincerest wish that this English edition will help to deepen understanding of Japanese society among an English readership.

Inoki Takenori
January 2017

INTRODUCTION

Key issues

I wrote this book with several questions in mind. How are workers selected and trained in Japan? What principles of selection and training did Japan's schools, companies, government, and military utilize through the end of the twentieth century? What elements formed the core of systems for developing human resources as these institutions transitioned from their Edo-period heritage to the technologies and systems of the West?

From an economic perspective, the most straightforward answers to these questions lie in expanded opportunity and increased competition. How one evaluates a system will vary depending on whether the focus is on long-term competitiveness or specific short-term results. Setting such issues aside, however, there is little doubt that careerism is one of the mores characterizing modern democracy in Japan and the West. In industrial society, the home and religious organizations such as churches and temples have ceased to play a role in formal education; people now obtain skills and knowledge through schools and businesses. Careerism is among the principles that dominate these educational spheres, both within and outside of Japan.[1] Even so, careerism in Japan differs somewhat from that of the West on at least two counts, namely, the breadth of opportunity and the harshness of competition. A desire to explore this difference in detail was a primary motivation for writing this book.

I also wished to reexamine a number of theories that have gained wide acceptance despite their shaky foundations. One example is the idea that Japanese companies allocate human resources based on seniority rather than ability. Employees in Japan are supposedly guaranteed promotions as they age, but can organizations and society truly develop and attain stability without fairly evaluating ability?

In the eighteenth century, the Tokugawa shogunate under Yoshimune established the *tashidaka* system, which provided talented low-ranking men with postings and stipends normally reserved for their social superiors. In the samurai class, while status was generally inherited through bloodlines, talented youth were sometimes brought into clans through adoption. Among merchant families too, it was not uncommon for a promising child to be adopted as a means of ensuring continuance of the family business, even when a biological child existed.

---

1. See Takeuchi (2005) for a lucid and broad description of "careerism" (*risshin shusse*).

While Japan's technical contributions are widely recognized, many cases of Japanese innovation remain unknown internationally, simply because they were not presented in the *lingua franca* of international academia. We should pay greater attention to the originality of domestic inventors like Tanaka Hisashige, Toyoda Sakichi, and Shimazu Genzō. While Japanese elementary school students are likely to read about the genius of Edison, they have few opportunities to learn about scientists and technological innovators from their own country. As one example, in the Genroku era (1688–1704), Seki Takakazu invented a method of calculation known as *tenzan*. Some mathematical historians consider Seki's work comparable to the discovery of calculus by Newton and Leibniz.

As a society, we Japanese have an excessive tendency to subscribe to the masochistic belief that our own social systems are illogical, outdated, and hostile to progress. A typical example of this is the assertion that Japan is in all areas "behind" the more "modern" nations of the West. Of course, some Japanese systems and customs have failed to keep up with the times — but many others are highly logical, and born of hard-earned empirical knowledge.

The aim of this book is a better understanding of the systems and customs of modern Japanese human resource development, unrestrained by commonly held beliefs. To that end, I emphasize my theory of expanded opportunities and harsh competition. While my focus is primarily on the educational and industrial spheres, I also touch on the government and military, because military organizations cannot be ignored in any discussion of nationwide human resource allocation.

The labor economics perspective

The academic interest underlying this book is the relation between education and economic growth. This relation is more complex than one might expect, and our understanding of whether it is causal remains insufficient. Affluence stimulates the aggregate demand for education services, and increased spending on education improves the quality of labor, thereby improving productivity and further increasing affluence. Even if we recognize such a bidirectional causal relation, however, questions remain as to which direction exerts the stronger influence, and how the mechanism connecting the two functions in detail. As in any academic discussion, clearly defining concepts and restricting the area of study are of primary concern.

Yet, before doing even that, we must critically assess whether we have correctly identified the problem at hand. It is particularly important to note that the framework for education and economic growth developed by

Simon Kuznets — who made important contributions to our theoretical and empirical understanding of modern economic growth — does not address issues related to human resources. Kuznets states that "All empirical knowledge is thus potentially relevant to economic production."[2] He refers only to empirical knowledge, with no particular emphasis on (formal, school-based) education, and his factor analysis for growth is rooted in the broad concept of "growth in the stock of knowledge."

Kuznets also added that even if school education is to some extent an investment, current national accounts treat it as consumption. Accordingly, the idea that investment-based differences in quality should be considered in measures of labor input is incompatible with the concepts and actuality of national economic calculations — expenditures such as those for education and healthcare are wholly or partially shifted from "consumption" to "capital formation" (investment), so unless capital depreciation amounts are deducted each year, such handling is inconsistent.[3]

"Years of schooling" is a convenient measure of school education, so research related to the impact of human capital formation (investment) on economic growth resulting solely from school education has served to confirm a causal relation between the two. Over time, scholars increasingly recognized the above-mentioned importance of clearly distinguishing and restricting concepts and targets of inquiry. For example, does "education" refer to elementary or more advanced education? Academic or vocational education? In addition to school education, should we also consider on-the-job training?

It is also important to consider the impact of education on the type of labor in question. Does it affect agricultural productivity, or only non-agricultural productivity? Within the manufacturing industry, have we considered the kinds of knowledge necessary for handling specific types of technology (machining, assembly, equipment, etc.)? Are we interested in labor performed by the rank-and-file, or by the leadership and managers, and if the latter, mid- or top-level staff? The list goes on.

So long as these issues are not specifically addressed, it is impossible to make general statements about the authenticity or validity of the problem at hand. Concepts and theories from labor economics are useful in targeting topics for discussion.

---

2. Kuznets (1968, p. 61).
3. Kuznets (1971), chapter 2.

Human resource development is a long-term issue

The topics addressed in this book are deeply connected to human mental and physical well-being. Even if we restrict discussion to physical well-being, there is certainly value in exploring a country's long-term approach to human resource selection and development, and the effects of that country's customs and educational system on the affluence of its population. Reflecting on modern Japan's economic development in light of its history of human resource formation should provide some degree of self-validation and guidance for what to preserve and what to avoid in the future.

This too provided impetus for writing this book. We must not accept narrow perspectives when considering the long-term meaning and effects of education and training. In recent years, I have found myself increasingly concerned with issues such as immediacy and practicality. For this reason as well, I sought self-validation through reflection on twentieth-century Japanese economics and our methods of human resource development.

Japan's "miraculous" period of postwar economic growth was driven by strong private capital investment and robust consumer demand. The positive feedback cycle of investment inducing further investment was not only a result of external demand (exports), but also of bold investment from a domestic private sector equipped with advanced technologies and a highly skilled labor force. This was a period of ever-increasing international acclaim for Japanese production technologies: whereas "Made in Japan" had once implied shoddy workmanship, it now became synonymous with the highest quality.

In actual economies, technological innovation is neither a necessary nor sufficient condition for economic growth. Ultimately, tying new technologies to increases in productivity requires a skilled labor force that has undergone thorough education and training. Japan still has workers with advanced skills acquired in the workplace, and experienced managers and supervisors who customarily foster skill development through fair evaluations of worker competence and effort. However, the arrival of post-industrial society has pushed manufacturing industries to the economic sidelines, weakening long-term perspectives on human resource development through skill improvement.

Indeed, if we focus strictly on employment, manufacturing industry workers now account for only around two-tenths of Japan's overall labor force. From an input–output analysis perspective, however, a surprisingly large number of tertiary industries and job types can only exist given the products of the manufacturing sector, such as high-performance machinery and equipment. Dismissing the manufacturing sector thus ignores the high

The Shizutani School. (Photo: Association for the Preservation of the Shizutani School)

CHAPTER 1

EDUCATION IN THE EDO AND MEIJI PERIODS

Japan has long valued education. Perhaps no other country has gone farther in pursuing and deepening knowledge, attaining skills, and emphasizing the importance of moral and physical education.

The Edo-period Satsuma domain, for example, is known for its credo that "our people are our bulwark." Its core educational principles of "don't lose, don't lie, don't bully" urged clansmen to excel in battle, seek impartiality, and consider others;[1] by restating these concepts using the more modern terms "competition," "fairness," and "welfare," it is evident that they formed a solid foundation for the establishment of an exemplary society. The educational policies of the Satsuma domain emphasized a balance between these three provisions, and in that sense they were quite modern.

When examining systems for human resource development in modern Japan, we must be careful not to view the importance of Meiji-period reforms without recognizing their continuity with practices of the Edo period. The Meiji Reformation did indeed revolutionize Japan's political systems and further its relationships with foreign countries (the United States, Great Britain, and continental Europe in particular), and as a result induced dramatic changes in Japanese culture and society. Nonetheless, while various Japanese customs and practices disappeared during that period, in many ways the changes did not alter the essence of Japanese society. The field of education is no exception: despite some substantive changes, there has been an unfortunate emphasis on superficial modifications.

1. From provincial and private education to "schools"

Systems for selecting and educating clansmen
Let us first briefly review the types of educational institutions that existed in the Edo period.

Japan in this period was a caste society, and clansmen, samurai, and commoners (farmers, artisans, and merchants) were educated separately. Individual domains established schools for the education of clansmen and their

---

1. For example, the Official Guide to the Kagoshima Tourism and Culture Test states that "Shimazu Tadayoshi and Yamada Arinaga were highly dedicated to the education of vassals and their children ... conducting clan education by dividing clansmen by age into *chigo* (six or seven to mid-teens) and *nise* (mid-teens to mid-twenties) and having older students instruct younger ones. Children improved body and mind by engaging in outdoor activities, practicing swordsmanship, studying the Confucian classics, and memorizing poetry. Shimazu and Yamada emphasized discipline and taught youth not to 'lose, lie, or bully,' a spirit of education that was preserved after the Meiji Restoration. In the Satsuma domain, there were very few public schools for commoners." (Kagoshima Chamber of Commerce and Industry, 2005, p. 68).

children. Even today, some high schools still bear the name of the domain school from which they originated, such as Shūyūkan Senior High School in Fukuoka and Denshukan High School in Yanagawa.[2] There were several motivations for establishing domain schools. Most importantly, the formation of the Tokugawa shogunate necessitated systems for educating and selecting students as a means of establishing ruler legitimacy. This view is supported by the fact that most domain schools appeared in the mid-seventeenth century, following the establishment of the shogunate, and disappeared or were refashioned in 1871 after the domains were abolished and government authority was centralized. An estimated 260 domain schools existed throughout Japan at the time of the Meiji Restoration.[3]

The subjects taught at domain schools varied over time, but centered on reading, writing, and Confucian teachings aimed at cultivating character. At the Kōjōkan School in the Yonezawa domain, for example, the core curriculum was the Confucian classics from around age ten, and from ages fifteen to twenty-five added historical studies. Boarding students listened to lectures on classical Chinese history, and occasionally polished their literary skills through poetry critiques.[4]

As Japanese military and diplomatic affairs grew increasingly opaque in the late Edo period, schools began to teach practical subjects better suited to the political situation. Many domain schools introduced into their curricula not only Western subjects such as medicine, astronomy, surveying, and herbalism, but also Western military science and martial drills.[5]

At first, the children of nobility predominated in domain schools, but gradually the children of mid- and lower-ranked clansmen entered as well, and eventually even upper-class commoners came to be admitted in locations like the Kanbe, Shimabara, and Ashimori domains.[6] These trends accelerated toward the end of the Tokugawa shogunate, due to the need for domains to raise militias. Ages of admission changed too; while at first boys started their education following their coming of age at around fifteen, by the end of the Edo period they were entering school between the ages of seven

---

2. In many cases it is difficult to determine the lineage of domain schools, because some were closed while others were reestablished but inherited no more than a name from their predecessor. However, many schools that survived the Meiji Restoration likely did so as elementary schools and (old system) junior high schools.

3. Umihara (1996).

4. Yamagata Prefectural Museum (1998).

5. The list of school subjects by Kasai (1960, p. 246) provides a quantitative description of annual changes in educational content. Ishikawa (1972, p. 115) presents the same table. Of particular note is the fact that all schools established since the first year of the Meiji period included Western studies as a topic of study.

and nine (formal education at the time was, of course, limited to males).

Thus, over the two-century history of the domain schools we see a change from exclusivity in preference of the elite to increased inclusion. The educational emphasis also shifted from Confucian studies to Western and practical studies. What remained unchanged, however, was that the educational circumstances of boys and girls were quite distinct.

The *terakoya*

A form of private elementary school called the terakoya played an important role in educating commoners and increasing literacy and transmitting knowledge among townsfolk. The origins of these schools extend much farther into the past than those of domain schools. New terakoya continued to be created even after a public school system was established in the Meiji period, and others established in the Edo period continued to operate in some parts of Japan, an indication of their roots in popular demand for educational institutions teaching practical skills.[7]

Education at terakoya focused on the "three Rs" of reading, writing, and arithmetic (in the form of abacus usage), and this clearly played a central role in the spread of science and industry. Public education not only improves logical processing ability and makes communication easier, but also shapes thought patterns and emotions. In most cases, people can't think creatively or make good decisions in atypical situations unless they've mastered certain conventions. Creative ideas and discoveries do not arise from a blank slate, but rather presume a certain level of common knowledge — namely, the "three Rs."

As the scale of society increases, it becomes impossible to transmit government orders and announcements by word of mouth; writing must be employed, in the form of documents or public notices. Edo-period townsfolk required not only practical knowledge for their daily lives, but also computational and predictive abilities, which greatly influenced the success of their businesses. Farmers, too, depended on the 3 Rs to calculate land taxes and town dues and protect themselves from the dishonesty of feudal lords and town leaders. This meant that their overlords did not always welcome

---

6. This of course does not represent full equality of opportunity in education, but merely a trend in that direction. As Umihara (1996, p. 51) writes, "Admission of low-ranked samurai and vassals remained highly discriminatory with regards to seat allocations and admittance to dormitories. Commoners in particular had to go to great lengths to establish their credentials, and the courses and lectures they could attend were prescribed. It was not uncommon for education of samurai and commoners to take place at different times in order to prevent comingling to the extent possible." See chapter 9 in Kasai (1960) for further details.

7. For exemplary research related to education in the Edo period, see chapters 7–9 in Dore (1965), which provide a clear description of education from the commoner's perspective.

the spread of education, and indeed there is no sign that the shogunate or domain leadership promoted education for commoners.

As the economic power of townsfolk increased, however, and as national defense gained importance, education for commoners inevitably spread. Many terakoya were established in the Tenmei (1781–1789), Kansei (1789–1801), and Tenpō (1830–1844) periods, as well as in later years. At their peak, there were an estimated twenty thousand such schools.[8]

Instructors at terakoya were typically town leaders or low-ranking samurai, but also sometimes intelligentsia such as Buddhist or Shinto priests, doctors, and calligraphers. Commoners ran the schools most often, followed by samurai and priests.[9] Some schools even allowed coeducation of boys and girls.

Instructional materials consisted of elementary textbooks called ōraimono. Originally, the term referred to collections of correspondence from the Heian (794–1185) and Kamakura (1185–1333) periods, but it later became a generic term for the texts used in pre-Meiji elementary education. For example, the most common ōraimono in the Edo period was titled Teikin-ōrai ["Correspondences for Home Education"], and is said to date to the Muromachi period (1336–1573). The book featured paired letters and replies for each month as a format for presenting vocabulary relevant to the daily lives of samurai and commoners and the industries and products they interacted with, along with narratives and notes regarding their origin. These texts were broadly disseminated in the Edo period, both in their original paired-letter format and in annotated and illustrated editions. In Europe, the first widely read children's text is said to have been Johann Amos Comenius's Orbis Sensualium Pictus, which was published in 1658. Even from a global perspective, then, elementary education based on textbooks and lectures started very early in Japan.

Incidentally, the illustrated Orbis Pictus was rooted in ideas similar to those behind the Japanese oraimono, in that both were resources for systematic education combining language and facts. The Japanese language textbook Tangozu, published in the early Meiji period, is said to have been an imitation of Orbis Pictus.[10]

---

8. According to Ishikawa (1972), who refers to revisions to 1892 reports by the Ministry of Education, 10,831 private elementary schools were newly established. The classification of private schools for commoners and other private or domain-supported schools is problematic, however, so the number is generally reported as 20,000 to 30,000. In any case, 20,000 does not seem to be a significant overestimate.

9. See Ishikawa (1972), chapter 4, section 4 for details.

10. See the translator's endnote, "The Significance of Orbis Pictus," by Inokuchi Junzō in Comenius (1995) for a more in-depth description.

Gōgaku and *shijuku*

Another type of institution for formal education was the gōgaku, operated privately but under the supervision and protection of the shogunate or domains (who also created some gōgaku of their own).[11] Most were established in Western Japan during the Bunka–Bunsei period (1804–1830). The gōgaku varied in terms of format and educational approach, with some targeting samurai while many taught Chinese studies, reading, and calligraphy to the children of commoners and townsfolk. Their approach to education fell somewhere between the individually operated terakoya and the official domain-supported schools; the elementary schools established as a result of Meiji educational reforms are said to have been modeled mainly on gōgaku. Gōgaku operated directly under the shogunate included the Fukagawa, Kōjimachi, and Azabu Schools for young learners, all of which were managed by the Shōheizaka School in Edo's Yushima district, a semiofficial institution founded through a donation by Tokugawa Iemitsu as a private school for a noble family. In time, however, this school came to be viewed as a national academy of sorts — a status that was further established when Matsudaira Sadanobu's Kansei Edicts declared that the neo-Confucian teachings of Zhu Xi, which the Shōheizaka School emphasized, were the only "true education" in Japan.

Domains established many gōgaku schools as well, starting with the Shizutani School, founded by Okayama domain daimyo Ikeda Mitsumasa, which accepted both samurai and commoners from within and outside of the domain. The school taught not only standard fare like the classic Confucian works and materials for young learners by Zhu Xi, but also Japanese language studies, poetry, and Chinese texts such as The Commentary of Zuo, The Book of Han, Records of the Grand Historian, and The Hundred Schools of Thought and its commentaries. Mitsumasa's decision to establish the school is said to have been influenced by Kumazawa Banzan and Nakae Tōju, who converted Mitsumasa to Confucianism. Even in the Meiji period this school produced many notable figures, including Miki Rofū, Masamune Hakuchō, and Ōhara Magosaburō.[12]

---

11. There were, in fact, two types of gōgaku: those for domain clansmen and vassals, and those for commoners. See Ishikawa (1957) for details.

12. Ishikawa (1957); Association for the Preservation of the Shizutani School (2003). The lecture hall of the Shizutani School has been designated a Japanese national treasure, and is regarded as an educational structure unlike any other from the Edo period. Upon visiting it, I was quite impressed by its magnificence. Executive Committee for the 330th Anniversary of the Shizutani School, Shizutani School Archives Catalog Subcommittee (2000) includes many photographs of the building.

Some gōgaku schools were founded by local volunteers, and did not receive the protection or guidance of domains or the shogunate. At a type of private school called a shijuku, an individual managed the school and taught students according to his own academic, philosophical, and moral framework. These shijuku contributed to the emergence of specific schools of thought resulting from a focus on specific areas of study. While the terakoya were institutions for elementary schooling, the shijuku were places for passing on more advanced studies and military arts.

Shijuku heads were often popular Confucian scholars, followers of Western thought, or skilled artists, and in many cases were Confucian officials in the shogunate or domain government. Students were typically young acolytes of the founder or his studies, and generally met at the founder's home. There were an estimated 1,500 such schools throughout Japan.[13] Well-known older schools include Nakae Tōju's Tōju Academy, Itō Jinsai's Kogidō and his son Tōgai's Horikawa-juku, and Miura Baien's Baien-juku. Schools for Western studies such as Seibold's Narutaki-juku and Ogata Kōan's Teki-juku (sometimes called Tekiteki-juku) also produced many notable figures.

My former employer Osaka University, and particularly its School of Medicine, traces its origins to Ogata's Teki-juku and the Kaitokudō School, which was founded to educate the townsfolk of Osaka. Ogata was an Edo-period physician and Western studies scholar who opened a school for Western studies in Osaka's Kawaramachi district in 1838, after completing his studies in Nagasaki. Five years later, he moved it to what at the time was called the Kaisho district, and is currently known as the Kitahama district in Osaka's Chūo ward. Students from across Japan gathered to receive the strict instruction that characterized Teki-juku. Counting only those whose names are known, over 600 students studied at the school, including many notable figures of the Meiji Restoration: Ōmura Masujirō, Takeda Ayasaburō, Sano Tsunetami, Fukuzawa Yukichi, Hashimoto Sanai, Ōtori Keisuke (who also studied at the Shizutani School), Nagayo Sensai, Takamatsu Ryōun, Mitsukuri Shuhei, Hanabusa Yoshimoto, and others.[14]

The Kaitokudō School, which is the other institution viewed as a precursor to Osaka University, was founded in 1724 by a group of Osaka residents called the godōshi ["five comrades"]. Its status is said to have rivaled the Edo-period Shoheizaka School, producing notable merchant-class scholars such as

13. Ishikawa (1972, pp. 168–184) tallies 591 schools in the 23 provinces described in vols. 8 and 9 of Nihon kyōiku-shi shiryō (History of Education in Japan), and mentions that there must have been many more in the remaining 40-plus domains; there were at least 30 in the Hekikai district of Mikawa province alone.

14. See Umetani (1996) for a roster of Teki-juku students by their home prefecture.

Nakai Chikuzan and his brother Riken, Tominaga Nakamoto, and Yamagata Bantō. Kaitokudō was a private school, and while shogun Tokugawa Yoshimune strongly supported its establishment, the Osaka merchant families who founded it bore most of the financial burden. The school was destroyed in the bombing of Osaka in 1945, but its library escaped the flames, and the 36,000 books and other materials contained therein were donated to Osaka University upon the establishment of its School of Letters in 1949. For this reason, Kaitokudō is seen as the foundation upon which Osaka University's liberal arts program was built.[15] In several other cases as well, shijuku later developed into universities.

Some shijuku strongly resembled political collectives; the Risshi School (Tosa domain) and Shōka Sonjuku (Chōshū domain) are typical examples. Shōka Sonjuku was founded by Yoshida Shōin to serve samurai-class families, but it also accepted their infantrymen, retainers, and vassals, who were unable to enter the domain-supported Meirinkan school, as well as the children of antiques dealers, fishmongers, and others in the merchant class.

However, as the political activities of its students gradually intensified, Shōka Sonjuku began to lose its original character as an institute of learning for commoners and low-ranking samurai. By the time activists like Kusaka Genzui and Takasugi Shinsaku began their studies there in 1857, much of the curriculum focused on current affairs. As a result, the school produced a number of sonnō-jōi ["revere the Emperor, expel the barbarians"] activists and Meiji Restoration political figures. Some Meiji-period political leaders such as Itō Hirobumi and Yamagata Aritomo were influenced by founder Yoshida Shōin himself, but when the Chōshū daimyo imprisoned Shōin for his extreme ideology and actions in 1858, his direct involvement with Shōka Sonjuku ended. The school nevertheless remained open until the late nineteenth century.[16]

In 1875, civil rights activists in northern Kyoto established the private Tenkyō Gijuku school, which admitted elementary-school graduates or those with an equivalent education. The school gradually came to teach a combination of libertarian political ideals and Fukuzawa Yukichi's *Minkan keizairoku* (Popular Economics).[17]

One particularly impressive shijuku that I once visited was the Kangien School in the city of Hita, Ōita prefecture. Hita was an Imperial holding in

---

15. See chapter 5 in Wakita and Kishida (1997) for a description of Osaka University's modern reconstruction.
16. Naramoto (1969).
17. Kyoto Prefectural Tango Regional Museum (1975) provides an account of how Tenkyō Gijuku became a base for anti-government movements.

the Bungo province, but the Edo-period Confucian scholar and poet Hirose Tansō established the Kangien School there as a boarding school in the early nineteenth century. The school was noted for accepting anyone who could pay its tuition, regardless of social rank, background, or age. In addition to Chinese classics, the school taught the natural sciences, including mathematics, astronomy, and medicine. Students sat for tests each month and were divided into nine rankings according to the results. Kangien was at one time the largest shijuku in Japan, educating nearly five thousand students before it closed in the late nineteenth century, including Takano Chōei, Ōmura Masujirō, Kiyo'ura Keigo, and Asabuki Eiji.

Hirose Tansō's most notable contribution as an educator was his development of an educational system that produced individuals rooted in their local community but active across regional boundaries. Prevented from traveling by poor health, Tansō instead consorted with the literati who visited Hita from the capital and elsewhere, including Rai Sanyō, Tanomura Chikuden, Takashima Shūhan, and Kawaji Toshiakira. He devised educational innovations that emphasized cooperation, sociability, and friendship in learning, such as forming a student government and assigning tasks to those living at the school.[18]

Later, in the early Meiji period, the Risshisha ["self-help movement"] political association established a shijuku called the Risshi School as a base for libertarian activism. The school was intended to embody the core ideals of Risshisha founders such as Itagaki Taisuke and Kataoka Kenkichi, namely, "developing human knowledge, fostering character, promoting welfare, and advancing freedom." Its instructors included graduates of Keio Gijuku (now Keio University) and educators from the domain-supported school in Tosa. Many more movements rooted in political ideals and centered around shijukus followed, and continue in some form even today.

Family schools and merchant worksite training

So far, I have discussed schools as an element of cultural heritage passed down from the Edo period to the Meiji, but there is no reason to limit discussion of education to schools alone. Indeed, it would be a serious oversight to ignore the vital role of informal education in fostering human resources. Home education is of particular importance, followed by education and training supported by industry or employers. Leaving industrial training to chapters 2, 5, and 6, which consider the situation in Japan after full industrialization, let us here limit the discussion to Edo-period educa-

---

18. Hirose (1973).

tion in homes and merchant houses.

Children were trained extensively at home on matters of etiquette, regardless of their social station. From the youngest ages, all children were taught manners, and how to apply them in daily life. In particular, court nobles distanced from politics needed to learn not only social niceties, but also arts and talents specific to their own family, which were traditionally taught at home. The kakun [written statements of family codes] of samurai and merchant homes reflect this, their central purpose being the maintenance and management of ancestral properties and heritage.[19]

During the long peace of the Edo period, the samurai class increasingly emphasized cultivation through arts like Japanese and Chinese poetry and calligraphy, and many commoners who had succeeded in industry took up scholarship and writing. These families — and merchant families in particular — formalized their family codes and devoted significant effort to educating their progeny to "retain trust, bring honor to the family name, and produce assets" as workers in the family business. Not only family members but apprentices, too, received this type of training.[20]

The heads of merchant households were responsible for the education, oversight, and physical well-being of their apprentices. By the late seventeenth century, major merchant houses like Mitsui, Sumitomo, and Kōnoike employed many apprentices, who by the Genroku period (1688–1704) accounted for around a quarter of the 330,000 people living in Osaka. These leading houses established kakun and promoted the thorough education and training of their apprentices through a system of promotions, raises, and establishment of business branches.[21]

In many cases apprentices came from the same region as their masters, but from branches of the family involved in farming. To summarize the promotion structure, boys were first apprenticed at age twelve or thirteen and would perform household chores such as babysitting, cleaning, or serving as attendants to their master. At around age fifteen or sixteen they would take a new name, formed from the first character of their family name plus a suffix of "-kichi" or "-matsu." They would then start assisting with business-related tasks, such as running errands, packing goods, or receiving payments. These were not salaried positions — apprentices received only small allowances

---

19. Yasuoka (1998). Yasuoka (1984) provides a transcript of a family code.
20. See Kitajima (1962). Ōkita (2005–2006) provides an easy-to-understand description of this in the case of merchants in Matsuzaka.
21. Chapter 3, "Merchant family apprentices and workers," in Saitō (1987) compares changes in the hiring and employment structures of male sales-related workers in Osaka and Edo, providing an analysis from the perspectives of internalization and dual structures.

in the summer and at New Year's, along with new work clothes — and smoking and drinking alcohol were forbidden. At night, after completing their work duties, they would study the 3 Rs and penmanship.

Apprentices came of age at age seventeen or eighteen, at which time they were promoted and issued a cotton kimono and haori coat with the family crest at a celebration hosted by the head of the household. The apprentice was now considered a full-fledged clerk, and so was provided with food, clothing, and a salary. Work responsibilities became more focused, gradually incorporating accounting and finance tasks under the instruction of the head clerk. This phase generally lasted until around age twenty-seven or twenty-eight, but in some cases could extend almost to age forty. This was also a period of training in basic commercial activities such as sales, customer relations, and purchasing. Further advances brought higher wages and bonuses, and achievement-based systems of advancement eventually propelled some workers to the middle-management position of head clerk or, when multiple head clerks were present, their manager.

These advancements were by no means automatic; those deemed unlikely to climb the rungs of advancement were sent home. "Rank 1" apprenticeship lasted for the first seven or eight years, and chances for "rank 2" and "rank 3" advancement were provided every few years thereafter (shogunate law forbade extending "rank 1" apprenticeships to more than ten years). This "up-or-out" system of periodic personnel evaluation suggests that the time spent as an apprentice at a major trade house was one of fierce competition. Indeed, only around one out of twenty apprentices at the top houses made it to the level of clerk.[22]

Such systems for on-the-job training and internal promotion that combined long-term education and training with selection are very similar to the methods of human resource development employed in post-industrial Japan, which will be described later. In that sense, the systems for educating and training apprentices that were developed by Edo-period merchant houses (not to mention samurai families, farmers, and artisans) remain in place to some extent even today.

Internal labor markets centered on systems for promoting workers were already well-formed by the Edo period, and the research of Chimoto Akiko explores how those systems changed and were absorbed into new systems as employment was modernized in the Meiji period and later. Chimoto uses the case of Mitsui to discuss unified hiring practices for apprentices, and to

---

22. See Nakai (1966). Volume 2 of Ōkita (2005–2006, p. 45), too, provides an easy-to-follow commentary.

show how their skills were developed and how a competitive selection and winnowing process led to the long-term employment of elite workers.[23] During the period of social and economic change that spanned the Meiji Restoration, Mitsui transformed itself into a player in the modern-day industry of banking and finance, and during that process reshaped its previous apprenticeship system into a modern employment system. It is possible that this provided the template for all systems of long-term employment and human resource development in Japan.

But how did major merchant families like Mitsui, Kōnoike, Daimaru, and Shirokiya acquire and allocate apprentices amongst themselves, and how did they allocate and promote these apprentices internally?[24] While the above discussion has considered trading houses in general, the skills required of workers of course varied according to the business they were in. Moneychangers needed to learn not only how to deal with promissory notes, but also how to balance account books. Clothiers needed knowledge of their product along with skills related to purchasing and sales. They obtained these skills and knowledge through on-the-job training, which made the occasional hiring of workers from outside the company difficult. Monopolistic merchant guilds set basic employment policies that made it nearly impossible to change employers, and employers in turn were forbidden from poaching apprentices from other houses. This was a key factor behind the "internalization" of labor markets for apprentices.[25]

Chimoto's research focuses on the systems by which apprentices were selected and trained. More apprentices were cast aside than were promoted, suggesting harshly competitive internal labor markets and strict ability-based selection rules. The "elite" apprentices who were selected enjoyed long-term employment, and older apprentices with sufficient ability could be rewarded with opportunities for independence by starting new branches of the family business, or even taking over existing ones in a process of non-hereditary succession. Apprentices were thus presented with an interesting multiplicity of career paths.[26]

The birth of elementary education

During the Meiji period, Edo Japan's various forms of public and private schooling were consolidated into a unified system founded upon elementary education. The abolition of the domains and their replacement by

---

23. Chimoto (1998a).
24. Chimoto (1998a).
25. Chimoto (1986).
26. Yasuoka (1968).

prefectures in 1871 transformed Japan into a modern, centralized nation, and laws enacted the following year established its first nationwide system for primary education. By the end of the twentieth century, this education system would come to be recognized as one of the best in the world.

Let us consider a specific example. In an afterword to Japanese Education Today, a report by the U.S. Office of Education Research and Improvement, former U.S. Secretary of Education William J. Bennett writes that, in Japanese schools, "It is possible to deliver to virtually all children a comprehensive education that starts with the '3 Rs' but also incorporates history, science, art and music, physical education, practical studies, and the beginning of foreign language study. This can be done through a balanced and integrated curriculum that is substantially the same for all youngsters..." He also states that "If Japanese schools do any one thing with greater care and persistence than other nations of whose education systems I have knowledge, it is to forge the kinds of habits that their society deems right."[27]

Of course, this is not to imply that Japanese education is without fault. As Bennett writes, "There are aspects of Japanese education, perhaps especially at the college level, that do not impress me, that would not be appropriate in the American context, or that contravene other principles we value." Even so, Bennett's words suggest that compulsory education in Japan, and primary education in particular, has beyond a doubt produced extremely good results as evaluated from a global perspective.

To understand how Japan achieved these results, let us take a closer look at how the nationwide system for primary education was created.[28]

The Meiji government published the Introduction to the Education Order in August 1872, one day before promulgation of its Education Order, as an easy-to-understand explanation of that order's goals. The document was highly critical of the feudal educational systems of the Edo period, and positioned schools as institutions for aiding individual advancement, productivity, and prosperity. It also declared school education a right of all citizens, girls and women included. The costs of education would be borne by its beneficiaries and shared equally among those living in each school district (with the exception of nationally supported schools).

The Education Order divided Japan into eight university districts, each hosting its own university. Each university district was subdivided into 32 junior high school districts, for a total of 256 junior high schools. Each

---

27. OERI Japan Study Team (1987).
28. The following description of Japan's modernized system of education is based on Ministry of Education (1972) and Ministry of Education (1992).

junior high school district was further divided into 210 elementary school districts, each district having a population of around 600 persons, for a total of 53,760 elementary schools. These school districts were at first separate from general administrative districts.

As a result of this massive school-building project, by 1875 around 2 million students (1.5 million boys and 0.5 million girls) were attending 24,000 schools nationwide. School enrollment had officially reached around 35% of all children, but attendance records indicate the actual figure was closer to 26%. However, due to an over-reliance on private funding and problems related to labor loss (particularly for farming households) resulting from mandatory school attendance, the Code of Education was revised in 1879.

Even before the new Ministry of Education began directing the construction of new schools, prosperous merchants had already developed a modern elementary school system in Kyoto; by 1869 the city had 64 elementary schools, making it the first elementary school district in Japan. While these schools were not much larger than the terakoya schools, they combined the functions of what today we would call ward offices, neighborhood police stations, and fire departments, making them something akin to school-district-scale local governing bodies. Besides the 3 Rs, these schools taught The Analects of Confucius and The Mencius, as well as the syncretic Confucian–Buddhist–Shinto religious philosophy of Ishida Baigan.[29] Texts by Fukuzawa Yukichi describing Western institutions and world geography were also reportedly used. Reflecting on his visit to these Kyoto schools in the spring of 1872, Fukuzawa wrote that "The joy I have experienced in seeing the people establishing schools for the education of all — something I have longed to see for so many years — is like that experienced when returning to one's home town and meeting with old friends."[30]

From an "Education Order" to a "School Order"

The substantive work of revising the Education Order was done by David Murray, an American advisor to the Ministry of Education, and the Ministry's Tanaka Fujimaro.

Murray was a professor of mathematics and astronomy at Rutgers College who came to know Mori Arinori when the latter was serving as the first Japanese ambassador to the United States, which led to Mori recommending Murray as an advisor. Murray emphasized the importance of educating girls and women, and helped establish the Tokyo Women's Normal School

29. Kyoto Municipal Museum of School History eds. (1998, pp. 34–47).
30. Fukuzawa (1991).

(now Ochanomizu University). He is also known for helping to reorganize the University of Tokyo as a modern university. Murray was critical of the extreme uniformity enforced by the Education Order.[31]

Tanaka Fujimaro had visited the U.S. and Europe through his position with the Ministry of Education, as a member of the Iwakura Mission in 1871 (during which time Niijima Jō, then an exchange student at Amherst College, served as his interpreter and assistant). The experience helped shape his image of the ideal form of a revised Japanese education system. After becoming Vice Minister for Education in 1874, Tanaka effectively became the chief executive in the Ministry, due to the frequency of Minister post vacancies. He returned to the United States in 1876 to further investigate the educational systems there, after which he published his report Educational Law in the United States (Ministry of Education, 1878).

Murray and Fujimaro's revision of the Education Order was fundamentally an attempt to apply educational theories that were prevalent in the United States at the time. The Education Order was revised two more times, in 1880 and 1885. Mori Arinori became the first Minister of Education following inauguration of the Cabinet system in 1885, and after taking that post he abolished the Education Order in favor of issuing individual regulations for each type of school. The term "School Order" therefore encompasses a number of decrees, such as the Imperial University Order, the Normal School Order, the Middle School Order, and the Elementary School Order.[32]

Of these, the Elementary School Order was extensively revised in 1900 to establish four (and, in 1908, six) years of free compulsory education with a standardized curriculum. This law remained in place for over forty years, until the National School Order was enacted in 1941. Due to the introduction of compulsory education, elementary school enrollment in 1902 exceeded 90% of all children, and 98% by 1909. Considering that when the first nationwide school system was implemented thirty years earlier, elementary schools had on average only one or two teachers and forty to fifty students, that approximately 40% of schools were in temples and 30% in private homes, and that enrollment rates were around 30%, this represents remarkable progress.[33]

We can determine illiteracy rates and elementary school graduation rates in Japan from this time through the start of the Sino-Japanese War by examining schooling data obtained from twenty-year-old men who

---

31. See Yoshiie (1998) regarding Murray. I am unaware of any recent biographies of Tanaka Fujimaro, but Kano (2005) provides vital information.
32. For the timing of the above events, see Kishimoto and Kaigo (1980, pp. 309–336).
33. School enrollment rates are from Umihara (1996) and the table in Ministry of Education (1972, p. 31).

Table 1. Academic ability of individuals taking conscription exams   (%)

Level / Test year	University	High school/technical school	Junior high school	Upper elementary school	Ordinary school or below	Illiterate
1891	–	–	–	11.4	62.0	26.6
1902	–	0.1	2.1	15.8	65.2	16.8
1912	0.3	0.7	4.4	32.3	59.4	2.9
1926	0.1	0.4	9.5	40.3	48.9	0.8
1936	1.6	2.7	11.3	59.3	24.8	0.3

Note: Test takers were men who had reached twenty years of age in the previous year and thus were eligible for conscription.
Source: Yearly editions of the *Annual Statistics Report of the Ministry of the Army* in Kumagai (1994).

underwent conscription inspections. As Table 1 shows, the illiteracy rate in 1891 was 26.6%, but by 1912 it had fallen to 2.9%.

The revised Elementary School Order established a common curriculum for all elementary school students in Japan, regardless of their status, class, affluence, or gender. All children were taught ethics, language, arithmetic, and gymnastics, and the goal of developing human resources from among the entire national populace became firmly established as government policy. Notably, Western countries were not far ahead of Japan in establishing modern compulsory education systems that taught all children a common curriculum. For instance, compulsory education laws were enacted in Massachusetts in 1852, the U.K. in 1870, and France in 1882.

It is important to note that the economic environment created by industrialization promotes a transition to systems that consider childhood education not simply as a matter of custody, but of national interest. During the industrialization process, the nation's demand for the mass production of workers through compulsory education meshes well with worker demands for education as a right of all citizens, thereby leading to the establishment of modern systems for compulsory education.

2. Transfer of foreign knowledge and skills to Japan

Foreign advisors

There are various ways to propagate knowledge and skills. Using written words and symbols is one common method of transmitting information, but some information is difficult to express through symbols. In many such cases, the most effective way to pass on knowledge is to physically go to a new place and demonstrate it. Studying abroad in more advanced nations or inviting specialists from those nations to visit one's country can be effective strategies for acquiring new or advanced knowledge. In Japan, the Meiji government took the latter approach by hiring foreign advisors.

Both the Meiji and prefectural governments, as well as many private companies, hired foreign advisors with specialized skills to obtain their guidance and advice. By 1900, over 4,000 such advisors were in the employment of the national and regional governments, and nearly 8,000 foreigners are estimated to have been on private company payrolls. Let us consider some of the situations in which these foreigners were hired in order to gain an overview of their characteristics.[34]

Foreign advisors were employed in a wide range of fields, including politics, law, the military, diplomacy, economics, finance, industry, transportation, education, academia, and the arts. In the early stages most of these advisors were hired by governmental agencies, but the practice later extended to private firms as well, with particularly many hires in 1874 and 1875. Early on, advisors often filled technical and academic positions, with academic hires becoming remarkably numerous (and technical positions conversely declining) in the 1880s and 1890s. British nationals made up the overwhelming majority of engineers; approximately 80% of the six hundred or so modernization consultants hired by the Ministry of Industry were from the U.K. The large number of German instructors was also notable. Specialists came from other major countries of the West as well, including France, the U.S., and Italy.[35]

Countries were selected for their areas of expertise within particular technical and academic fields; for example, British consultants were brought in to assist with railways, communications, and lighthouses, French for shipbuilding, and Americans for education and land reclamation. The cultural and technological characteristics of these countries of first contact strongly influenced the development of their respective fields in Japan.

Inviting foreign consultants to Japan did not always result in an immediate transfer of knowledge and skills, however. The human resources and preparedness of the inviter were of equal importance to the invitation itself, since someone on the receiving end had to be capable of accurately

---

34. The following discussion is based on the statistical analyses in chapter 4 of Umetani (2007), which were performed on data taken from the Nihon teikoku tokei nenkan (Japanese Imperial Statistical Yearbook).

35. See Umetani et al. (1968–1976) for comprehensive information and discussion from a specialist's viewpoint. The overview by Umetani divides foreign advisor employment into sixteen fields: medicine, industry, music, diplomacy, land reclamation, education and religion, finance, the military, construction, traffic, natural sciences, the humanities, political and legal systems, the arts, communication, and regional culture. This section draws on information and analysis from Umetani et al.'s series, along with additional material related to personages of particular interest.

understanding the new knowledge being presented. Individuals with the foresight and leadership skills to make full use of new knowledge — in other words, cooperative yet independent pupils — were also essential.

Another key factor was preparedness for receiving these foreign advisors in an appropriate (not to mention economical) manner. Advisor salaries varied according to experience, but many received in excess of a Cabinet minister's monthly salary of 600 yen per month, making this an extremely lucrative job. By comparison, elementary school principals at the time received monthly salaries of 50 yen, and male instructors in the upper elementary grades received 10 yen. Of course, some Japanese criticized the extravagant salaries and cost of providing accommodation and transportation for foreign advisors, some of whom were employed due to misguided adoration of the West. In other cases, a lack of forethought and research resulted in the employment of persons ill-suited to the task at hand. Such cases were rare, however, and in general, exceptional persons with authority in their field provided much-needed guidance and advice.[36]

The breadth of expertise and diversity of educational background that these foreign advisors had is also noteworthy, especially when compared to the narrower scientific and technical specialization of modern experts in today's highly educated society. Well-known examples include Ernest Fenollosa, who came to Japan as a professor of political economics, but subsequently became a scholar and champion of Japanese art, and Raphael von Koeber, who taught both music and philosophy at Tokyo Imperial University. The varied background and career of the Frenchman Paul Brunat, who was hired as an advisor to the Tomioka Silk Mill, is also remarkable. Brunat was not educated at one of France's prestigious Grandes Ecoles; rather, he worked at mills in France and Spain, and arrived in Japan as an inspector of raw silk for a French trading company. A proponent of introducing Western-style silk production, he was hired as a technical consultant for the installation of new equipment at the Tomioka mill, after which he left for Shanghai to help Russell & Company build a silk mill, which he eventually came to manage. In Shanghai he played a variety of roles far beyond that of a simple consultant for silk production, such as helping to extend the French Concession and build new roads.[37]

---

36. Foreign advisor salaries through 1871 are from the "Full List of Foreign Advisors" in Meiji Cultural Studies Association (1928) vol. 16 (vol. 17 in the reprinted edition), Foreign Cultures. The comparison with Cabinet minister salaries is based on Umetani (2007).

37. Verbeck (1978) provides historical underpinnings for a detailed understanding of the social relationships between foreign advisors and Japanese politicians, bureaucrats, and other foreign advisors.

Japanese pupils

This section presents several individual cases that highlight how the systems discussed above functioned as human networks of pupils, collaborators, and successors.

The Meiji-period advisor Guido H.F. Verbeck, who was also an instructor at Kaisei Academy, is sometimes called "the father of modern Japanese construction."[38] Verbeck was a Netherlands-born American who came to Japan as a missionary for the Dutch Reformed Church. Even before the Meiji Restoration, he taught English, French, Dutch, and German in Nagasaki and Saga. His students included Ōkuma Shigenobu, Itō Hirobumi, and Yokoi Shōnan. After being invited to serve as an advisor to the Meiji government, he made great contributions to Japan's new educational, legal, and administrative systems. In June 1869, Verbeck recommended through Ōkuma the formation of a foreign envoy mission, and with the support of Iwakura Tomomi the Iwakura Mission to study the systems and cultures of Western countries was realized.

The Hepburn School in Yokohama, founded by Verbeck's contemporary Clara Hepburn, wife of the prominent missionary James C. Hepburn, was the precursor of Meiji Gakuin University and Ferris University.[39] Verbeck himself helped found Meiji Gakuin University.

Some of these advisors played an influential religious role. Many Japanese joined James Hepburn and other Protestant and Dutch Reformed missionaries such as Samuel R. Brown and James H. Ballagh to form the "Yokohama Band." The group primarily comprised the children of deposed Shogunate supporters who had come to Yokohama to learn Western studies and Christianity (Protestantism). Some members contributed to the founding of the United Church of Christ in Japan, including Ogawa Yoshiyasu, Okuno Masatsuna, Oshikawa Masayoshi, Ibuka Kajinosuke, Uemura Masahisa, and Yamamoto Hideteru. Shimada Saburō, too, should be remembered as a proponent of the liberalist movement in Japanese Protestantism. Besides the Yokohama Band, groups of youth formed under Congregationalist and Methodist leaders in Kobe, Shizuoka, Matsue, and Hirosaki.

The "Kumamoto Band" and "Sapporo Band" also produced many notable figures. The Kumamoto Band formed under Congregationalist pastor L.L.

---

38. Hepburn (1978) provides important materials that reveal his high aspirations and candid humanity.

39. Doshisha Sanmyaku Editorial Board (2003).

Janes in 1871, after Janes was invited to found the Kumamoto Western School. Most members came from samurai families but had failed to find positions in the central government following the Meiji Restoration. Under Janes's leadership, they sought to replace the previous domain system with a new Japanese state that looked to Christianity for its moral basis and political philosophy. Soon after the band's establishment, many of its young members — including Miyagawa Tsuneteru, Ebina Kisaburō, and Tokutomi Iichirō — transferred to Doshisha Academy, where they became central figures. Many went on to take leadership positions in the Japanese intelligentsia as clergy, teachers, officials, and politicians.[40]

The Sapporo Band was comprised of followers of Sapporo Agricultural College instructor William S. Clark who signed his "Contract for Believers in Christ" and became his spiritual successors. Clark came to Japan in 1876 on invitation from the Japanese government. Although he remained for only eight months, during that time he led many of his students to baptism by Methodist missionary Merriman C. Harris. Sapporo Agricultural College inherited Clark's spiritual legacy and educated many of the workers needed to reclaim the Hokkaido frontier. Many graduates became prominent figures in Japan's religious and educational spheres, including Itō Kazutaka (who was active in the fisheries industry), Satō Shōsuke (later president of Hokkaido Imperial University), Uchida Kiyoshi, Ōshima Masatake, Nitobe Inazō, Miyabe Kingo, Uchimura Kanzō, and Hiroi Isami. Incidentally, Ōshima became an instructor at Yamanashi Junior High School as well as a Christian minister who strongly influenced Ishibashi Tanzan.[41]

As the above examples illustrate, the activities of foreign advisors and the Christian thought that they brought with them were powerful factors behind the development of the moral and political attitudes of Japan's youth during the Meiji era.[42]

Legal advisors
Foreign advisors were also active in establishing Japan's modern legal

---

40. Tomioka City Board of Education (2010). Regarding the revolutionary nature of the technology introduced at the Tomioka Silk Mill, see chapter 6 of Kiyokawa (1995).
41. Ōshima (1993). Note that the first edition was published in 1937 by the Imperial Board of Education Publications Department.
42. Ogawara (2013) investigates connections between the politics and beliefs of Christian civil rights activists through discussions of Kataoka Kenkichi, Honda Yōichi, Katō Katsuya, Muramatsu Aizō, and Shimada Saburō. Inoue (1991) provides further research on Shimada Saburō.

systems. In addition to the above-mentioned Verbeck, Prosper G. Gross helped found Japan's police system, Francis S.G. Piggott swayed opinion toward a British-style constitution, and Georges H. Bousquet was involved in preparations for treaty renegotiations. Here, however, I would like to touch on the contributions of Gustave E. Boissonade, Karl F.H. Roesler, and Albert Mosse.

Following the Restoration, the Meiji government initially modeled its new penal code on that of France. Etō Shinpei and the French foreign advisor Bousquet were central to this endeavor. After Boissonade arrived in Japan, he and Bousquet helped train many Japanese lawyers as instructors at schools such as the Meiji Law School (now Meiji University) and the Tokyo School of Law (now Hosei University). At the time, the Law School of the Ministry of Justice primarily taught French law, while schools supported by the national government researched and taught British law. Seven students who attended special lectures by Boissonade and Bousquet went on to study in France, including Inoue Shōichi. Other graduates such as Isobe Shirō later became instructors at the Law School of the Ministry of Justice, while others like Kabuto Kuninori became prominent judges.[43]

Over a period of ten years, Boissonade directed the crafting of Japan's civil code, which was enacted in 1890 alongside a commercial code drafted by Roesler. Enforcement of these codes, however, was delayed due to controversy. Similar controversies occasionally arise today, and bring to light interesting conflicting opinions regarding what constitutes a "Japanese" society and family system.[44]

In the 1890 case, a "delay" faction strongly opposed the implementation of the new civil and commercial codes. This faction consisted chiefly of the Barrister's Club of the Imperial University School of Law, which was composed of graduates who favored British law and were led by Egi Makoto and Hozumi Yatsuka. The above-mentioned Isobe Shirō and Kishimoto Tatsuo led the opposing "enact" faction, which espoused a "natural law" theory asserting that the principles of French law were universal and thus applied equally well to Japan. This faction ultimately lost out to the delay faction, which held that Western law was ill-suited to Japan. After extensive

---

43. Kabuto Kuninori's autobiography (Kabuto, 1982) describes how Boissonade came to Japan at the invitation of the Ministry of Justice, stayed for twenty-two years, and after departing was awarded the Order of the Rising Sun and a lifelong annuity of two thousand yen. When Boissonade died in Antibes, the Japanese government expressed its deep gratitude for his contributions by holding a memorial service and erecting a statue in his honor.

44. See chapters 4 and 5 in Umetani (1971).

revisions, the civil code was finally enacted in 1898, and the commercial code was enacted the following year.

With the exception of laws relating to families and inheritance, the Meiji (Boissonade) civil code has remained in effect through the present day. This, as well as a similar case in the United States, illustrates the extent to which the French civil code spread throughout the world. This code is said to survive today in the former French colony of Louisiana, in contrast to the common-law systems generally practiced in other U.S. states.[45] Incidentally, Roesler, who drafted Japan's original commercial code, also contributed significantly to Japan's constitution as an advisor to Itō Hirobumi and Inoue Kowashi. The same is true of Mosse, whose lectures helped shape the laws that provide the basis for Japan's local self-governance system. Mosse's memoirs provide a good example of the deep respect that foreign advisors of the time had for the Restoration-era Japanese politicians and officials who were absorbing the cultures the advisors represented.[46]

Education for engineers

This section describes some of the most prominent foreign advisors in industrial fields.

Many foreign specialists came to Japan to lead projects to create government districts, schools, factory modernization plans, flood control systems and harbors, and water and sewage systems. Examples include Paul Brunat (Tomioka Silk Mill engineer), Gottfried Wagener (ceramics manufacture), Edmund D. Morel (railroad and telegraph system construction), and Richard H. Brunton (lighthouse construction).[47]

These specialists also established educational institutions to pass on their skills to Japanese successors. One example is the School for Industrial Studies, opened on the advice of chief railroad engineer Thomas R. Shervinton with a faculty largely comprised of foreign advisors. In addition to railroad technologies, the school taught mathematics, surveying, drafting, mechanics, civil engineering and construction, mechanical engineering, and transportation. The curriculum encompassed a broad range of scientific principles and technologies directly applicable to modern industry, thus laying the foundation for future independence from foreigners.[48]

---

45. Some scholars assert that, strictly speaking, the Napoleonic Code and the civil code practiced in Louisiana share a common origin in the Spanish Civil Code.
46. The collected letters of Mosse (1995) provide a wealth of interesting information about him.
47. Brunton and his team of British engineers introduced technologies and systems that reportedly shaped the tradition of Japanese lighthouses. See Brunton (1986) for details.

Other advisors provided vital information regarding the "soft" aspects of government, such as administration. Examples include Alexander A. Shand, an advisor to the Ministry of Finance, and National Mint Director Thomas W. Kinder.

I have already mentioned Murray and Clark's influence on formal education, but Henry Dyer's contributions to technical and vocational education are equally noteworthy.[49] Dyer did not attempt to transplant a particular Western model of education in Japan. Rather, he argued that two methods for teaching engineers predominated at the time. One was the "Continental approach" practiced in France and Germany, which focused on teaching scientific principles. The other was the "British approach," which engaged students in hands-on learning as trainees at actual production sites. Dyer taught a combined model that judiciously fused these two methods; the application of this model in Japanese engineering schools was highly praised in an 1877 issue of Nature.

After returning to his native Scotland, Dyer gave a lecture on engineering education at the Glasgow and West of Scotland Technical College, where he extolled the virtues of Japanese industrial education, saying "Japan has provided the United Kingdom with many important lessons."[50] Specifically, he noted these schools' adoption of the "sandwich method," in which engineering laboratories combined scientific principles with practical studies.

Yamao Yōzō, who assisted in the creation of the Ministry of Industry, was among those who pushed for Dyer's invitation. Dyer's pupils include Takamine Jōkichi (discoverer of the enzyme takadiastase), Tatsuno Kingo (architect of Tokyo Station and Bank of Japan buildings in Tokyo and Kyoto), and Tanabe Sakurō (chief engineer of the Lake Biwa Canal project).

Modern science and academics

Foreign advisors also greatly contributed to the establishment of modern medicine in Japan. Physicians such as Engelbert Kaempfer, Carl Peter Thunberg, and Philipp Franz von Siebold pioneered the introduction of Western medicine during Japan's period of national isolation. German internist Erwin von Bälz came as a foreign advisor and took a post as instructor at the Tokyo School of Medicine (precursor of the University of Tokyo School of Medicine), where he taught the foundations and clinical

---

48. Yamada (1968, pp. 112–118).
49. See chapter 1 of Miyoshi (1983) for details of Dyer's experiments.
50. Ibid., p, 31.

application of medicine and performed examinations. Julius K. Scriba, who helped found modern surgical practice in Japan, also hailed from Germany. Bälz and Scriba were the first foreign instructors at the Tokyo School of Medicine. It is no exaggeration to say that the twenty-six years Bälz spent working as an internist in Japan provided the foundation for modern Japanese medicine.

A diary entry by Bälz from 18 April 1900, around the time of his departure from Tokyo Imperial University, suggests that his feelings toward the School of Medicine were increasingly conflicted due to the growing independence of the Japanese medical field:

> I took a very important step today, giving notice of my intended retirement from my position at the university. I shall, therefore, not be there for the twenty-five years' jubilee festival. Of course I am sorry to take this course, but the way in which the foreign professors are being treated has gradually become intolerable to me. I have known for a long time that in the medical faculty there has been a movement towards independence. I understand and sympathize with the Japanese point of view. [....] Then, within the last few days, I learned that the plans for the new hospital and outpatient department were practically finished although I have never been consulted about them. This was really too much. I went to the rector and told him I wanted to resign — to sever my connexion with the university, in the most friendly way possible. [....][51]

Many foreign physicians were also employed outside of Tokyo. For example, the Kyoto Prefectural Hospital at the Kyoto Prefectural School of Medicine (now the Kyoto Prefectural University of Medicine) got its start in 1872 by hiring Junker von Langegg, Constant George van Mansveldt, and Heinrich Botho Scheube as doctors and educators.[52]

American Edward S. Morse taught zoology and physiology at the Tokyo University Faculty of Science, where he instructed many students and helped to establish zoology and archaeology as modern sciences. British Japanologist Basil H. Chamberlain spent thirty-eight years in Japan researching Japanese language and classical literature. One of his notable pupils was Ueda Kazutoshi, who learned the fundamentals of linguistics from Chamberlain, and after continuing his studies in Germany, became a

---

51. Bälz (1932, pp. 122–123).
52. Morimoto (2011).

professor of philology (linguistics) at the Imperial University.

While perhaps arriving in Japan a bit late to be considered foreign advisors, Raphael von Koeber and Lafcadio Hearn had a distinct influence on the humanities and arts of Japan. Koeber arrived in 1893 and spent twenty-one years as a philosophy instructor at Tokyo Imperial University (he also taught piano at the Tokyo National Music School). He served as an agent of Western culture during the period of "cultivationist" thought that arose in Japan in the Taishō period (1912–1926). His students, many of whom he became personal friends with, included the literary figures Iwamoto Tei, Takayama Chogyū, Tanabe Hajime, Ishihara Ken, Watsuji Tetsurō, Kuki Shuzō, Iwashita Sōichi, and Kubo Masaru. His music students included Kōda Rohan's sister Nobu.[53] Natsume Soseki attended Koeber's art lectures, and wrote several short pieces about him, including "Teacher Koeber."[54]

The Greece-born Englishman Lafcadio Hearn also left an indelible impression on Japanese culture. After arriving in Japan in 1890 he became an English instructor at the Shimane Prefectural Common Middle School and Normal School in Matsue, and went on to teach British and American literature at the Fifth Higher Middle School in Kumamoto, Tokyo Imperial University, and Waseda University. His writings on Japan and its people are filled with careful observations and keen insights that continue to garner him many readers today.

Hearn's students in Matsue included Ōtani Masanobu, Ochiai Teizaburō, Azukizawa Yasaburō, and Ishihara Kikutarō. In Kumamoto he taught Murakawa Kengo, Kuroita Katsumi, Akahoshi Tenta, Yasukōchi Asakichi, and Totoki Wataru. At Tokyo Imperial University, his admirers included Osanai Kaoru, Kuriyagawa Hakuson, Togawa Shūkotsu, Yoshizawa Kenkichi, Uchigasaki Sakusaburō, Ishikawa Rinshirō, and Tanabe Ryūji. This roster makes apparent the extent of the effect that this single exceptional foreign instructor had on Japan's youth.

Music

When Isawa Shūji was posted to the Institute of Music in 1880, he invited to Japan Luther W. Mason, under whom Isawa had previously studied music

---

53. Takii and Hirataka (2012) present Nobu's diary over eight months in 1909 and 1910, during which time she resided in Europe following her departure from the faculty of the Tokyo National Music School. The diary provides important insight into the high level of sophistication of female musicians, as well as the campus politics at the Tokyo National Music School. Most importantly, it shows that studying music is not simply a matter of acquiring skills, but of experiencing good music.

54. Takahashi (1984).

in Boston. Mason helped popularize Western music in Japan, as did the above-mentioned Raphael von Koeber.[55] Japanese and Western music are based upon completely different theoretical systems — in linguistic terms, different vocabularies and grammars — so going from one to the other is similar to learning a new language. Music in Europe developed as a part of people's lives in royal courts, churches, and theaters. It was therefore important not only to invite music teachers from Europe, but also to send Japanese students to Europe, and particularly to Germany, where they could experience music in the daily context from which it arose.

I once had an interesting experience that relates to this point, which I would like to mention here. The Swiss tenor Ernst Haefliger developed an interest in modern Japanese songs and performed them in many concerts and albums. His recordings include works by Yamada Kōsaku and Kitahara Hakushū, such as Kono michi ["This Road"], Machi-boke ["Stood Up"], Pechika ["The Fireplace"], and Karatachi-no-hana ["Orange Blossom"]. Haeflinger sang Japanese lyrics translated into German, so my initial impression of his work was somewhat off-putting. After listening repeatedly, however, I unexpectedly came to appreciate these recordings not only for their melody, translated lyrics, and vocal virtuosity, but also because the music suits Haefliger's skills as a singer quite well. Yet perhaps this is to be expected, given that Yamada Kosaku, the composer of these famous songs, learned Western musical techniques and aesthetics in Germany. Yamada traveled to Germany in 1910, at age 24, and resided there for four years studying late Romantic music.[56]

Taki Rentaro also traveled to Germany, on invitation by Koeber, to study piano under Robert Teichmüller. His stay was brief but intense. Narita Tamezō, famous for his Hamabe-no-uta ["Song on the Beach"], studied in Germany as well. Given the number of Japanese who studied Western music in Germany, the fact that a German musician performed Japanese songs is not particularly exotic. Indeed, it may have been the German influence that attracted Haefliger to these songs in the first place. When I played Taki's Hana ["The Flower"] for a German, he told me it reminded him of a German folksong.

The origins of much modern Japanese music thus have significant

---

55. Kikkawa (1965).

56. Also note that after Mason returned home in 1882, German (Prussian) Franz Eckert, who had come to Japan as director of the Imperial Japanese Navy band, took over instruction. Eckert spent twenty years in Japan, during which time he introduced a wide variety of European music. This likely had a large influence on the development of Japanese musical styles.

connections with German culture. Many of the songs in Japan's Songbook for Elementary Schools were written by Mason and Isawa, who selected melodies from Western European songs and freely added Japanese lyrics. Niwa-no-chigusa ["Flowers in the Garden"], which takes its melody from the Irish folksong The Last Rose of Summer, exemplifies this blending of East and West.[57]

Arts and crafts

Foreign advisors also profoundly impacted Japanese arts and crafts, and helped produce many ambassadors of Japanese culture. As mentioned above, Ernest F. Fenollosa was an American scholar of Oriental art, but for the first eight years after his 1878 arrival in Japan, he lectured on political science, economics, and philosophy at Tokyo Imperial University on introduction by E.S. Morse. Fenollosa became increasingly interested in Japanese culture and eventually began promoting traditional Japanese painting. Together with Okakura Tenshin, a former university student of his, and others, he formed a movement to encourage the creation of this type of artwork. In 1886, he traveled to Europe with Okakura as a member of an expedition sponsored by the Meiji government to survey Western arts, and later helped found the Tokyo School of Fine Arts (now the Tokyo University of the Arts). In 1904, Okakura became curator of the Asian art department at Boston's Museum of Fine Arts, where he played a key role in introducing Japanese art to the world — and even to Japan itself — through English works such as The Ideals of the East, The Awakening of Japan, and The Book of Tea. Today, too, foreign appreciation of Japanese art occasionally prompts the Japanese to reevaluate its worth.

Foreigners hired to teach at the art school of the Ministry of Public Works included sculptor Vincenzo Ragusa, painter Antonio Fontanesi, architect Josiah Conder, and draftsman and architect Giovanni V. Cappelletti.

Ragusa introduced modeling techniques and taught fundamental skills such as how to carve marble and fashion molds from plaster. His pupils included Ōkuma Ujihiro and Fujita Bunzō. Fontanesi improved Western-style painting technique in Japan by attracting students such as Koyama Shōtarō, Matsuoka Hisashi, Asai Chū, Goseda Yoshimatsu, and Yamamoto Hōsui. Conder established the foundations of Western architecture in Japan through his many successors, who include Tatsuno Kingo, Katayama Tōkuma, and Sone Tatsuzō.

---

57. Nomura (1971) provides an overview of the introduction of Western music to Japan through military bands, foreign advisors such as Mason, and government-supported music schools. Inose (1994) is another useful reference.

Italian engraver and painter Edoardo Chiossone assisted the Ministry of Finance's Printing Bureau in developing printed money, stamps, and checks, and deserves credit for providing Japan with the advanced printing technology required to produce paper money. Before Chiossone's arrival, Japan outsourced printing of its money, primarily to Chiossone's former employer, the luxury playing card printer Dondorf–Naumann of Germany.[58]

The importance of technology transfer through relocation

The physical movement of people plays an extremely important role in the diffusion of skills and technology. For an industrial technology to take root in a new land, not only formal technical training but also individualized, specific on-site training is required. This type of training strongly affects the efficiency — and even the possibility — of knowledge transfer.

Technologies are in essence diffused through imitation, but in many cases new technologies are incorporated gradually into traditional production techniques. It is in fact rare for a given innovation to be adopted without being modified according to the resources, related technologies, personal preferences, and social systems of the adopters. While modifications and improvements are usually needed, however, the extent of modification varies widely.

According to U.S. economic historian W.C. Scoville, diffusion of technology occurs via two paths: "diffusion by radiation," in which observers watch and imitate skilled workers, and "diffusion by migration," in which skills and technology are diffused along with skilled workers who relocate to new places.[59] The two paths are similar in that they involve direct human participation. For example, scholars and writers can conduct tours to observe foreign factories and workplaces. Alternately, select, highly skilled workers can be relocated, as Jean-Baptiste Colbert did when he established several privileged enterprises in France by bringing foreign lace makers and glassworkers into the country. Human capital can also relocate in large numbers through migration.[60] Migration is a particularly important method of diffusion. Mass human movement brings not only new skills and technologies, but also lifestyles, ideologies, and new types of economic activity. Migrants bring in capital as well. Setting aside questions relying on human capital movement and differences in the economic standards of the

---

58. Kumamoto (1976) provides a roster of many of the pupils who studied arts and crafts under Chiossone and other foreign advisors.
59. Scoville (1951).
60. La Force (1964).

migrant's origin and destination, there is no denying that migration greatly affects the efficiency and speed of technology transfer.

Study abroad

The alternative to importing specialists is exporting students. By studying at overseas schools, students acquire both skills and knowledge of the societies that produced them. The broad goals and effects of international study have long been recognized, and since the Meiji period many Japanese students have headed to foreign countries to study in a variety of fields, as discussed above with regards to music. Indeed, this has been the case since ancient times, when Japanese traveled to China for a similar purpose.

"Travel is the finest schooling," as the saying goes — or, as Augustine of Hippo phrased it, "The world is a book, and those who do not travel read only one page." Of course, travel alone is insufficient to guarantee true learning; discovery and enlightenment come not merely from seeing new sights, but from acquiring "new eyes." True learning (as well as teaching) comes from an inner fire.

While study abroad does not have the same level of impact as mass relocation, it occurs over long periods, and, so long as students are carefully selected, can be an extremely effective means of technology transfer.

In Japan, the Tokugawa shogunate sent students abroad for the first time in 1862, to study in the Netherlands. Competing domains such as Chōshū and Satsuma, too, sent promising youth to study in the Netherlands, Russia, England, France, and the United States (sometimes, during periods where overseas voyages were forbidden, in secret).[61] The Meiji government promoted overseas study as part of its cultural policy, and in 1870 issued a proclamation demanding that domains annually nominate one to three students (according to the domain's economic production) for study at the Southern College of the [Meiji government-sponsored] University, which specialized in Western studies.[62] This school eventually evolved into the modern-day University of Tokyo.

The best-known overseas student from this time was Tsuda Umeko, who greatly contributed to English language and cultural education in Meiji- and Taishō-era Japan. Tsuda arrived in the United States in 1871 at age seven as one of five young girls accompanying the Iwakura Mission. She lived with an American family in Washington, D.C. until her graduation from high school, then returned to Japan in 1882 and taught English at a women's

---

61. Watanabe (1977–1978).
62. Karasawa (1974).

school for the nobility. She returned to the U.S. in 1889 to study at Bryn Mawr College, and in 1900 opened the Women's Institute for English Studies in Tokyo. Her father was the agronomist Tsuda Sen, who introduced Western farming methods to Japan and was well versed in Western culture, due to a previous trip to the U.S. in 1867 alongside Fukuzawa Yukichi.[63]

Several other students were also selected by the new government to accompany the Iwakura Mission and study abroad. As the case of Tsuda Umeko illustrates, these early students were chosen from a limited segment of society. Only individuals with a certain perceived dedication to the public good were permitted to go, and being a child of the nobility or intellectual elite took precedence over academic ability. Some students thus did not perform to expectations, and criticisms of the program's costs (one thousand yen per student per year) led to its suspension in 1871 and its abolishment in 1873. In its place, a scholarship for overseas study through Tokyo Kaisei Academy was established in 1875 for students with exceptional academic ability who could not otherwise afford to study overseas. Participants included Hatoyama Kazuo, who attended Yale University, and Komura Jutarō, who attended Harvard. While this improved the overall caliber of students sent overseas, numbers remained low through the end of the nineteenth century. Looking just at students sent by the Ministry of Education, numbers reached double digits following the end of the First Sino-Japanese War, but even in the best of years only forty to fifty students were sent. As a general trend, students with public funding went to Germany and became instructors and researchers, while self-financed students went to the United States and exhibited large disparities in academic ability.[64]

Approximately 24,700 publicly- and privately-funded students studied abroad during the Meiji period. It is difficult to determine in detail what these learners brought back to Japan and the precise ways in which they contributed to Japan's culture and economy. What is clear, however, is that almost all those who studied abroad eventually returned to Japan. This contrasts starkly to the "brain drain" experienced by many developing countries in later years.

In the 1960s, for instance, many scientists and engineers from Asian and

---

63. Takahashi (2002).
64. See Ishizuki (1972) for details of overseas studies during the first seven years of the Meiji period. Appendices to that work list students' names, departure and return dates, level and field of study, destination country and area of origin, subjects studied before and during study abroad, and career after returning to Japan, as collected from various documents, records, and citations. Data related to these students' careers after returning to Japan are particularly interesting.

African nations studied at laboratories and universities in developed nations, and many remained in those countries after completing their studies. This represents a loss of human resources for their country of origin, or at least a lost return on investment in education; in either case, the loss for the home country was significant. In that regard, the students who studied abroad in Meiji-period Japan had an extremely large social and economic effect on their country.

Female silk factory workers. (Photo: Jiji Press)

CHAPTER 2

INDUSTRIALIZATION AND THE
LABOR FORCE

This chapter examines how expanding Japanese industrialization affected methods of industrial education and corporate training. Differences in industry and job type make generalizing about industrialization difficult, particularly with regard to its early stages.[1] Clearly, however, industrialization improved productivity, and that increased the number of workers engaged in manufacturing in Japan, which in turn led to an increase in facilities for collective training and classroom learning at both schools and factories. Managers divided and specialized manufacturing processes to further improve productivity, and used trial and error to develop efficient methods for teaching job skills.

Adam Smith's *The Wealth of Nations* opens with the example of how division of labor greatly enhanced efficiency in the manufacture of pins, as factories divided the process into separate tasks and assigned workers to specialize in each one. Smith then goes on to describe how technological advances resulting from division of labor and collaboration within firms lead to division of labor and collaboration in the overall market, thus promoting the growth of national wealth. It is particularly noteworthy that while Smith admits to individual differences in talents, predispositions, and qualities, he states that "The difference of natural talents in different men is, in reality, much less than we are aware of,"[2] and that such differences are the effect, rather than the cause, of division of labor. This view on education and training contrasts with that of scholars dating back to Plato, who took the position that innate human differences were the fundamental reason division of labor arose. Plato's view was perhaps formed by the strictly defined social hierarchy of his day, in which restricted labor mobility made appropriate division of labor difficult.

If human knowledge and skills are not severely constrained by innate qualities, then education and training play a decisive role in individual growth and the wealth of society overall. This raises the question of who should bear the costs of education. To this day, no satisfactory answer has been found.

In *The Wealth of Nations*, Smith suggests that wages should reflect the cost of the education needed to acquire the position: higher skill requirements equate to a need for workers to invest more in training, and this is one reason why experienced workers are paid more. Smith also addresses problems related to the technology and regulations of his day. He criticizes

---

1. Odaka (1993b) presents thorough investigations of various industries, using historical depictions of pre-World War II industry leaders and a survey of postwar companies to develop a history of corporate training since the Meiji period.
2. Smith (1904, p. 17).

apprenticeship systems and argues that mechanized technologies will make long apprenticeships and training periods of more than a few weeks unnecessary.

A closer examination of industrial training systems is instructive toward understanding the types of knowledge and skills that mechanization and industrialization made necessary. In this chapter, I focus on corporate training in Japan during the Meiji period (1868–1912) and succeeding decades.

1. Sites of industrial education and labor

Industrial schools

Developing modern Japanese industry required a particular type of workforce. Because Japan's traditional handicraft industries differed in content and operational style from modern industries introduced from abroad, fostering technicians and other skilled workers for these new industries was a pressing concern. From the late Edo to the early Meiji periods, technicians were trained primarily at government-run factories. As described in the previous chapter, technology transfer generally occurred through the hiring of foreign advisors who worked alongside traditional artisans and served as their instructors. From around the time of the First Sino-Japanese War (1894–1895), when the framework for general education was being established, the Meiji government began promoting industrial education in earnest with the goal of modernizing industry. Several institutions had already been established in the latter half of the 1870s, including the Mitsubishi Merchant Marine School and the Mitsubishi Commercial School. By the 1880s, the Ashikaga Textile School was teaching daily classes in linguistics, mathematics, and chemistry, in addition to its industrial curriculum.[3] The number of industrial schools again increased markedly during the industrialization that followed the Russo-Japanese War (1904–1905).

In many cases private firms contributed to the establishment and funding of academic and industrial schools, but it was only after Japan seriously committed to industrialization that industrial schooling was systematized and officially positioned within the educational system. In 1899, the government issued the Vocational School Order with the goal of establishing schools to educate industrial, agricultural, and commercial workers to fill mid-level positions. This law divided industrial schooling into seven broad categories: schools for mechanical and electrical training, schools for

---

3. Odaka (1993b, pp. 71–72).

apprentice training, schools for teaching needlecraft to girls (apprentice schools at first, but later vocational schools), agricultural schools, fisheries schools, commercial schools, and merchant marine schools. The first merchant marine school was the above-mentioned Mitsubishi Merchant Marine School, founded in 1875 through a government grant aimed at producing crews capable of working international shipping lanes, and transferred to government control in 1882. The Kobe Merchant Marine School was established in 1920.

Even in these industrial schools, however, only around a third of the curriculum was directly related to industry; the remainder was the same curriculum taught in general-purpose middle schools, with, for example, the same time allocated to studies of mathematics and foreign language.[4]

In addition to these general industrial schools and more specialized schools teaching advanced skills such as medicine, dentistry, and foreign language, "vocational supplementary schools" also played an important role, particularly for agriculture. The groundwork for these schools was laid in 1893 with the Vocational Supplementary School Regulations. Although they served working youth who had completed elementary school, they did not offer the junior high school curriculum; rather, they provided a supplementary elementary education and a chance to develop vocational skills. These schools were modeled on the Fortbildungsschule ["continuing education schools"] of Imperial Germany, which provided further education to graduates of the Volksschule, where compulsory primary education occurred. This was a separate educational track from the Gymnasium, which were elite institutions for high-school education leading directly to university.[5] Inoue Kowashi, who served as minister of education in the second Ito administration, promoted a two-track Japanese system of standard and vocational education modeled on this German system. Inoue is viewed as having greatly improved elementary school enrollment rates.[6]

Vocational supplementary schools offered six to eight hours of night classes per week, thus catering to working youth who wanted to attend junior high school but were unable to do so for economic reasons. Since

---

4. National Institute of Education (1974, p. 248).
5. The Fortbildungsschule were the predecessors of the Berufsschule ["vocational schools"] established in 1920. Today, after completion of primary education (Grundschule) around age ten, students decide whether to continue in vocational (Hauptschule or Realschule) or academic (Gymnasium) training, so this system has not changed in essence since the days of Imperial Germany. Hisamoto (1986) provides an accessible description of German vocational training based on primary sources.
6. See Kino (1995) for details.

these schools were not actually junior high schools, however, they did not provide opportunities for further educational advancement.

Concurrent with Japan's development of a heavy chemical industry following World War I, the number and attendance of supplementary schools greatly increased. By 1925, there were 15,316 supplementary schools attended by over one million students. While these schools certainly provided vocational education for the heavy chemical industry (with emphasis placed on vocational and civics education over supplementary primary education), most were located in rural communities, and hence were largely viewed as night schools for farming villages. In 1935, for instance, around 12,000 of the approximately 15,000 supplementary schools had an agricultural focus. Even so, the low agricultural productivity of the time suggests that these schools did little to directly support scientific approaches to farming.

In 1926, the vocational supplementary schools were combined with the newly created youth training centers, and in 1935 these were rebranded as "youth schools" by the Youth School Regulations. Under this system, after graduation from "ordinary" (compulsory elementary) schools, students studied a "normal" curriculum for two years, followed by "main" studies for three years (girls) or five years (boys). Upper elementary school graduates could start from "main" studies, which could be followed by further study of specialized subjects. Pre-World War II junior high school education was a dual-track system leading either to academic or vocational schooling, similar to the German system.[7]

Training artisans

It is difficult to quantitatively assess the types of labor that various segments of the industrial sector were applying to production activities in late-Meiji Japan. Furthermore, an overwhelming portion of the Japanese labor force was still engaged in agriculture at this time; of a total population of approximately 36 million in 1880, over 29 million (80%) were farmers.[8]

The 1909 edition of the Factory Statistics Tables lists the industry types, number of factories, number of workers, and production levels in Japan at the time. According to these tables, the industrial worker population at the time was just over 740,000. Industry was focused on textiles, mainly the spinning and weaving of silk and cotton. Other notable industries were metal products and refining, shipbuilding, machine manufacturing,

---

7. National Institute of Education (1974, vol. 5, pp. 267–294).
8. Umemura et al. (1988, pp. 4, 107).

ceramics, and chemical industries such as fertilizer and pharmaceuticals manufacturing.[9]

To ensure a labor force with appropriate skills, factory owners not only invited foreign technicians and artisans to Japan, as discussed in the previous chapter, but also improved their competitiveness by training existing skilled workers, key "artisan" engineers in particular.[10]

Odaka provides detailed information on the role of foreign advisors. With regard to the shipbuilding industry in Japan, he describes the vital importance of guidance from Westerner advisors, as well as the important role that Japanese artisans played in the transfer of Western shipbuilding technology. He also notes that that while the influence of Japanese artisans waned around World War I, they retained a key place in the shipbuilding industry until just before Japan's period of rapid economic development following World War II.[11] He goes on to divide Meiji- and Taishō-period (1912–1926) artisans into six types:

1. First-generation artisans who continued to work as independent private companies following the Meiji Restoration. The Miyata Corporation, for example, began in the Edo period as a group of gun blacksmiths, but later developed into a bicycle manufacturer.

2. First-generation artisans who were employed at shipbuilding facilities and other industrial centers that wished to make use of their skills, and thereby learned new trades through instruction from Western technicians. Examples include Ueda Torakichi, Furukawa Shōhachi, and Yamashita Iwakichi, all of whom were sent to the Netherlands in the Edo period and joined the Yokosuka Navy Yard upon their return to Japan.

3. Artisans trained in the Meiji period who opened private factories as independent operators. An example is Okamoto Shōzō, who created a bicycle manufacturing plant following his apprenticeship as a blacksmith.

4. Artisans who underwent master–apprentice training but later established independent operations, such as Yoshikawa Tsuruhiko, who trained

---

9. See Odaka (1984, 1993a) for detailed graphs and tables presenting the number of foreign advisors invited in this capacity. Odaka (1993b) surveys the history of the companies and corporate leaders listed in the Hitotsubashi University Institute of Business Research's *Honpō kigyōsha-shi mokuroku* (Bibliography of Japanese Entrepreneurial History) (Special Bibliography 3, 1969), and in chapter 3 investigates vocational training in the mining industry by area in prewar Japan.

10. Odaka (1984, 1993a).

11. Odaka (1993a).

with the clockmaker Seiko.

5. Those who continued artisan work while also participating in factory training programs, particularly at government-operated factories. For example, Yasui Kenkichi, the founder of Brother sewing machine, was also a supervisor at the Atsuta artillery arsenal.

6. Those who became artisans after completing factory training programs. This was the most common situation after the Taishō period, and was particularly common in the metals processing and machinery manufacturing industries. Many of the workers at NSK immediately after its founding in 1916, for instance, were former Navy shipyard workers.

The role of military arsenals

Odaka's classification makes clear that programs at facilities such as naval shipyards played a large role in the training of artisans after the Meiji Restoration. Below, I outline the nature of these government-run facilities.

Until the end of World War II, military arsenals were factories where the Japanese army and navy manufactured and repaired weaponry including warships, aircraft, explosives, and fuel. Arsenals also produced the special types of steel and other metals used in military hardware. The first arsenals created by the Meiji government were the Imperial Army's Tokyo Artillery Arsenal (1868) and Osaka Artillery Arsenal (1870) and the Imperial Navy's Yokosuka Shipyard (1872), which was originally built by the Tokugawa shogunate. Weapons manufacture thus began immediately after establishment of the Meiji government.[12]

Scientific discoveries are in general the product of human curiosity and a drive to make life easier, but the application of newly discovered knowledge to industrial activity — in other words, innovation — has historically been motivated primarily by either profit or warfare. We cannot ignore the link between military and industrial technologies, given that one generally stimulates the other (with military technology most often driving the development of industrial technology). Indeed, it is innovation in military

---

12. Miyake (1993) provides a detailed narrative of the development of weapons manufacturing technology at the Osaka Artillery Arsenal from the time of the Satsuma Rebellion (1877) through the First Sino-Japanese War (1894–1895), and subsequent expansions of the facility's manufacturing scope to include automobiles, water-supply pipes, and other items. He also describes steel production, wartime weapons development, and technology transfer to the private sector. Tomita and Nishibori (1983) provide an account of how the transfer of industrial technology can simultaneously result in unexpected transfer of culture to various fields.

technology — from bows and chariots to gunpowder, chemical weapons, jet planes, radar, and hydrogen bombs — that has most profoundly altered human history.

Japanese military arsenals were on the cutting edge of domestic technology, and at times offered evidence that Japan was becoming the technological equal of other nations. Mass production of weaponry such as the Murata rifle and 7 cm mountain and field artillery had already begun by the First Sino-Japanese War. (The Murata rifle was developed by Murata Tsuneyoshi in 1880 based on similar European designs, and was one of the most advanced guns of its time.)

Japan expanded its arsenals during the Sino-Japanese and Russo-Japanese Wars, establishing manufacturing systems that allowed for fully domestic weaponry production and steel refining. In 1910, the Imperial Navy completed construction of its battleship *Satsuma*, another example of Japan attaining world-class standards in military technical prowess. The Kure Naval Arsenal, in conjunction with the government-operated Yawata Steel Works, grew into a massive facility that performed full-scale production of steel, weaponry, and warships.

Such massive arsenals became something like towns in their own right. The site of the Kure Naval Arsenal, for example, was until 1889 a small fishing village on the east side of Hiroshima Bay. The area experienced rapid growth following its development by the Navy, and the population swelled along with the arsenal and aircraft production facilities. By World War II, Kure had a population of over 400,000. The same is true of Sasebo, which in 1886 was a desolate village on Nagasaki Bay with a population of only 4,000. The population grew steadily after establishment of a naval district and port there, and by the end of World War II over 300,000 people lived in the town.

The Tokugawa Shogunate built the Yokosuka Steel Works deep within the bay at Yokosuka in 1866, and the Meiji government passed this facility on to its navy as the Yokosuka Ship Yard. It became a naval arsenal in 1903, following which more facilities were constructed, making it the largest Imperial Navy port in Japan. It continued to grow until 1907, when it was officially incorporated as the second city in Kanagawa prefecture (following Yokohama). In addition to private shipbuilding firms like the Ishikawajima Shipyard (now IHI Corporation, formerly Ishikawajima–Harima Heavy Industries Co., Ltd.) and the Uraga Dock Company (now Sumitomo Heavy Industries, Ltd.), Yokosuka also hosted the headquarters of the Tokyo Bay Fortress, firmly establishing its image as a military-industrial town. Here too, increased population indicates increased employment opportunities.[13]

The Maizuru Naval District was established in Higashi-Maizuru in 1901, somewhat later than the cities described above. It was the fourth military port in Japan, and the first on the Sea of Japan. This area too became a concentration of various military facilities, but also rapidly developed into an industrial port city with the founding of private firms such as Gunze Silk Manufacturing Co., Ltd. (now Gunze, Ltd.) in 1920 and Hinode Spinning (later Daiwabo Co., Ltd.) in 1938. Both population and employment continued to increase through the end of World War II.[14]

Trainee systems in military arsenals

Military arsenal trainees were selected and trained using particular methods.[15] In the case of Yokosuka, the arsenal distributed an entrance prospectus to elementary schools within and near the city. Applicants were tested for physical and academic aptitude, and generally admitted starting with those who had the highest scores. Trainees studied academic subjects during the mornings every other day, and spent their remaining time in on-the-job training. Subjects included arithmetic, science, English, and Japanese, as well as drafting, algebra, geometry, applied mechanics, ethics, and electrical or marine engineering. After three or four years of on-site training, trainees were required to work at the facility for a similar period of time. Experienced technicians and engineers served as instructors at each factory. Trainees who demonstrated exceptional academic ability and work skills were admitted to the Naval Engineering School or the Munitions Worker Training School, where they furthered their studies and had the opportunity to advance through a series of ranks until becoming a naval engineer or assistant engineer. Following employment, pay raises and bonuses were offered twice a year, according to individual performance.

Training programs evolved later in large private firms than they did in military arsenals, primarily in the Taishō period. Before that, many companies had factory-based apprentice schools, such as the Mitsubishi

---

13. Sakane (2010–2014) presents a multifaceted, detailed analysis of the rise and fall of naval ports. See the first volume in the series for information regarding the port at Maizuru, discussed below.

14. The Maizuru Naval Arsenal opened in 1903, but the weaponry and shipbuilding arsenals that preceded it were established in 1901. Following the Washington Naval Treaty of 1923, the Maizuru Naval District was reduced to designation as a third-echelon naval port, and the naval arsenal became a navy construction department. The latter regained its status as a naval arsenal in 1936 and the former as a naval district in 1939 (Maizuru City History Compilation Committee, 1982).

15. See Meiji Documents Publishing Committee (1966) for details on the Yokosuka Naval Arsenal through 1897. The description below is based on Yokosuka Naval Arsenal (1983).

Factory Preparatory School and Hitachi's Apprentice Training School, and frequently combined training at company factories with training at external facilities.

By 1935, the importance of on-the-job training was emphasized at all levels. At many facilities, the most experienced engineers were delivering subject lectures for two to three hours each day, and section leaders who were most familiar with job practices were selected as instructors.[16]

2. Labor conditions and labor disputes

Cotton spinning

The number and scale of factories in Japan in the early twentieth century, which is considered the start of Japan's accelerated industrialization, provides important background information for discussion of labor conditions and disputes. One instructive dataset is the *Kōjō tsūran* (Factory Overview: 1902) (1904, 1906 editions) compiled by the Ministry of Agriculture and Commerce, Department of Commerce and Industry,[17] which lists 33 government-owned and private factories employing over 1,000 workers. Among the government facilities, military arsenals were by far the largest, with each of the above-mentioned arsenals at Yokosuka, Sasebo, and Kure having more than 5,000 workers. Only two private factories were of this scale: the Mitsubishi Ship Yard at Nagasaki (5,058 workers) and the Ashio Copper Mine operated by the Furukawa Corporation in Tochigi prefecture (7,224 workers).

Of the 33 non-mining factories with over 1,000 workers, 20 were cotton-spinning mills, a good indication of how important this industry was to Japan's "industrial revolution." Table 2 lists the names of these factories and the number of workers at each. The ratio of male to female workers is particularly interesting; women were the core labor force, making up 80% of all factory workers. This stands in stark contrast to mines and military arsenals, which were almost completely staffed by male workers.

---

16. *Minaraikō no saiyō narabini yōsei hōhō* (Methods for the Training and Employment of Trainee Factory Workers) (Japan Industry Association, 1935). Regarding years of engineer training and the presence of apprenticeship programs, Odaka (1993b) provides tables of data for industry sub-categories from the *Nihon shokugyō taikei: Kōgyō-hen* (Compendium of Japanese Occupations: Industrial Edition) (Occupational Placement Service, 1936–1942) indicating whether they employed conventional technologies, which had the longest training periods, and which had apprenticeship programs.

17. Matsuda, Arita, and Kimura (1990) present statistical tables organized by number of engineers and form of factory ownership, based on a factory statistics database reconstructed from the *Factory Overview: 1902*.

Table 2. Large silk and spinning factories in 1902

Factory	Location	Workers	Ratio of men to women (%)
Settsu Spinning Co.	Osaka	3,778	21.1 : 78.9
Kanegafuchi Spinning Co., Hyōgo Branch	Hyōgo	3,689	17.6 : 82.4
Osaka Spinning Co.	Osaka	3,208	22.7 : 77.3
Tokyo Gas Spinning Co.	Tokyo	3,191	17.5 : 82.5
Japan Textile Co.	Osaka	3,066	28.5 : 71.5
Settsu Spinning Co., Hirano Factory	Osaka	2,381	34.2 : 65.8
Owari Spinning Co.	Aichi	1,958	14.8 : 85.2
Mie Spinning Co., Tsu Branch	Mie	1,947	17.3 : 82.7
Kanegafuchi Spinning Co., Miike Branch	Fukuoka	1,890	18.0 : 82.0
Amagasaki Spinning Co.	Hyōgo	1,849	22.3 : 77.7
Kanegafuchi Spinning Co.	Tokyo	1,842	17.4 : 82.6
Koriyama Spinning Co.	Nara	1,840	20.2 : 79.8
Mie Spinning Co., Aichi Branch	Aichi	1,738	14.0 : 86.0
Tokyo Spinning Co.	Tokyo	1,685	18.3 : 81.7
Mie Spinning Co.	Mie	1,681	13.7 : 86.3
Tokyo Muslin Textile Co.	Tokyo	1,655	8.0 : 92.0
Kurabo Industries Co.	Okayama	1,383	14.5 : 85.5
Okayama Spinning Co.	Okayama	1,319	21.1 : 78.9
Hosoito Spinning Co., Osaka Branch	Osaka	1,309	20.0 : 80.0
Meiji Spinning Co.	Osaka	1,236	20.7 : 79.3
Osaka Joint Textile Co., Tenma Factory	Osaka	1,200	20.0 : 80.0
Okaya Silk Co.	Nagano	1,152	10.4 : 89.6
Hokkaido Hemp Co.	Hokkaido	1,106	23.8 : 76.2

Source: Overview of Factories (Ministry of Agriculture and Commerce, 1902).

In 1897, the cotton spinning industry was second only to the silk industry in terms of exports, with approximately 30% of industry output exported. In 1899, capital in cotton spinning companies accounted for 25% of all capital in industrial firms, and spinning companies employed 16% of the labor force. Factors behind the rapid development of this key industry included the high productivity of its female workers and the low wages they were paid. Furthermore, factories replaced spinning mules with easier-to-operate ring-frame spinning machines, installed electric lighting and other new technologies, and introduced daytime and nighttime shifts, which increased employment opportunities for many young women relocating from rural farming villages.

The situation was similar in the silk industry. The low price of Japanese silk had helped increase exports to Europe after Japan's ports were opened in 1859, and from the mid-1880s, the United States became Japan's largest trading partner in silk. The quality of Japanese silk remained inferior to that of European products, however. It was not until the early 1900s that Japan was able to export high-quality yarn silk for warp weaving, pushing it ahead of Italy and then even China to become the world's largest silk exporter in 1909.

By 1894, mechanical devices were replacing manual spinning wheels, although the older devices remained in use beyond 1910.[18] Mechanical spinners allowed for silk production in factory systems, but still required significant labor input. This labor was generally supplied by young women, who were housed in company dormitories, worked long hours, and were paid according to their output.[19]

Valuable information about the working and living conditions of female laborers at this time is presented in the 1903 edition of the *Shokkō jijō* (Conditions of Factory Workers) report[20] and journalist Yokoyama Gennosuke's 1899 book *Nihon no kasō shakai* (Lower Class Society in Japan).

The former is based on interviews and data that the Ministry of Agriculture and Commerce collected in 1900 from thirteen industries (including cotton spinning, silk spinning, and weaving) to better understand the conditions of factory workers in order to establish factory regulations.[21] This investigation forced a reassessment of the long hours and late nights that laborers were forced to work in the textile and other major industries in Japan. The government had previously attempted to regulate working conditions at factories, but factory owners and proponents of a free market fiercely opposed regulation as unneeded and harmful, so progress was minor. The *Conditions of Factory Workers* report, however, led to enactment of the Factory Law in 1911 to protect laborers and public health. It took effect in September 1916, but because it only limited working hours to twelve-hour shifts (including one hour of break time), it perhaps failed to meet international standards of the time.

The *Conditions of Factory Workers* report and other documents supply the following information about spinning mill workers around 1897:[22]

1. Approximately 20 to 30% of female spinning mill workers were in their early teens, about 40% were in their late teens, and about 40% were over twenty.
2. Standard shifts were twelve hours long, including three breaks total-

---

18. See Kiyokawa (2009) for a discussion of the modernization of spinning technology in Japan, including comparisons with China and India.
19. Hunter (2008) provides an extensive review of the Japanese literature, and presents a critical, multi-faceted analysis of the working conditions for women in Japan's prewar textile industry.
20. Ministry of Agriculture and Commerce, Department of Commerce and Industry (1998).
21. The first volume in particular provides a detailed description of the educational backgrounds of workers at cotton spinning mills during this period, and shows that very few had graduated from ordinary school.
22. The "Conditions of Spinning Mill Workers" section in Sumiya (1970) largely duplicates the "Conditions of Cotton Spinning Mill Workers" section in *Conditions of Factory Workers*, but the former is far more critical of the conditions for female workers. See the "Commentary" by Sumiya.

ing one hour. Shifts began at 6:00 am and 6:00 pm.

3. The report states that it became common for women and girls to work overnight shifts because "the spinning industry was highly profitable, leading to the addition of nighttime work hours."

4. The practice of housing spinning mill workers in dormitories in large cities (with almost no workers commuting) began in the Echigo and Ecchu districts in the Kanto [eastern Japan] region, and in the Echizen, Kaga, Hiroshima, Sanuki, Awa, Tottori, and Hyōgo districts in the Kansai [western Japan] region. Hiring areas were prescribed for each factory, with, for example, the Tokyo Gas Spinning Company recruiting in the Echigo district and the Tenma Spinning Company recruiting in the Tottori district. Hiring areas for spinning mills in Osaka were prescribed at the municipal district level.

5. Employment contracts generally required the following:
   i.   An employment period of three to five years.
   ii. Assurance of no employment relationship with other currently operating mills.
   iii. A guarantee that that mill's confidential technologies would not be disclosed during employment.
   iv. Agreement to follow the mill's rules, both present and future.
   v.   Agreement that, barring exceptional circumstances, the worker could not terminate employment.
   vi. Acknowledgement that the mill could terminate employment at its discretion, for any reason and without prior notification.
   vii. Acknowledgement that failure to abide by mill rules or the conditions of the employment contract could result in reduced wages or forfeiture of unpaid wages or savings.

As the above contract requirements show, there was a clear imbalance of power in the worker–employer relationship. This raises the question of how long laborers could bear working under such circumstances. Table 3 shows length of service at three spinning companies in Osaka as of 1900.

The state of the "lower class"

Yokoyama's *Lower Class Society in Japan* is also frequently cited as a source of information on working conditions at the time. Originally from Toyama prefecture, Yokoyama left the Toyama Ordinary Junior High School to study law in Tokyo, after which he began working as a journalist for the *Mainichi Shimbun* newspaper. He also contributed to the Ministry of Agriculture and Commerce investigation of factory working conditions, discussed above. *Lower Class Society in Japan* is a detailed, well-reported account

Table 3. Lenght of service of factory workers in October 1900

Company	Osaka		Settsu		Tenma	
	Men	Women	Men	Women	Men	Women
Less than 1 yr.	253	710	146	989	88	417
Less than 2 yrs.	150	621	312	585	59	278
Less than 3 yrs.	119	480	260	480	31	139
Less than 4 yrs.	106	376	51	338	0	94
Less than 5 yrs.	70	209	35	115	59	141
Less than 7 yrs.	26	18	19	33	22	35
Less than 10 yrs.	24	13	0	0	5	13
More than 10 yrs.	26	16	0	0	0	0
Total	774	2,443	823	2,540	264	1,117

Source: Textile Federation reports (Sumiya (1970)).

of his travels in Tokyo, Osaka, Kobe, Kiryu, Ashikaga, and Maebashi, during which he observed the lifestyles and labor of farmers and factory workers in the general merchandise, textile, silk, and spinning industries.

An earlier work of equally high quality was Hosoi Wakizō's *Jokō aishi* (The Tragic History of Female Factory Workers), an account of female workers in the spinning industry during the latter half of the Taishō period.[23] Hosoi left school at age thirteen, during his fifth year at an ordinary elementary school, and took a job as a junior weaver. For the next fifteen years, until 1923, he worked at textile mills including the Kanegafuchi Spinning Company (Kanebo) and the Toyo Muslin Kameido Factory. His book is based on these experiences. It is today considered a classic work describing the lives of female laborers in Japan's spinning and textile (but not silk) industries in the 1920s.

The Tragic History begins with an account of the difficulties that factories had in finding female laborers following the First Sino-Japanese War, which led to mills competing for workers and establishing systems of forced remittance of salaries to male family members. It also describes how this "era of free competition" for female workers led managers at large spinning mills to improve conditions in an effort to improve worker retention. Factories began to set up clinics that provided free health care and medicine to dormitory-housed workers, and offered services to commuting workers and their families at below market prices. The book even praises the Kanebo Company for providing in-home health services for its workers. Factory daycare and kindergartens were provided nearly free of charge for those living in company housing. Many factories also established systems to aid workers in difficult situations.

The Tragic History has frequently been used in Japan to back up arguments

23. Hosoi (1980).

that female employees were poorly treated in the past. However, in any country where rapid industrialization occurs, examples abound of children and women being misused as a labor force. As I argue in this book, the textile industry played a key role in Japan's industrialization, and women made that possible. Comparing the sweat and tears of the textile workers described in *The Tragic History* with the conditions at English factories that Marx decries in *Das Kapital*, it is hard to say which was more dehumanizing. Perhaps the only honest answer is that they were equally bad.

In most cases, female spinning-mill workers are described as young, unmarried women from farming villages who are forced to work long hours for low wages to support their poor families. However, it is important to put the lives of these women into the context of conditions for other factory workers in Japan at the time.[24] Debates over Japan's Factory Law pointed out that all industrial workers at the time — both men and women — were working long hours for low wages. Not until the early Shōwa period (1926–1989) could a male head-of-household who worked at a factory earn sufficient wages to support his family.[25]

Even so, *The Tragic History* leaves readers with several overall impressions. One is that working conditions were improving. The book describes harsh restrictions on the freedom of boarded workers, such as limitations on leaving the factory premises, rules about what workers could eat or read, and censoring of private communications. The Omi Kenshi Dispute of 1954 demonstrates that such problems persisted to some extent even after World War II. As we have seen, however, the increasing difficulty of retaining female workers resulted in factories not only raising wages and paying increasingly large end-of-contract bonuses, but also improving welfare facilities. In the nineteen years between 1903 and 1921, the average daily wage at spinning mills increased from 36.8 to 149.2 sen for men and 23.5 to 114.6 sen for women, a four- to five-fold increase.[26] Commodity prices are estimated to have increased by 250% during this period, so by a simple calculation this represents a doubling of real wages.

Little reliable data exists regarding changes in the educational background of factory workers, but some fragmented records are available. Table 4 presents the results of an Osaka Board of Education survey conducted in November 1897 on the educational background of spinning and textile mill workers. In both cases, approximately 70 to 80% of workers were

---

24. Iijima (1949).
25. Chimoto (1998b).
26. Hosoi (1980, pp. 139–140).

Table 4. Educational level of factory workers in 1897

		Uneducated	Some education	Graduated ordinary school	Total
Spinning (7 factories)	Men	757 (7%)	1,520 (13%)	403 (4%)	11,142 (100%)
	Women	3,427 (31%)	4,313 39(%)	722 (6%)	
Textile (4 factories)	Men	61 (3%)	192 (10%)	99 (5%)	1,831 (100%)
	Women	726 (40%)	687 (38%)	66 (4%)	
(Reference) Letterpress	Men	6 (5.5%)	14 (13%)	74 (68%)	109 (100%)
	Women	6 (5.5%)	9 (8%)	–	

Source: Osaka Board of Education (Sumiya (1970)).

Table 5. Educational background of spinning mill employees in the mid-1920s

Educational backgroun	Men		Women	
	Number	%	Number	%
Did not complete compulsory education	220	15.5	3,000	41.6
Completed compulsory education	480	33.9	2,640	36.6
Did not complete elementary school	155	10.9	81	1.1
Completed elementary school	274	19.3	79	1.1
Entered junior high school or above	43	3.1	5	0.1
No schooling	245	17.3	1,405	19.5
Total	1,417	100.0	7,210	100.0

Source: Hosoi (1925).

either wholly uneducated or had not graduated from elementary school. For comparison, the table also presents data for the letterpress printing industry, where nearly 70% of workers had graduated elementary school.

Table 5 shows data collected by Hosoi from two or three factories, allowing comparison of the educational background of the workers investigated in *Conditions of Factory Workers* with those in the subsequent generation (the 1920s) described in *The Tragic History*. Educational attainment improved significantly during this single generation, particularly for female workers, with 80% having graduated from elementary school by the 1920s.

Female factory workers and corporate education

The most important form of corporate education for female factory workers in the 1920s was private elementary schools established within large spinning mills. These schools provided education for young women who had not yet completed compulsory education, and taught the same curriculum as public schools. Study materials such as textbooks were provided without charge. Instruction lasted for two hours in the morning (for night workers) or evening (for daytime workers), after work shifts were completed. Workers were required to complete the ordinary elementary school curriculum. Some factories also established high schools for girls, which taught subjects including sewing, flower arrangement, tea ceremony, etiquette, cooking, dyeing, artificial flower craftwork, embroidery, kimono care, and dance.

Male factory workers were taught Japanese language, mathematics, and other preparatory subjects, with a focus on spinning and mechanical techniques. Some mills, such as Kanebo and Toyo Muslin, established institutions that provided the equivalent of a junior high school education. *The Tragic History* explains that these schools "provided further technical education for leaders arising from the factory floor and improved the level of education in factories; they thus played a dual role in both providing industry with workers and improving education levels by providing training for graduated youth through practical experience."[27]

The preceding discussion has described the treatment of factory laborers in Japan from the end of the nineteenth century through the 1920s, with an emphasis on the female workers in the spinning and silk industries who greatly supported Japan's industrialization. The recruitment methods for female factory workers and the welfare facilities that factories established became a model for future Japanese industries. During this period, many other new and existing industries, including machinery, shipbuilding, clocks, glass, tiles, pharmaceuticals, and sundry goods such as matches and brushes, were also expanding. Even so, the textile industry was disproportionately large in terms of the employment opportunities it provided, and the scale and productivity of this industry was without question the primary engine behind Japan's industrialization. The labor of young women was the foundation of the textile factories. It is thus interesting to consider the process by which the spinning industry transitioned from employing commuting workers to lodging workers, and how spinning companies improved dormitories and other labor and living conditions in an effort to address labor shortages. The eventual result was the emergence of internal education and training systems for fostering experienced female workers, not unlike apprenticeship systems.[28]

Kurashiki Spinning Works president Ōhara Magosaburō provides an interesting example of how welfare standards were raised for female workers in the textiles industry. Ōhara was highly acclaimed for implementing

---

27. Hosoi (1980, p. 27).
28. Chimoto (1999).

many innovative reforms, including abolishing "lodging systems" that largely amounted to indentured labor, introducing personnel divisions responsible for the hiring and allocation of workers, establishing elementary schools for the education of young workers, and building distributed worker dormitories and company-operated cafeterias and general stores.[29]

The July 1919 issue of the critical journal *Kaizo* listed the results of a poll asking "Who should be dispatched from Japan to the Commission on International Labour Legislation?" This referred to the first such meeting, held in November 1919 in Washington, D.C. as dictated by the Paris Peace Conference that followed the end of World War I. The poll aimed to gather recommendations from various industries as to who should represent the government, employers, and laborers at this meeting. Alongside nominations of notable figures such as Yosano Akiko, Yamakawa Hitoshi, Minobe Tatsukichi, and Uchida Roan were the names of unknown male and female factory worker representatives from Kanebo, as well as from the glassworking and machine finishing industries.

The economist Fukuda Tokuzō, an active public speaker at the time, asserted that only Kanebo's Mutō Sanji or Kurashiki Spinning's Ōhara Magosaburō could represent the capitalists, and wrote a long recommendation for them. Ōhara in particular was described as having a high degree of understanding of workers' issues at the time.

Ōhara was eager to improve the working and living conditions of laborers even before he became president of Kurashiki Spinning, and worked to abolish lodging systems during this period. He asserted that improving working conditions would increase productivity while benefitting both employers and employees, and believed there was a need for scientific investigation into where the point of mutual benefit was.

Such ideas are considered common sense today, but the influence of Marxist thought, which denied any possibility of mutual benefit between workers and employers, made them incomprehensible to many. Current labor economic theory posits the "efficiency wage hypothesis," which states that while good working conditions and high wages increase the cost of labor, they also improve worker productivity, and that when the latter effect exceeds the former there is an overall benefit. Ōhara believed in the importance of returning that benefit to society.

These ideals led him to found the Ōhara Institute for Social Research and

---

29. See Ōhara Magosaburō Biography Publishing Committee (1983) and Kaneda (2012) for biographies of Ōhara Magosaburō. See Inoki (2006) for an overview of Ōhara as an administrator.

its Kurashiki Institute for Science of Labour. Tokyo Imperial University professor of economics Takano Iwasaburō (brother of pioneering Meiji-period labor union activist Takano Fusatarō) was invited to direct the Institute, a situation made possible because he had left his university over the issue of who to send to the Commission on International Labour Legislation. The Institute attained fame through its investigative research on labor issues, but later was decried as a "den of leftist scholars." Despite this, Ōhara did not interfere with Takano's operation and management of the Institute.

Ōhara also established the Kurashiki Institute for the Science of Labour, and entrusted Teruoka Gitō to lead it. The institute performed critical research on the American scientific management methods of Frederick Taylor and provided important results related to community health and the physiology and psychology of labor.[30]

The birth of labor unions

The industrialization of Japan was not as rapid as that of Southeast Asia today, but it nevertheless resulted in significant social change. Overreaching and cutting corners are inherent to rapid change, and labor–management relations are no exception. In the case of mining, an important export industry in Meiji Japan, workers had been demonstrating and rioting over poor labor conditions since the 1870s.[31] The Takashima Mines in Nagasaki are a representative example, having experienced multiple large conflicts.

At the time, mines generally implemented a contracting system called "boarding," in which the company itself did not directly manage labor, but instead delegated worker recruitment, work supervision, and lifestyle management to a contracted individual called the "boarding leader." In 1897, coal miners at the Takashima Mine went on strike to protest their treat-

---

30. Despite the many reforms in this period, there remained much room for improvement. Between the late Taishō and early Shōwa periods, *Rōdō kagaku* (Labor Science), the official publication of the Kurashiki Institute for the Science of Labour, published a series of papers by Japanese industrial psychology pioneer Kirihara Shigemi on "menstruation and worker ability," and during World War II these papers were compiled into a book of the same title (Toyo Shokan, 1943). The papers debated whether, with sufficient mental training and development, women could provide labor equivalent to men, and suggested the impracticality of attempts to leverage "inherent" female labor capacity. See Katayama (2012, pp. 315–323).

31. It is difficult for those living today to imagine the harsh conditions and frequency of accidents in the coal and metal mines of this time. According to chapter 10 of *Kōzan hensai* (Mining Accidents) (Ministry of Agriculture and Commerce Bureau of Mines, 1907), there were 6,281 cave-ins, explosions, and floods in 1906, resulting in 695 fatalities and 6,238 injuries. The Innai Mine Fire in January and the Nagasaki Takashima Coal Mine Gas Explosion in March of that year respectively resulted in 103 and 307 deaths.

ment by boarding leaders, long work hours, and low wages.

Coal was a primary Japanese export, and mining was a significant source of employment. According to Ministry of Agriculture and Commerce statistics, in 1901 there were 146,000 mine workers, of which 75,000 were coal miners. Working conditions were squalid and dangerous. Injuries were common, as were maladies such as gastrointestinal disease, respiratory disorders, trachoma, conjunctivitis, tuberculosis, and beriberi. Despite these conditions, wages were lower than in other industries.

Although labor unions were recognized under the "freedom of association" guarantee in the prewar Meiji Constitution, there were no laws establishing their legal status, so their legal positioning was unclear. Authorities were therefore extremely sensitive to the "disturbances of the peace" that often accompanied strikes, and overreacted in many cases.

Strikes were common not only in the mining industry but also in the textile and railroad industries and at military arsenals. For example, in March 1898 engineers and stokers at Nippon Railway (the first private railway in Japan, which today forms the JR Tohoku Line) launched a widespread strike over wages and demands for status recognition, stopping train service between Tokyo and Aomori. The strike succeeded in winning better worker treatment, and resulted in the creation of the Nippon Railway Kyōseikai, a labor union of approximately one thousand stokers, engineers, and other regular employees. This was a "closed shop" union organized solely within the Nippon Railways Company, with union membership a requirement for employment. (Other unions of the period, such as those for experienced steel and printing industry workers, were open to anyone in the relevant industry.) Nippon Railway Kyōseikai was a combative union, and was shut down in 1901 under the Public Order and Police Law of 1900, following claims that a union member had caused a train accident.

In the early twentieth century, protests became frequent at major heavy industry sites like artillery arsenals, shipyards, and naval arsenals. There is a common misconception, both within and outside of Japan, that Japanese labor–management relations have always been cooperative, and that unions have simply bowed to the will of companies. I would therefore like to examine the nature and severity of several of the particularly important protests that took place prior to World War II (I will discuss the postwar era in later chapters).

During the economic downturn that followed the Russo-Japanese War, labor disputes broke out frequently in the heavy industries. In February 1906, there was a major dispute at the Ishikawajima Shipyard, followed by incidents at the Kure Naval Arsenal and the Koishikawa Arsenal in August.

Table 6. Labor disputes following the Russo-Japanese War

Year	Number of disputes	Number of participants
1904	6	879
1905	19	5,013
1906	13	2,037
1907	57	9,855
1908	13	823
1909	11	310
1910–1916 avg.	50	5,740
1917	398	57,309
1918	417	66,457
1919	497	63,137

Source: *The History of Labor Movement in Japan*, vol. 10 (Labor Movement Data Committee, 1959, pp. 440-441).

The following year saw further disputes at Mitsubishi's Nagasaki Shipyard in February and at the Yokosuka Naval Arsenal from April through June. These were primarily the result of staff cuts and lowered wages due to the poor economy, but workers were also dissatisfied with corporate culture, including allegations of management bribe-taking.

In August 1912, Suzuki Bunji and fifteen companions formed the *Yūai-kai* (Friendly Society), a labor union in the spirit of a mutual aid society. The society's activities expanded steadily through World War I. With the Russian Revolution of 1917 and the rice riots of 1918, democratic and socialist ideals gained currency among workers. Protests increased in 1918 and 1919 (Table 6), and in 1919 the much enlarged Friendly Society renamed itself the *Dai-nippon Rōdō Sōdōmei Yūai-kai* (Japan General Federation of Labor, Friendly Society). During the 1920s, anarchist radicals like Ōsugi Sakae exerted a strong influence on labor union members, including those at the Shibaura Engineering Works, Ishikawajima Shipyard, Ikegai Ironworks, and Niigata Engineering Co., which led to the rapid development of highly militant union movements.

Intensified protest

The intensity of labor disputes continued to increase in the 1920s, during which time several dramatic incidents occurred. Asahara Kenzō's *Yōkoro no hi wa kietari* (Everlasting Fire at the Blast Furnace) (1930) describes a strike by 13,000 workers who left their jobs at the government-operated Yawata Steel Works to demand better treatment (inclusion of bonuses and allowances in base salaries, shortened work hours, etc.). The strike lasted for over one month.[32]

The largest strike in prewar Japan was the Kawasaki–Mitsubishi Kobe Shipyard Strike, which involved approximately 30,000 workers and lasted from 25 June until 9 August 1921. The strike took place in Kobe — Japan's largest industrial zone at the time — and involved collaboration between workers at three Kawasaki Shipyard factories and the three primary Mitsubishi companies who engaged in "factory management tactics" in pursuit of their rights to organize and bargain collectively. The companies responded with a lockout, and following violent confrontations with the police, strike organizers admitted defeat. As a result of the strike, the companies involved replaced full labor unions with a system of factory committees.

Similar factory committee systems had been established in the U.K. during World War I with the goal of improving labor–management relations in order to develop cooperative wartime production systems. In Japan, the growth of labor movements after World War I led government and business leaders to jointly establish the Kyōchōkai ["Cooperation and Harmony Society"], a private organization for investigating labor issues and promoting social policies.

There were two types of factory committees: "alliance-type" committees that cooperated with government officials and the Kyōchōkai to avoid confrontation whenever possible, and "council-type" committees that only included workers and did not allow the participation of company management.[33] In *The Tragic History of Female Factory Workers*, Hosoi wrote of the latter that "Current Japanese factory committees are famously powerless and worthless. About the only one worth mentioning is the Factory Council at Toyo Muslin's Azuma and Kameido factories."[34]

In 1927, female factory workers at the Dainippon Spinning Company's Hashiba Factory went on strike with the slogan "Free the caged birds!" On 12 June, a "banzai brigade" of approximately ten strikers broke into the factory and severed its power lines. The company responded with a lockout, and eventually confined over 2,800 female and 800 male workers to their dormitories.

The longest strike in prewar Japan occurred at the Noda Soy Sauce Company (now Kikkoman) over a period of 216 days between fall 1927 and April 1928.[35] Unrest first began in 1922, when 170 coopers involved in the fabrication of soy sauce brewing casks went on strike demanding that kickbacks to master coopers be abolished. This was followed by worker demands for higher wages and improved welfare and treatment, to which the company

---

32. Asahara (1930) contains some redacted text, but is a highly interesting resource describing 33 years of his life and the social and political background of his time.
33. Kaneko (2014).
34. Hosoi (1980, p. 391).
35. Noda Soy Sauce Company (1940).

responded with union-busting tactics such as switching to contracts with non-union carriers. In September 1927, all employees went on indefinite strike. The company fired striking workers and hired thugs and right-wing radicals to apply pressure, but in April 1928 it rehired 300 workers and reimbursed them some back pay. Notably, this strike was initiated over demands for organization and collective bargaining rights, but the agreement that ended the strike did not address these issues.

Japan's economy worsened further in the early Shōwa period, and bankruptcies, downsizing, and businesses closures increased concerns about employment. Few reliable employment statistics exist from this period, but the Social Affairs Department of the Home Ministry performed a nationwide survey in March 1930. Of the 6.9 million persons surveyed, approximately 315,000 reported not having a job, which by simple calculation suggests an unemployment rate of only 4.5%. Assuming an equivalent number were unemployed but not actively seeking a job, that raises the figure to 9%. Compared to unemployment rates of 20 to 30% in the U.S. and Germany at the time, Japan's situation was relatively good amidst a global depression. As if in response to this, labor movements started showing signs of losing momentum.

Nevertheless, major strikes did occur in 1930 at Fuji Gas Spinning Company's Kawasaki factory and at Kanegafuchi Spinning (Kanebo) Company factories. The Kanebo Company had considered a strike unlikely due to its "familistic management," but this proved untrue.[36] The direct cause of the strike was a 23% cut in non-salary compensation resulting from curtailed operations due to the poor economy. In April of that year, union members at the Yodogawa and Kyoto factories went on strike, soon followed by employees at Kanebo's main production facility in Hyogo, where all machines were stopped. The company stood firm, however, and twenty days later the strike ended with the labor representative apologizing to management. Among the approximately 36,000 workers at Kanebo's sixteen factories, only around 6,800 took part in the strike.

The strike at the Fuji Gas Spinning Company featured an unusual occurrence.[37] In November 1930, at the height of the strike, a member of the Kanagawa Combined Union expressed his support by staging an impromptu sit-in atop the 40-meter smokestack at Fuji's Kawasaki factory, taking with him a supply of food and a red flag. He spent five days, ten hours, and

---

36. See Okabe (2001) and Kawai (2005) regarding Mutō Sanji's ideals of "paternalistic" labor management.
37. See Hashimoto (1997) for a detailed account of this event.

twenty-two minutes in the sky before being brought down, covered in soot, following the company's capitulation in negotiations; Fuji had decided to act before the Emperor's train was scheduled to pass near the smokestack.

The economic situation was particularly dire in 1931, which was the prewar year with the largest number of strikes. The Great Depression had resulted in strikes not only at large companies in industries like spinning, coal, and urban transport, but also at medium-sized and small companies, including some in farming villages. Indeed, data from the time suggest that farming communities were more severely affected by the depression than industrialized areas. While general prices fell by less than 20% in 1930, the prices of agricultural products fell by between 40 and 60%. The silk industry, too, was severely affected: while a 60-kilogram bundle of silk sold for 1,330 yen in September 1929, the price had fallen to 540 yen by October of the following year. This placed extreme pressures on silkworm farmers, who made up approximately 40% of the 5.6 million farming families nationwide.

The labor strikes described above demonstrate the tenuous nature of labor–management relations in prewar Japan. Furthermore, historical fact shows that Japanese workers were not deferential to their employers, but instead united to assert their individual rights. History also shows that delays in government social policy and a lack of labor union laws subjected Japanese laborers to extremely competitive conditions. Japanese labor–management relations thus do not present an unbroken history of cooperation, nor could workers in the past expect government labor policies to protect them.

3. Skills and length of service

Traditional theories of economics and labor–management relations held that labor unions negatively affect productivity because they instigate labor disputes, and that unions distort resource allocation by demanding higher wages irrespective of market conditions. Over time, however, evidence began to emerge that unions sometimes increase productivity. Notably, labor unions provided a forum for workers to express dissatisfaction, which in turn lowered turnover (or, conversely stated, increased length of employment) and raised productivity. By contrast, economics textbooks typically assert that perfect labor mobility (the ability for workers to move at any time to areas of high marginal productivity) promotes the equalization of marginal productivity and minimization of costs, and is therefore a necessary condition for profit maximization. On the surface, then, it would seem that lowering worker turnover should not increase productivity, because it increases the number of immobile workers.[38]

Nevertheless, improving employee retention rates has been a top concern of management since the earliest periods of industrialization. When Japan was developing its heavy industries during World War I, the lack of workers, and particularly experienced workers, was a serious problem. This shortage intensified worker poaching between companies, prompting firms to take whatever measures they could to reduce worker mobility. This often took the form of newly created or resurrected systems for retirement and welfare benefits that improved with length of service. Laborers in turn came to recognize the importance of staying at one company due to the opportunities for skill development doing so provided. It was therefore clear to all involved that the experience gained through continuous employment at one company had long-term benefits for both workers and management.

Adverse effects of labor mobility

The economy greatly affects worker mobility and retention rates. Generally speaking, a strong economy bolsters the labor market and increases transfer rates, while a weak economy lowers the demand for labor and decreases transfer rates. When considering labor statistics, it is therefore important to consider the economic conditions when they were obtained. In the following section, I use a range of statistics to examine employee turnover rates in Japan between the two world wars.[39]

Japan is sometimes assumed to have always had lifetime employment due to its feudal history or the value its culture places on loyalty, but the discussion below demonstrates just how far that popular belief is from the reality of the labor market in the 1920s.

High employee turnover

The Survey on Length of Service[40] provides data for 1927, a year of financial crisis and growing social unease in which workers likely had difficulty transferring to better jobs. Even so, this survey indicates a relatively high turnover rate of three percent per month at twenty-three machinery factories. Because this is a monthly average, it equates to approximately one in

---

38. Freeman and Medoff (1979) first examined labor unions and worker mobility from the perspective of productivity. See Muramatsu (1984) and Tomita (1993) for empirical research related to the situation in Japan.
39. The following is based on Inoki (1998).
40. Osaka Municipal Central Employment Agency (1927).

three workers relocating in a one-year span. Awareness was growing that for employers, such high turnover rates meant increased expenditures on worker recruitment and training, and for workers, they meant disruptions in daily life and training, lowered wages, and an increased risk of industrial accidents. This caused employers to take a heightened interest in company policies that would lengthen terms of employment, such as adjusting wages according to length of service, giving retirement bonuses, and providing education in order to improve workers' mental and physical well-being and stabilize their daily lives.

The Survey on Length of Service targeted all workers who had found positions through the Osaka Municipal Central Employment Agency. We must therefore take into account the facts that respondents had all found jobs through an employment agency, and the agency itself had only been established seven or eight years prior to the survey. However, data from the first survey in 1925 shows that only 4% of the approximately 120,000 respondents were working for the same employer they had worked for eight years prior. The mining industry had the highest retention rates (40%), but rates in the commercial and miscellaneous sectors were as low as 20%. Approximately 95,000 persons had changed jobs, accounting for 75% of the total.

Unemployment among factory workers

Shokkō eizoku-saku ronshū (Essays on Long-term Employment Policy), edited by Uno Riemon, an important figure in industrial education, provides statistics from a few years earlier.[41] In the introduction, Uno insists that while significant attention had been paid to unemployment following World War I, the true problem was worker retention at factories, and the fact that workers did not become attached to any one company. "Japanese workers lose their jobs when they only serve as temporary labor. Were they to remain in place long enough to master a skill, they would not so easily become unemployed," he writes. He goes on to state that most unemployed people at the time were unskilled workers; companies did not fire skilled workers even when conditions forced them to close factories, preferring to continue paying them wages even when there was nothing for them to do.

The *Essays* suggested that failure to promote long-term employment hindered skill formation, and some form of preferential treatment based on years of service was needed to improve worker retention. The process by

---

41. Uno (1920).

which Japanese companies developed such systems is an important topic. Later in this chapter, we consider one aspect of these systems: retirement bonuses.

Short employment periods

Let us next consider the length of employment in a few important industries between 1924 and 1927, as presented in the "Working Conditions by Occupation" report.[42] This data does not come from employment agencies, but rather from individual companies, so disparities between industries may exist. Other problems with this report include uncertainty regarding the number of companies surveyed and the sampling methods used, but the information nevertheless provides a broad picture of conditions at the time.

The average length of employment in the chemical industry was only three years. The machinery industry was somewhat better, at five years. The report states, "Normally, cohesion among workers in large machinery factories is strong, with some form of organization or union present. Small factories also tend to have special relationships between workers and owners, somewhat reducing the mobility rate of experienced workers." This supports the above supposition that unions lower employee turnover.

Ship and vehicle manufacturing factories had the longest employment terms among factories in the machinery industry, at over nine years. Among shipbuilding factories, well-established naval arsenals had particularly long average employment terms of twelve years. Many ship and vehicle factories already had systems in place for promoting long-term employment, with bonuses paid each year following the fifth full year of employment, and retirement benefits that increased with the number of years served.

Finally, I would like to touch upon the situation in the silk and spinning industries, which employed many women. Reports by placement offices indicate that in 1920, 23 silk factories employed 10,433 women as silk reelers and another 1,232 as re-reelers. The data for spinning factories is from 1928 and uses only a single-digit sample size, making direct comparison difficult, but the average for male workers and commuting female workers was about six to seven years. In contrast, practices promoting stable employment started to become prevalent in the silk industry in the 1920s, and there seems to have been recognition that length of service and employee turnover rates were much better than in the spinning industry.

Policies to promote long-term employment included monetary and commodity rewards, wage increases, vacation time, and severance pay benefits

---

42. Osaka Municipal Central Employment Agency (1924–1927).

that increased with the length of service, but the main policy impacting worker retention was retirement allowances. In a May 1932 report titled "The Status of Retirement Allowances,"[43] Machida Tatsujirō represents his co-authors in stating that while retirement allowances are used for a variety of incentives, their primary function is to serve as a special form of salary that promotes skill development and stabilizes length of employment.

Such measures seem to have paid off in terms of lowering employee turnover. This was demonstrated during the period of economic recovery that started in 1933, when employee turnover rates at large companies remained low despite renewed labor shortages due to growth of the heavy chemicals industry.[44] The high retention rates likely contributed greatly to the improvement of skills in companies and factories.

4. Research & development and engineers

The previous section considered the role of long-term employment in improving job skills, but research and development occurring far from the factory floor also had significant indirect and long-term impacts on productivity. The pursuit and application of industrial science is deeply connected with industry growth. This section reviews how universities, other institutes of higher learning, and research laboratories developed systems for advancing science in Japan, how the nation supported these systems financially, and how private firms contributed to the process.[45]

Hara Takashi and the University Ordinance

The end of World War I in 1918 boosted Japan's economy and led to major changes in its university system. The Terauchi cabinet resigned in the aftermath of the rice riots of the summer of 1918, and Hara Takashi formed the first cabinet led by a party politician (Hara was the first Japanese Prime Minister to hold a seat in the House of Representatives without a noble title). Rapid industrialization was making the need for widespread education painfully clear, and the Hara cabinet issued policy statements promoting education, together with national defense, industry, and transportation infrastructure. The cabinet also implemented more specific measures, including the University Order and a revision to the Higher School Order, a plan for the establishment and expansion of higher schools, and policies

---

43. Kyōchōkai Department of Labor (1932, pp. 1–3).
44. Odaka (1984, p. 205).
45. Sawai (2015) describes the contributions of engineers between and after the world wars, along with an analysis of the political and economic conditions of the time.

to expand large institutions of higher education.[46]

As economic conditions improved after the war, the number of students hoping to continue their studies rose alongside industry demand for workers. As a result, the government allocated 44.5 million yen to increase the number of departments at the Imperial University, build new academic, vocational, and commercial high schools, and convert medical schools into full universities.

Twenty-two new private universities were founded during the Taishō period alone. Private universities licensed in 1920 include Keio University, Waseda University, Meiji University, Hosei University, Chuo University, Nihon University, Kokugakuin University, and Doshisha University — all of which existed previously as vocational schools or institutions of higher learning with well-established histories that already bore the "university" appellation. In the nearly twenty years from this time until the start of the Pacific War, the number of schools for higher education increased 250%, and the number of students pursuing higher education increased 370%. During this period, the reorganization of colleges specializing in a single field resulted in the founding of the Tokyo University of Commerce in 1920, Kobe Commercial University, the Tokyo Institute of Technology, the Osaka Institute of Technology, the Tokyo University of Literature and Science, and the Hiroshima University of Literature and Science in 1929, and medical universities in Niigata, Okayama, Chiba, Kanazawa, and Nagasaki. Public universities founded in this period include prefectural medical universities in Osaka (1919), Aichi (1920), Kyoto (1921), and Kumamoto (1922), and the Osaka University of Commerce (1928).

Challenges for university graduates

The Great Depression hit Japan in earnest in 1930, causing severe job displacement. The growing number of individuals with higher education did not escape this trend; the number of jobs for college graduates declined sharply, and according to some sources even disappeared entirely. The *Tokyo Asahi* newspaper reported that of approximately 2,000 students who graduated from Tokyo Imperial University in March 1929, only around 30% were employed in 1930.

College graduates had already begun encountering serious difficulties in finding jobs in 1927 and 1928. Ozu Yasujiro's movie *I Graduated, But...*,

---

46. See volume 1, chapter 2 of Amano (2013) for details of the "Plan for the Establishment and Expansion of Higher Schools." Both volumes of this work provide exemplary research on the history of higher education in Japan.

released in April 1929, is often cited as evidence that this problem predated the Great Depression.[47] In one scene, the newly graduated protagonist visits a tailor for a fitting. He shows the tailor his diploma, and wryly laughs about how he had spent all his time since the age of eight taking test after test just to obtain this piece of paper. But even after getting his new suit and a letter of recommendation, none of the companies he applies to have a job for him. In the end, it is the dedication of his wife that encourages him to persist in his job hunt until he finds employment.[48] The film depicts not only the powerlessness we feel when unemployed, but also, as the title suggests, an ironically comical view of the low value of a college degree. In actuality, however, the conditions at the time were quite serious, and led to increased social unease and dissatisfaction among Japan's intelligentsia.

Junior high school admissions also declined markedly at this time. Junior high school was seen as no more than a bridge to more advanced studies; a junior high school diploma itself was viewed as lacking any economic value. Parents therefore concluded that if their children were going to continue with education beyond primary school, learning a trade would provide more economic benefits. Attendance at vocational and normal schools greatly increased as a result.

A newspaper report[49] on a 1930 survey by the Social Affairs Department of the Home Ministry presents several relevant figures. As of May 1, employment rates were 9.2% for college graduates, 14% for junior college graduates, and 23.4% for junior high school graduates. There were 6,939 applicants for jobs at banks with over one million yen in capital, of which only 745 were hired. Similarly, only 716 of 4,432 junior college graduates were hired, and 1,343 of 5,051 junior high graduates. It is difficult to interpret these numbers, but — with regards to the banking industry at least — it is evident that there were many college graduates and not many jobs for them. The opening of an "employment agency for the educated classes" in Tokyo provides further evidence of this situation.

As we will see later, universities expanded again in the 1960s, when Japan's economy was experiencing accelerated growth and once again suffering a shortage of engineers. In 1957, the Ministry of Education drew up plans for supplying industry with much-needed engineers by attracting

---

47. Only around 10 minutes of this movie remain, so its full content can only be surmised from its script.
48. Film Arts Company (1982). Ozu went on to produce other films addressing problems related to attending university and establishing a career, such as *I Flunked Out of School, But...* (1930), *University is a Fine Place* (1936), and *Only Son* (1936).
49. *Asahi Shimbun* newspaper, 11 June 1930.

Table 7. Postwar college and university advancement rates (including prospective students studying for exams)   (%)

Year	Total	Men	Women
1955	10.1	15.0	5.0
1965	17.0	22.4	11.3
1975	37.8	43.0	32.4
1985	37.6	40.6	34.5
1990	36.3	35.2	37.4
2000	49.1	49.4	48.7

Source: Ministry of Education, Science and Culture (various issues).

more students to science and engineering programs beginning in 1961. When the first generation of baby boomers started entering higher education around 1965, the number of students studying at this level increased greatly (Table 7). Private universities continued to increase their capacity to accommodate this influx, to the point where talk arose of "higher education inflation."

Advances in science and technology

As described above, prior to World War II Japan experienced an over-supply (or premature expansion) of individuals with higher degrees in relation to the demands of industry. It is therefore interesting to consider the situation in research laboratories, which were the primary entities for scientific and technological research. Practical applications are neither necessary nor sufficient conditions for spurring scientific research. Following World War I, however, countries around the world came to recognize that technological research was critical to national military strength and economic power. Chemical products in particular had increasingly come to determine military strength. In Japan, the Special Nitrogen Research Laboratory was established in 1918 and later combined with the Tokyo Industrial Laboratory. The Army Institute of Science and Technology and the Naval Technology Laboratory were established in 1919 and 1923, respectively.

In 1829, long before these laboratories were established, Fukuzawa Yukichi donated land to found the Institute for Infectious Diseases in Tokyo's Shiba Park. He was motivated by his interest in promoting the medical sciences, and his desire to support the research of Morimura Ichizaemon, Nagayo Sensai, and Kitasato Shibasaburō, the last of whom had just returned to Japan after producing excellent research results under the guidance of Robert Koch at the University of Berlin.[50] Fukuzawa considered supporting academic research to be part of his job as a journalist and

---

50. See Fukuda (2008) for a recent biography of Kitasato.

intellectual. Two years later the Institute for Infectious Diseases borrowed land from the Ministry of Home Affairs, to which it now belonged, and moved to the Atago district in Tokyo's Shiba ward.

The Institute produced world-class research by scientists such as Shiga Kiyoshi and Noguchi Hideyo, and in 1899 was converted into the National Institute of Infectious Diseases under the Ministry of Home Affairs (in 1967 it became the Institute of Medical Science at the University of Tokyo). In 1902, however, the Institute came into conflict with researchers at Tokyo University over the detection of cholera bacteria, and this expanded into a conflict between the Ministry of Education and the Ministry of Home Affairs. In 1914, the Institute was transferred without consultation to the Ministry of Education as an organizational part of the University of Tokyo. Upon hearing this, the Institute's director Kitasato Shibasaburō turned in his resignation, as did many sympathetic researchers and laboratory staff. Kitasato and his former coworkers then founded the Kitasato Institute.[51]

This highly publicized dispute was not just a conflict between individuals, but a sign of fierce confrontation within the government regarding whether academic research should be conducted by public or private entities. The debate rested on further disagreements regarding academic authoritarianism and the struggle between authority and freedom of research.

In 1917, at the suggestion of Shibusawa Eiichi and Takamine Jōkichi, the Institute of Physical and Chemical Research (RIKEN) was founded as a semi-private research institute supported by donations from the Imperial Household, the government, and private sources. It was the largest facility of its type in prewar Japan, and performed the highest levels of research. Young scientists such as Yukawa Hideki and Tomonaga Shin'ichirō came to RIKEN to study under Japan's top researchers of the day, including Nagaoka Hantarō, Honda Kōtarō, Suzuki Umetarō, and Nishina Yoshio. At its peak, RIKEN comprised 33 laboratories and around 1,800 researchers. It was organized into individual laboratories, some of which were headed by faculty at the Imperial University. Laboratory heads controlled budgets and personnel, and could freely determine their own research goals, creating what some called a "scientist's paradise." This did not protect laboratories from financial difficulties, however, so third-generation Institute director Ōkochi Masatoshi established the RIKEN Kogyo Company, which converted

---

51. This dispute with the School of Medicine at Kitasato's alma mater of Tokyo Imperial University arose from criticism of a theory by that school's Ogata Masanori regarding a microbial origin of beriberi, and is said to have limited Kitasato's research opportunities after returning to Japan. This dispute also likely influenced Fukuzawa's support of Kitasato.

RIKEN discoveries into industrial applications and used income from patent licensing fees to financially support research. Ōkochi also developed many other RIKEN-affiliated organizations, eventually turning it into a mammoth research conglomerate comprising 66 companies and 121 factories.[52]

Many other laboratories were also founded at this time, including the Iron and Steel Institute at Tohoku Imperial University (1919) and the Aviation Research Institute (1921) and Earthquake Research Institute (1925) at Tokyo Imperial University. These institutions, too, were home to exceptional scientists and promoted organizational research.

The most outstanding research at the time did not always come from elite technologists in university engineering departments, however. One famous example is the development of the Mitsubishi Zero fighter plane. This project was headed by Horikoshi Jiro, a young engineer at the Mitsubishi Internal Combustion Engine Company and a graduate of the Aviation Laboratory in Tokyo Imperial University's Engineering Department. While he had spent some time researching aircraft fuselages at companies such as Junkers in Germany and Curtiss in the U.S., part of the reason why he was provided a position as lead designer at such a young age was that few researchers at the time specialized in aeronautical engineering, and the aeronautical industry itself had only just begun engaging in independent research. Against this background, the young Horikoshi undertook the challenge of developing the Zero with a team of inexperienced assistants who were not even college graduates. They succeeded in producing the most technologically advanced fighter plane available at the start of World War II.

Japan was not the only country where scientific and technical innovation was coming from sources other than highly educated researchers at universities or research facilities. For example, the English scientist Michael Faraday started out life as a bookbinding apprentice with little formal schooling, yet made great contributions to our understanding of electromagnetism and electrochemistry. Fellow Englishman Henry Bessemer learned metallurgy while working at his father's metal processing plant and went on to develop innovative methods for refining steel. Even Thomas Edison was uncomfortable with school education and started his career at seventeen years old as a nighttime telegraph operator at a Canadian train station.[53]

Sawai Minoru's *Systems of Research and Development in Modern Japan*

---

52. See Saitō (1987, 2009) for exemplary research on the industrial face of RIKEN. Miyata (1983) describes RIKEN before World War II.

53. See Amano (2005) for an analysis of the relation between academic background and academic achievements.

is an extensive treatment of how research was performed in Japan before, during, and after World War II. It provides details on how university engineering departments and specialized industrial schools produced researchers, and describes the research programs at laboratories in public and private mining concerns and army and navy research programs, as well as national policies for promoting science and technology. Sawai's impressive research also demonstrates through case studies such as that of the optics industry how military technologies originally developed by the army and navy during World War II were transferred to the public sector in the 1950s.[54]

Think tanks

Think tanks also performed research, but they had different characteristics from the scientific and engineering institutes described above. Think tanks rely not on large-scale industrial equipment but rather on brainpower (and, in recent years, computer power) to develop national and corporate strategy. The first think tanks arose in the late nineteenth century and included Edison's Menlo Park, the Franklin Institute, and Arthur D. Little.

In Japan, the Manchuria Railway Research Department was an early think tank that conducted pioneering research on national policy in Japan. Its parent company, the South Manchuria Railway Company, was founded in 1906, the year following Japan's victory in the Russo-Japanese war, with Goto Shinpei as its first president. It officially opened in 1907 when its headquarters relocated from Tokyo to Dalian, and the research division was established in the same year. Following the Russian Revolution in 1917, the research division became a think tank that functioned like an "economic GHQ" for the nation.[55] Far beyond functioning simply as a research organization, it played important roles in proposing and implementing national policy, and was the center of Russian studies research and Japan's advance into East Asia. Following Japan's defeat in World War II, Manchuria Railway Research Department staff became academic researchers or social activists. Their influence on postwar Japanese thought is exemplified in the research of Kobayashi Hideo.[56]

The Mitsubishi Economic Research Institute, another think tank, was

---

54. Sawai (2012).
55. See Kobayashi (2005). Note that the new paperback edition (2015, Kodansha Gakujutsu Bunko) contains supplementary information regarding the company's pre- and post-WWII history. See Yamada (1977) for a complete history of the Manchuria Railway Research Department.
56. Kobayashi (2005), chapter 5.

Table 8. Primary sources of funding for research organizations   (%)

Year	Private firm	Public organization	University
1970	60.7	12.3	27.0
1980	59.9	14.6	25.5
1990	70.9	11.6	17.6
2000	66.7	13.6	19.7

Source: Japan Management and Coordination Agency (various issues).

established in 1932. Other prewar private research organizations include the Shōwa Research Association (1933) and the East Asia Institute (1938), both of which performed research that influenced national policy, and the Ōhara Institute for Social Research (1919), which focused on social policy. The Shōwa Research Association, a brain trust headed by Konoe Fumimaro, was a large-scale policy research organization with various field-specific divisions. This organization resurfaced for a time in postwar Japan as the Shōwa Study Group.[57] The East Asia Institute was established as a think tank affiliated with the Cabinet Planning Board for the purpose of information gathering and research in preparation for the war with the U.S. and the U.K. It is noted for employing many leftist researchers who were denied work elsewhere due to suppression of free speech at the time. These researchers left a distinctive Marxist influence on social science research that continued to have an impact after the war ended.[58]

Following the war, not only think tanks but also research facilities for basic science gradually transitioned from public to private management. Many corporate research laboratories were founded, and as Table 8 shows, the level of research greatly improved as absolute and relative funding increased.

---

57. See valuable exchanges in the dialogue between Gotō Ryūnosuke and Sakai Saburō at the end of Sakai (1992), as well as the "Commentary" section by Itō Takashi.
58. Hara (1984).

The battleship *Yamato* under construction at the Kure Naval Arsenal.
(Photo: U.S. Naval Historical Center)

CHAPTER 3
THE MILITARY AND INDUSTRY

The military provides national defense and emergency response, while industry supports daily life. Given that one presumes the extreme circumstances of war or national emergency and the other the tranquility of peacetime, we might expect the two to have completely different methods of human resource selection and training. Yet in fact, they are deeply connected. The training methods used by the military are fundamentally similar to those of corporations, and the two compete for human resources within the same pool of candidates. The relationship between the two sectors is by necessity cooperative, due to the movement of employees — especially those with technical skills — back and forth between them; military technology often stimulates private innovation, and technicians serve as agents for that transfer. Furthermore, Japan spent nearly half of the fifty-year period from the Sino-Japanese War through the end of World War II engaged in warfare, so no discussion of human resource development in modern Japan would be complete without touching upon issues related to war and the military.

The previous chapter described how military arsenals that manufactured weapons used various methods to train engineers. This chapter begins with a discussion of how the prewar Japanese military recruited and promoted members of the armed forces, and of the broad opportunities and fierce competition that characterized the training process. I then outline how technology was exchanged between the military and industrial sectors, as well as the effects of technological research by the Imperial Army and Navy on Japanese industry. I conclude by considering how the military and warfare affected social mobility, a point that is particularly important with regard to prewar Japan due to the large number of students who received junior high school and high school educations as soldiers and sailors.

In simple quantitative terms, from the end of the First Sino–Japanese War (1895) through the end of the Meiji period (1912), the Imperial Japanese Army Academy admitted between 700 and 1,000 students per year, and the Imperial Navy Academy another 100 to 200. This represents a dramatic expansion accompanying the strengthened role of the military following victory in the Sino-Japanese War. By comparison, approximately 2,200 students entered high schools and technical schools annually during this time, so the ratio of students opting for a military education was quite significant.

This ratio tipped even further toward the military upon the start of the Pacific War. In 1944, the 59th class of the Army Academy boasted 2,850 students, and in 1942 over 1,000 students entered the Navy Academy, while approximately 6,000 students entered public high schools each year during this period. Enrollment further increased during World War II, with 4,700 Army Academy students and 7,800 Navy Academy students enrolled in 1945. The following section describes the institutional features that enabled such large numbers of students to receive military educations.

1. Selection and training methods of the Imperial Army and Navy[1]

The Imperial Army Cadet School, Academy, and College

The Imperial Army College was established in 1883 as an educational institution for the training of army staff and high-ranking officers. As compared to the highly technical curriculum of the Imperial Navy College, which was intended to "provide staff officers with basic knowledge," most subjects taught at the Army College were quite practical.[2] Required courses included general military tactics, fortress defense, naval tactics, military history, staff duties, foreign languages, and equestrian skills. Many courses focused on case studies, requiring students to consider what they would do as an officer under a given set of circumstances.

This systemization of military education through the Army College altered the leadership of the Imperial Army, which had previously been regionally dominated by a series of individuals from the old Chōshū domain — Yamagata Aritomo, Katsura Tarō, Terauchi Masatake, and Tanaka Giichi (similarly, the Navy was led by individuals from the Satsuma domain). However, academic performance mattered at the new Army College and Army Academy, and failure to perform well made it impossible to attain a position of power in the Imperial Army. The establishment of these educational systems therefore made human resource selection and development in the army more equitable, while also strengthening its bureaucratic elements.

Officer training in the army conformed to the following basic system. While there were some changes over time, the Imperial Army Cadet School generally accepted students between the ages of 13 and 15. For three years, they lived in dormitories while preparing for officer candidate studies at the Army College. At the end of the nineteenth century, there were six cadet

---

1. Basic information related to the Imperial Army and Navy in this section is based on Ōhama and Ozawa (1995).
2. Yamaguchi (2000) provides a detailed quantitative overview of the careers of generals, admirals, and "unorthodox officers" of the Imperial Army and Navy, along with a detailed comparative analysis.

schools (in Tokyo, Sendai, Nagoya, Osaka, Hiroshima, and Kumamoto), each of which generally accepted fifty students per year. The Imperial Army Cadet School in Tokyo, which had previously focused on language studies, was renamed the Imperial Army Central Cadet School, and in 1920 became a preparatory school providing two years of further study for graduates of the regional cadet schools (along with graduates of traditional junior high schools). Cadet schools began accepting increasing numbers of students around the start of the First Sino-Japanese War, and cadet school graduates came to comprise approximately one-third of regular army officers. The entrance exam consisted of a physical exam and tests covering topics from the curriculum of the first year of ordinary junior high school. Education following admittance had little military content and was very similar to education at standard junior high schools, with the exception of the availability of foreign language courses for languages other than English (English and Chinese were added at the start of the Shōwa period (1926–1989)).

The Imperial Army Academy was the next step up after the Cadet School. In 1887, the academy adopted a German-style cadet system in which students passing the entrance examinations began their studies after six months (for Cadet School graduates) or one year (for junior high school graduates) of working within an Army corps. The entrance exams covered the ordinary junior high school curriculum, and successful applicants received officer candidate education from age 18 to 23. The curriculum began with approximately two years of "preparatory" education at the Central Cadet School, followed by approximately two years of core studies at the Imperial Army Academy. The curriculum during preparatory studies was highly generic, combining elements of the humanities and science courses offered at high schools, the only difference being somewhat less time spent in classroom lectures. Even so, students advancing to artillery and engineering specializations received roughly the same academic grounding as general high school graduates.

Notably, students from the Cadet School generally graduated from the Army Academy with higher academic standing than did those from other schools, and this disparity in academic achievement came to have a large impact on Army personnel policies. In particular, establishment of the school system and selection by class standing led to a pecking order within the Army based on educational background. This likely arose around the turn of the twentieth century. In 1887 the Cadet Academy provided students who entered with the equivalent of an upper elementary school diploma the soldier's equivalent of an ordinary junior high school education, and the Army Academy accepted students with an ordinary junior high school diploma or equivalent academic ability, so there remained some commonality with Ministry of Education schools. Starting around the turn of the century, however, the "or equivalent academic ability" clause was dropped from the list of acceptable qualifications for admission. Furthermore, only Army Academy graduates could become commissioned officers, and noncommissioned officers such as sergeants generally could not be promoted to commissioned status (though this did happen at times, such as when noncommissioned officers were promoted to special-duty second lieutenants, lieutenants, and captains).[3]

This shift toward emphasis on academic achievement came approximately ten years later than a similar shift among civil servants, but Hirota makes the interesting observation that in the business world, increased emphasis on formal education came even later.[4] While various interpretations of this timeline are possible, it likely signifies that the military took to using examinations for officer selection sooner than private firms, because academic ability at the time was generally demonstrated through examinations.

In contrast to the Imperial Army, the Imperial Navy abandoned preparatory schools in 1888 when the Naval Academy was moved to Hiroshima prefecture. These schools had in effect been a form of welfare for the children of war dead, but there seems to have been concern that a premature focus on specialized education would adversely affect basic education, eventually resulting in deficiencies in common sense. Such sentiments are evident in the following harsh criticism of the Imperial Army, delivered by Diet member Takahashi Korekiyo during 1936 budget negotiations:

> The Imperial Army alone refuses to accept students who have received a junior high school education, which instills in them what the normal person would consider common sense, instead putting children straight out of elementary school into regional cadet academies that provide a peculiar education divorced from mainstream society... Only those having received this sanctioned education are allowed to lead the Army, and it is nothing less than a national disaster that such leaders lacking in common sense are allowed to involve themselves in political affairs.[5]

The problem was not the content of education at Army Cadet School per

---

3. See Nomura (2006) for details regarding how the Army Cadet Schools were established and attained their positions of privilege.
4. Hirota (1987).
5. Fujimura (1992, vol. 2, p. 184).

se, which as mentioned above was nearly the same as at normal schools, but the fact that cadet schools were "divorced from mainstream society." Presuming that Takahashi knew his comments would eventually be leaked to the mass media, he appears to have been quite fearless in his battle against the morass of political domination by an Army incapable of economic or social logic.

The Imperial Army College fostered top-level officers and staff. Lieutenants and second lieutenants with at least two years' experience in service were selected to learn advanced strategy and tactics and other necessary specialized knowledge such as the social sciences and foreign languages. Studies continued for three years during peacetime, but a shortage of staff officers shortened this to two years around the time of the Manchurian Incident (1931). Further cuts followed, until the course of studies was only six months for the class of 1945.

Momose makes the following interesting observation: The Army College allowed all Army Academy graduates to take its entrance exam, and "admission was determined not according to grades in the Academy, but based on the results of post-graduation studies and job performance following Army commission. There were many opportunities to take the exam." He adds that "This was quite a fair and reasonable method for the selection of the elite, and the education provided over the three years following acceptance made for a decisive gap in specialized abilities over the non-elite."[6] In other words, training institutions created a wall between the military elite (high-ranking officers) and non-elite, but there was fierce competition for the opportunities on either side of the wall.

The Imperial Navy Academy and the Imperial Navy College
The Imperial Navy eventually established an academy equivalent to the Imperial Army Academy.[7] A school providing a similar level of naval education had previously been opened in 1873, just after the Meiji Restoration, by British Admiral Sir Archibald L. Douglas and his staff of 34 faculty.[8] In 1893 the school was admitting boys between 16 and 19, and the course of

---

6. Momose (1990, pp. 335–337).
7. Shinjinbutsu Oraisha Military History Archives (1996) provides many personal accounts related to education at the Imperial Navy Academy.
8. As a predecessor to the Naval Academy, the Naval Training Center was established in Tokyo's Tsukiji district in 1869 and renamed as the Naval College the following year, after the completion of its student hall, which was considered the best in Asia at the time. In 1888, following a proposal by Deputy Director Commander Ijichi Koichi, it was relocated to Etajima, an island off the coast of Hiroshima. Today, the school's lecture hall serves as an educational facility for the Japan Self-Defense Forces.

study lasted 3 or 4 years, with the final year spent aboard a training ship. Admittance was based on an entrance examination and a physical exam, and the curriculum included academic subjects (foreign language, physics, geometry, chemistry, and law), ethics training, physical education, and knowledge necessary for future service as a naval officer, such as gunnery, operations, navigation, and the use of torpedoes and mines. In 1928, cruise training was extended by eight months and psychology, philosophy, law and economics, accounting, Japanese, Chinese, history, and geography were added to the curriculum. Students began studying either French or German in addition to English. So far as the curriculum indicates, the Naval Academy resembled the Army Academy in that its course of education was not too far removed from that of ordinary schools.

After attending the Naval Academy, students continued on to the Naval College to receive advanced military training. While the schooling policy was slightly different, the goal of the Naval College was still to foster naval officers and engineers. "First-class" students studied for two years as majors or captains, "engineering-class" students studied for two years as engineering captains or lieutenants, "specialty-class" students for one year as majors or captains, and "irregular-class" students studied for various periods depending on their specialization (foreign language, science and engineering, law and economy, education, military studies, etc.). "First-class" students were primarily groomed to become the naval elite.

Like the Army College, the Naval College taught map-based strategy exercises and military geography, but because the navy generally did not require strategic decisions based on land formations, over one-fifth of studies could be devoted to other subjects, such as international law, languages, and historical statistics. Each year a small number of students was selected for intensive studies, and upon graduation these students were assigned to important posts where they played a vital role in shaping naval policy and strategy.

Naval College graduates of course had an edge in being promoted, but this was not an absolute requirement. Frequently cited exceptions include Admiral Nomura Kichisaburō, Katō Hiroharu (commander-in-chief of the combined fleet and chief of staff of the Imperial Japanese Navy General Staff), Vice Admiral Ōnishi Takijirō (commander of the First Air Fleet and "father of the kamikaze"), and Vice Admiral Ōtani Koshirō (noted mine and torpedo tactician and commander-in-chief of the Kure Naval District), none of whom were Naval College graduates. Sanematsu provides the following comments about Ōtani:[9]

9. Sanematsu (1993, p. 108).

Ōtani frequently stated that graduating from the Naval College was a waste of time. In his *Secret History of the Shōwa Navy*, Fukuda Ryōzō suggests that this attitude likely had something to do with Ōtani becoming president of that school… Nakazawa Tasuku, the former director of the Ministry of the Navy Human Resources Department, said "College graduation was a consideration for that post. College graduates lasted a couple of years longer than did non-graduates."[10]

The Naval College admitted very few students. Its first four classes, starting in 1898, had ten or fewer students enrolled in the first-class (officer candidate) program, and enrollment grew slowly, with classes from 1907–1913 having 10 to 17 students, and classes from 1914 through 1933 having only slightly more than 20. Starting in 1934, enrollment was around 30 students.

According to Sanematsu, the course schedule for students entering the Naval College in December 1926 included the following subjects: leadership (10 hours), strategy (406 hours), tactics (580 hours), military service (215 hours), military history (245 hours), military politics (265 hours), and general curriculum such as language studies, lectures, etc. (280 hours).

Navy admiral and Ministry of the Navy Research Section Chief Takagi Sokichi recalls his time at the Naval College as follows: [11]

> Of the many officers and instructors there, Captain Teramoto Takeji's lectures on gunmanship and Captain Kurokawa Kai's on strategy were particularly memorable, as were Army Captain Tani Hisao's lectures on land tactics, due to his keen consideration of military history… Of course, there were poor instructors too. For example, I had heard that Dr. Uesugi Shinkichi was a brilliant scholar in constitutional theory, but to a student in his thirties, even one like myself who wasn't a law specialist, he used ridiculous metaphors and gave simplistic lectures on theories of the divinity of the Emperor, so most students in my class just ignored him… Dr. Mitsunami Shinzō's overview of law included serious lectures, but he just drily read from the textbook. Dr. Endō Genroku's theories on international law were sketchy, and didn't seem very convincing with regard to current issues.

---

10. Ōtani was remarkable for being one of the few Naval College presidents who had not graduated from the first-class program. He is said to have changed his mind regarding the College being "a waste of time" after serving as its president.
11. Takagi (1995, pp. 97–98).

While it is difficult to determine whether these comments reflect a poor evaluation of the school's coursework in general, or if they are simply examples of particularly bad cases, it is evident that students' interests were more oriented toward leadership and tactics.

Military families

The "Annual Statistics Report of the Inspectorate General of Military Training" and "Department of the Army Statistics Report" provide interesting data related to the types of families military men came from. The occupations of the fathers and brothers of students admitted to the Imperial Army Cadet School changed over time. Most commonly, they were military officers themselves, but this only accounted for approximately 50% of students when statistics began being recorded in 1899, and by the start of the Second Sino-Japanese War in 1937, the percentage had fallen to around 30%, in part due to increased enrollment. The next most common professions were public officials and self-employment (primarily landowners), which gradually increased from 20% to 30%. While over 20% were farmers in 1899, this figure fell over time to below 10%.

Examining the same statistics for the Imperial Army Academy, the percentage of students from military families started at over 30% but fell to 14% in 1937, while the figure for public officials and self-employment held steady at around 20% for many years, but exceeded 30% starting around 1935. The percentage for agricultural occupations exceeded 40% between the end of the Meiji period (1868–1912) and the beginning of the Shōwa period, but starting in 1935 fell to between 26% and 27%.

However, it is impossible to determine which occupations produced the most students without considering the size of their respective labor forces. Hirota's "selection index,"[12] calculated as the occupation ratio of accepted students divided by the occupation ratio of employed persons overall, addresses this issue. The index shows that the contribution of agricultural families increased through 1926, suggesting deepening connections between military personnel and agricultural regions. The contribution of public officials and the self-employed conversely declined over this period, suggesting a lessening desire among children from these families to become military officers. Hirota also presents values that omit differences in junior high school advancement rates, which further support the argument that agricultural sector workers increasingly aspired to joining the military. Becoming a military officer was considered a viable path to success for the

---

12. Hirota (1997).

children of workers in modern urban sectors during the Meiji period, but clearly became a less attractive option in the Taishō period (1912–1926). A particularly small number of graduates from prestigious urban junior high schools (Tokyo Prefectural Daiichi Junior High School, Kaisei, Seijo, etc.) became Army officers in 1914 and 1915.

Ranks and promotion of officers

To examine how Imperial Army soldiers were promoted, I will first limit discussion to the commissioned officer ranks. Commissioned officers were classified as general officers, field officers, and junior officers (each with general, captain, and lieutenant ranks), while noncommissioned officers were sergeant majors, sergeants, and corporals. Below that were the enlisted ranks of private and private first class. Generals attained their rank through direct appointment by the emperor, lieutenant generals and major generals by general imperial appointment, and field officers and below through appointment by the prime minister. Noncommissioned officers were appointed by ministers or regional administrators.

Officer promotions during peacetime generally required succession through the ranks, with a minimum number of years required at each rank (four years for lieutenant generals, three years for major generals, two years for field officers, etc.), and promotion occurring only within the present field of specialization (artillery or engineer corps officers could not be promoted into accounting or medical divisions, for example). As a rule, promotions required nomination from immediate superior officers. Performance evaluations primarily considered service-related knowledge and skills, attitude toward duties, and personal character. Promotions were awarded in annual reviews in order of inclusion on a candidates list with approval by a promotions board headed by the army minister. There were also special promotions during wartime and in consideration of debilitating injuries suffered in public service.

Kumagai uses the Imperial Army and Navy's "Roster of Service Times" and "Officer Roster" to investigate military promotions, concluding that:[13]

> During the Meiji period, there was a clear difference between those officers who were rapidly promoted and those who were not. Until around 1887, promotions in the Imperial Army required passing an examination that included mathematics, and poor scores frequently blocked promotion, likely leaving many

---

13. Kumagai (1994, p. 245).

individuals unable to progress beyond a given rank. From the Taishō period on, however, both the Imperial Army and Navy allowed promotion to first lieutenant if the candidate had attended the Army Academy, and the Navy began simultaneous promotions of same-year classmates... In 1941, with the 44th Army Academy class, the Army too began simultaneous promotions of same-year students up to the rank of major.

Also of note is that the Imperial Army had a lower ratio of field officers to junior officers than did the Imperial Navy, suggesting that it was relatively difficult for an Army Academy graduate to advance to lieutenant colonel or major, due to the limited number of available posts. Kumagai states that "In the Imperial Army of the Taishō period, promotion from second lieutenant to major required around fifteen years, five years longer than the equivalent in the Navy."

Kumagai further uses the "Roster of Service Times" to quantitatively analyze how Army Academy graduates were selected as branch officers. Using as samples graduates from the 16th and 25th classes of the Army Academy who served as Imperial Army officers (generals, lieutenant generals, and major generals) during World War II, he investigates promotions of highly ranked individuals from the time when they were infantry colonels or lieutenant colonels. While promotion from colonel to lieutenant general was largely based on class ranking, Kumagai's methodology clarifies how individuals from within the same class were promoted from colonel.

Kumagai's analysis shows that from 1922 through 1932 (just before the start of simultaneous promotions of same-year students up to the rank of captain), Army Academy graduates were preferentially promoted to captain, that grades upon graduation determined precedence for promotion to first lieutenant, and that those who performed best at the Academy were the first to be promoted to major. Kumagai also identifies a similar trend of continued preferential promotion through the rank of colonel.

In contrast, the Imperial Navy did not seem to emphasize graduation from the Naval College. I used *Officer Histories*, volume nine in *A History of the Japanese Navy*,[14] to examine the academic backgrounds of the 77 individuals who served as Imperial Navy admiral between the Meiji period and the end of the Pacific War. I omitted those born before 1850 (Saigō Tsugumichi, Samejima Kazunori, Shibayama Yahachi, Tōgō Heihachirō, Itō Sukeyuki, Inoue Yoshika, Kabayama Sukenori, and Kawamura Sumiyoshi;

---

14. Society for the Preservation of Naval History (1995).

note that Uemura Hikonojō and Hidaka Sōnojō graduated from the Naval College). I also omitted Prince Arisugawa Takehito, Ijūin Gorō, Prince Fushimi Hiroyasu, and Prince Higashifushimi Yorihito because they received special instruction at the British Royal Naval College, the German Imperial Naval Academy, or the École Navale. This left 63 individuals. All were Naval Academy graduates, but approximately one-third (18) did not attend the Naval College. Of these, 11 (Katō Sadakichi, Kataoka Shichirō, Saitō Makoto, Shimamura Hayao, Dewa Shigeto, Nawa Matahachirō, Fujii Kōichi, Misu Sotarō, Yamashita Gentarō, Yamamoto Gonbee, and Yoshimatsu Shigetarō) were from the 10th class of the Naval Academy or earlier. The other 7 were admirals who did not graduate as part of the Naval College's 11th class or beyond. Included among these are Katō Hiroharu and Nomura Kichisaburō.

As this data shows, promotion rested on much more than class standing upon graduation from the Naval Academy. Kumagai performs a similar analysis to that described above for the Imperial Army, and finds a similar pattern of promotion from colonel to major general that follows order of class standing. Both the Army and Navy were significantly downsized at the end of the Taishō period, however, and so both the Army and Naval Academies had smaller enrollments. Systems for promotion underwent modification according to such changes in student numbers. Examining the relation between the class rankings of February 1913 graduates from the Naval Academy and their position as captain or commander in January 1936, Kumagai finds that many of those first promoted to captain had not graduated from the Naval College as "first-class" category students. However, even some who had average class standings upon graduation from the Naval Academy but who graduated from the Naval College were selected with high preference for promotion to commander or lieutenant commander.

In any case, it seems that at the lower officer ranks educational background and student rankings had a large influence on promotions, but at the level of field officer and above, graduation from the Naval College, together with performance while serving as a junior officer, had no immediate and strong effect on further promotion.

Promotion systems in the Imperial Army
The discussion so far has described promotion through the system of military ranks in Japan prior to World War II. As was true in many countries, a caste-like system existed in the earlier prewar years, whereby the royalty provided generals and the nobility provided lieutenant generals, while

major generals led the troops. This resembled the systems of Edo-period Japan that distinguished between shogun, daimyo, and samurai, with the noble ranks filling the highest-level posts.

The abolishment of caste systems in the Meiji period ended consideration of caste in military promotions. This led to a remarkably democratic system by international standards, with the exception of the United States and European countries (post-revolutionary France in particular had many commissioned officers who had risen up from the lower ranks).

In his historical novel *Clouds Above the Hill*, Shiba Ryōtarō presents a relevant episode that occurred in 1890, when the Imperial Navy's training vessel *Hiei* was returning 69 survivors from the sinking of the Ottoman frigate *Ertuğrul* to Constantinople. When the *Hiei* arrived in Singapore, local Turkish volunteers and religious leaders gave sizeable donations to the survivors aboard the ship. The lower-ranking officers and infantrymen collected these donations, and asked *Hiei* captain Lieutenant Sakamoto Hajime to hold the money for safekeeping, saying that they could not trust their superiors with such a large sum. From this, Sakamoto realized the extent of corruption among the Ottoman officers and ruling classes in general. However, unlike in Europe, nobility in the Ottoman Empire was not strictly hereditary, but rather was attainable even by capable commoners. Even a farmer could become a government minister, and as in Japan such positions could not be inherited.

In another scene, during his stay in Russia, Lieutenant Commander Hirose Takeo speaks with the head porter on a train. "I hear that you are a Navy officer," the porter says. "So what are you? A count? A marquis?" When Hirose replies that he is a commoner and became an officer by passing the requisite tests, just like all the other officers in the Japanese Imperial Army from the generals down, the porter assumes that he is joking.

While these are fictitious episodes, they illustrate an interesting problem: while the system of promotions in the Ottoman Empire was more democratic than the Russian system, it was accompanied by corruption among military officers. Principles of competition (or over-application of such principles) alone lead to corruption through the struggle for power. One of the benefits of systems of nobility is that selection occurs through heredity, not competition, making advancement with malicious intent less likely. On the other hand, the undemocratic, caste-like selection processes in the Russian army certainly undermined military morale. Neither system is perfect, each having its pros and cons.

2. Military technology and private firms

From fighter planes to bullet trains

Weapons technology advanced remarkably following the industrial revolution, to the extent that some degree of technological knowledge became necessary to grasp military strategy. Officer positions for military technology and communications were established to address this, and the Japanese Imperial Army and Navy undertook efforts to foster officer candidates with specialized technical knowledge. For example, the Army began accepting officer candidates with degrees in engineering and the sciences. However, it was Army and Navy research laboratories that played the most central role in technological research. This section focuses on the technology and personnel of the Naval Research Laboratory, and the contributions of both to the Japanese economy following World War II.[15]

The Naval Research Laboratory was established in 1923, following the Washington Naval Treaty of 1922, through consolidation of the Navy's warship and aircraft testing facilities and arms factories in Tokyo.[16] It was severely damaged in the Great Kanto Earthquake of 1923, however, and did not begin functioning as a research organization until 1930. The laboratory was headed by Hiraga Yuzuru, who later became the president of Tokyo Imperial University.[17]

Hiraga was eventually promoted to vice admiral. He designed battleships and cruisers, participating in the design of numerous famous ships, from the *Yamashiro* to the *Yamato*. He was also an avid educator, and most of the naval engineers during the Pacific War had received training from him. Among his protégés were Makino Shigeru and Matsumoto Kitarō, who helped rebuild the foundations of Japanese shipbuilding following

---

15. The Imperial Army Research Laboratory performed investigations, research, and testing for the Army. In 1942, organizations related to army weaponry, including the nine laboratories of the previous Army Technology Department, were consolidated and placed under control of the Army Weapons Administrative Headquarters (Toyama and Morimatsu, 1987).

16. In 1923, the Imperial Japanese Navy Technical Department, an extra-ministerial bureau of the Ministry of the Navy, was combined with the Naval Research Laboratory as a research organization. See Nakagawa (2010) for an accessible yet detailed description of the research performed there.

17. Hiraga graduated from Tokyo Imperial University at the top of his class with a degree in naval engineering. After graduation, he took a position at the Yokosuka Naval Arsenal, where he researched technologies for warship construction (he was later transferred to the Kure Naval Arsenal). His academic and professional accomplishments are an interesting reflection on various problems in Japanese society at the time. See Naitō (1999) for further details.

World War II.

Exports during Japan's period of rapid economic development were highly reliant on a merchant vessel developed in 1960 by Ishikawajima-Harima Heavy Industries Co., Ltd. that used "block construction" and "early outfitting" methods. Block construction involves separating ships into several parts, fabricating those parts in land-based factories, and assembling them in naval stocks. The method is made possible through extensive welding, and is limited by available crane capabilities and the size of assembly factories, but it significantly reduces the time and number of fabrication steps required for ship assembly. Working on land also allows for a more comfortable posture during welding, thus improving safety and task efficiency.

While Japan already possessed world-class shipbuilding technologies by the 1920s, fuselages and motors for aircraft were mostly imported until the 1930s. Japan caught up with the rest of the world through the decade-long efforts of the aircraft manufacturing division of Mitsubishi Heavy Industries to develop the Type-0 Carrier Fighter, better known as the Mitsubishi Zero. The technologies accumulated in that endeavor later led to development of the Tokaido Shinkansen "bullet train," which went into operation in October 1964.

The "Bullet Train Project" began at the start of the Second Sino-Japanese War, with the goal of reducing land transport time over the approximately 1,000 kilometers between Tokyo and Shimonoseki to under nine hours. The plan was cancelled due to the Pacific War, but it reemerged when transport became difficult in the 1950s due to congestion on the Tokaido Main Line. Rail transport was in decline at the time, but the plan nevertheless moved forward under the direction of Japan Railways head Sogō Shinji and chief engineer Shima Hideo. Plans called for completion in the short span of five years. This was an ambitious goal considering the numerous problems that needed to be addressed, including motor design, coping with wind resistance, designing wheels that could navigate curves at high speeds, developing new rail seams, and ensuring contact between pantographs and power lines.

Japan Railways likely set such a short timeline because it was confident of its own railway technology prowess. The company had accumulated power-line technologies for high-speed rail starting with the prewar Bullet Train Project, and many former Army and Navy engineers had flocked to Japan Railways following World War II, due to a U.S. Occupation ban on Japanese aircraft manufacture; 400 engineers worked at the company's laboratories at the end of the war, but just one year later the figure had climbed to nearly 1,500.

Among them were engineers who had solved the "flutter" problem in the Zero, a phenomenon by which high-speed airstreams caused vibrations that could destroy the plane's wings. The same phenomenon also occurs in fast trains, so this was familiar territory for the aircraft engineers. They also applied their experience in making the Zero's fuselage lighter. The result was the elegant, streamlined design that characterizes the Shinkansen.[18]

By applying these wartime aircraft technologies, Japan Railways completed the project on time. Just four months after a model line was finished in 1962, the Shinkansen set a new speed record of 200 kilometers per hour, and in March 1963 it broke that record by traveling 256 kilometers per hour. On 1 October 1964, ten days before the opening ceremonies for the Tokyo Olympics and exactly on schedule according to Chief Engineer Shima's timeline, the Shinkansen opened for commercial operations. This technological success overturned the "common sense" of the time that claimed railways were obsolete.

Engines designed for aeronautical use also had direct applications in cars and motorcycles. As mentioned above, the ban on Japanese aircraft manufacture shifted many talented aeronautics engineers to the private sector. One well-known example is the Subaru 360 city car, which entered production in 1958. Subaru was a division of Fuji Heavy Industries, which was created through the anti-zaibatsu dissolution of the Nakajima Aircraft Company, one of the most advanced airplane manufacturers in the world prior to World War II.

Optics technologies developed for use in battleship rangefinders led to camera lenses at least equaling those produced in Germany, and electronic quartz watches evolved from cannon fuse technologies. Many former naval technical officers turned to electromagnetic, signaling, and audio technology development after the war. Most were indeed Imperial Navy officers, the technological elite of the time who were offered high-ranking positions immediately out of college. The Navy had an estimated 7,000 such technical officers during the Pacific War.

Effects of World War II on human resources

Wars and military forces affect a country's human and physical resources in various ways, including by bringing together people with different social backgrounds, and by reallocating national resources necessary for the

---

18. See Horikoshi and Okumiya (1992) for details of the Mitsubishi Zero. Yoshimura (1968) is an excellent reference for readers who, like me, have little knowledge of aeronautical engineering.

organization and operation of the military. The latter in particular was seen in Japan following its 1943 defeat at Guadalcanal, when resources were mobilized for military use without consideration for private demand.

The number of factory workers peaked at 4.7 million in 1942, and thereafter steadily declined until the end of the war. Considering that there were over 6.6 million Japanese soldiers, military personnel, and non-military workers overseas at the end of the war, the Japanese economy clearly faced a stark labor shortage for the production of private-sector goods during that time.[19] Of the approximately 5.45 million army soldiers and 2.42 million navy sailors serving at the end of the war, 3.09 million soldiers and 450,000 sailors were in the Kuril Islands and Sakhalin, Korea, the Chinese mainland, various Pacific islands, and Southeast Asia.

Japan experienced extensive loss of life during World War II due to combat, urban bombing campaigns, and the nuclear bombs dropped on Hiroshima and Nagasaki. There were approximately 2.3 million military casualties due to combat and disease, and approximately 300,000 overseas and 500,000 domestic civilian casualties. Together this comes to over 3 million deaths, an inestimable tragedy. Japan of course also suffered the loss of national wealth — up to one quarter of its wealth, according to Economic Stabilization Board estimates.

This disastrous war had extensive consequences for Japan's human resources. The government introduced fixed pricing in 1939, significantly increasing black market economic activity. The Corporate Accounting Control Ordinance of 1940 limited retained earnings and dividends, and the Employment Restriction Ordinance of 1939 and the Labor Adjustment Ordinance of 1941 extended military control over corporate management to workforce allocation, severely restricting the transfer of workers away from factories producing military goods. In December 1943, all students eligible for national service were drafted into the military. In the previous June the Cabinet had established the "Guidelines for the Mobilization of Students for the War Effort," which called for third-year junior high school students and above to be allocated to labor for increasing the food supply, constructing national defense facilities, increasing production of emergency supplies, and strengthening transport capabilities. In July 1944, with

---

19. According to the United States Strategic Bombing Survey (1950), there were 630,000 soldiers in the Imperial Japanese Army and Navy in 1937, while Hashimoto (2000) estimates that by 1944 there were 5.37 million. These figures suggest the extent of the labor shortage at facilities for production of both military and private goods during that time. See Yamazaki (1995) and Tōjō (1995) for details. Tōjō's article includes a detailed analysis of labor mobilization at the Nakajima Aircraft Company.

Table 9. Labor force transfers between industries, 1940–1947 (taking manufacturing industry totals as 100)

Industry	Men/Women	1940.10.1	1944.2.22	1947.10.1
Manufacturing	Total	100.0	100.0	100.0
	Men	72.5	73.2	74.3
	Women	27.5	26.8	25.7
Metals	Total	10.0	10.2	12.0
	Men	9.2	8.7	10.6
	Women	0.8	1.4	1.5
Machinery and	Total	30.4	53.3	19.5
Equipment	Men	27.1	43.6	17.0
	Women	3.3	9.7	2.6
Spinning	Total	23.6	10.0	18.4
	Men	8.4	3.0	7.1
	Women	15.1	7.0	11.2
Chemicals	Total	8.4	7.4	10.5
	Men	6.2	5.2	7.8
	Women	2.2	2.3	2.7

Source: Umemura et al. (1988).

the war situation worsening, mobilization was extended to all students at national high schools and in the first two years of junior high school. Labor conditions became significantly harsher: the previous six hours per week of compulsory education and training was abolished, replaced by ten hours per day of labor, and both boys and girls in the third year of junior high school and above were required to work night shifts.[20]

The government made various other attempts to forcibly solve labor shortages. Limits were placed on employment in specific sectors, with males between the ages of 14 and 40 forbidden to work in seventeen labor segments, including as sales staff, ticket takers, and barbers. The labor supply was also expanded, for example by forming the Women's Volunteer Corps for group allocation to military factories.

Between 1939 and the war's end, approximately 800,000 Koreans and 50,000 Chinese from Taiwan, Manchuria, and northern China were shipped to Japan to supplement the labor force.[21] At this time, many Japanese working in nonmilitary industries were forcibly reemployed at factories producing military goods (see Table 9).

---

20. Experienced factory workers were sent to the battlefront, leaving behind only young, inexperienced workers. Chapter 6, section 3 of Nishinarita (1988) describes how the resulting dilution of labor increased the number of "delinquent workers."

21. See Nishinarita (1997) for a detailed analysis of the wartime employment structure of Koreans in Japan and related government policies.

Wartime wage systems

The war also affected wage systems. During the war, all salaries — including those for factory workers — were paid monthly. The most notable change this policy brought about was that previous bonuses and retirement benefits were largely ended. Also, factory workers and other staff began receiving wages under similar systems. It was also around this time and immediately following the war that systems for annual wage increases for workers and staff took root.[22]

Labor wages are generally based on piece rates or time rates, or, quite frequently, on some combination of the two. Piece-rate wages are directly tied to worker output, while time rates are (in the short term, at least) determined according to the amount of time spent working. Of course, different industries emphasize one or the other of these systems more heavily. Piece rates are theoretically applied when a direct measurement of output is possible, while time rates are used where such measurements are difficult. However, the actual case is more complex.

Both systems have pros and cons. Measuring only time raises the possibility of inducing negligence. Highly productive workers prefer piece rates, but precise measurement of output incurs monitoring costs for the company. There are several other fundamental flaws with simple piece rates. One is that production is frequently a team activity, even if we ignore sales and management, which makes measuring individual output difficult. Another is that piece rates encourage employees to work quickly, potentially lowering product quality. Piece rates can result in large variations in wages, and thus workers who desire a stable income may avoid them. As has become evident in socialist economies, efficient labor can result in a ratchet effect by which production quotas increase. This can prevent workers from seeking more efficient production methods.

Japan has long employed bonus systems as a method for partially alleviating the inherent problems related to piece rates. These bonus systems are not tied to individual worker performance, but rather to the "piece rate" of laborers as a group. They are a form of profit sharing, in that wages are partially tied to overall company performance in the marketplace. However, such bonus systems represent a distant incentive for individual workers, and are an incomplete solution that can lead to problems of free-riding. Even so, because bonuses are related to salaries and thus to length of employment, they clearly contribute to extending years of service and improving worker skills.

---

22. Odaka (1984).

Recall that we first saw an example of such bonus systems in chapter 1, when discussing the Edo-period merchants who awarded apprentices with new sets of clothing twice per year. Modern companies like Mitsubishi also awarded bonuses starting in the Meiji period. While the form of bonus systems varies according to era and country, they are fundamentally similar in their long-term rationale.

Workforce mobilization and the "contact effect"

Wars greatly affect domestic labor structures and allocations. Table 9 shows a simplified comparison of estimated industrial populations between manufacturing industry segments in 1940, 1944, and 1947. The manufacturing industry overall showed a net employment increase of over 1 million workers from 1940 to 1944, while the machinery and equipment industry, an important military manufacturing segment, had an increase of 2.22 million. Over the same period, the spinning industry conversely lost 820,000 employees. As Umemura points out, until immediately before the war the spinning industry was second only to the machinery and equipment industry in terms of number of workers, so its equipment and workforce was forcibly diverted to military applications. Table 9 shows an index of this change. While not listed in that table, commercial industries employed 2 million men and women, and service industries employed approximately 600,000; both saw declines in workers between 1940 and 1944.

Table 10 shows figures for labor mobilization at the end of World War II.[23] These numbers suggest that 6 million people had been conscripted as laborers.

As described above, World War II mobilized an enormous labor force, rendered it fluid, consumed it, and caused extensive destruction both within and outside of actual combat. Simultaneously, the huge organizations of the military and military factories brought together individuals who would never have had social contact during peacetime. While it is difficult to conceptualize and quantify these social impacts, many people who lived through that period have related how contacts made during wartime provided new opportunities.

For instance, Katō Kametarō, author of *Dreams of Roofing Tiles*,[24] a work that describes the techniques and spirit of a tile artisan, relates how meeting intellectual soldiers during military service taught him the importance of cultural and moral education. Yearning to discover the "words" to

---

23. *Ibid.*, p. 65.
24. Katō (1991).

Table 10. Labor mobilization at the end of World War II (number of persons).

Conscripted persons	6,164,156 (1,609,558 new conscripts in addition to 4,554,598 existing ones, including those in military companies)
Mobilized students (including for agriculture) Women's Volunteer Corp Imported labor Other general workers (mining, construction, and transportation industries)	1,927,379 472,573 356,890 4,183,271
Total	13,104,269

Source: Ministry of Health and Welfare (1945).

"scientifically" pass on to his successors the skills he obtained through extensive effort and talent, he began to study basic mathematics and physics and the histories of tile-making and architecture. The military also taught him that educational background does not necessarily serve as a measure of character or competence.

Koike Kazuo calls the powerful motivation for self-improvement that arises from contact with persons unlike oneself the "contact effect,"[25] and proposes that this effect formed the basis for increased competitiveness in academic realms following the war. Academic advancement rates increased markedly under the newly established higher education system, and competition both at schools and within companies formed the basis of postwar economic activity. In that sense, postwar Japanese society was without question a product of war.

Career soldiers in postwar Japan

Despite the harsh realities of the Cold War era, political tensions in Japan were less severe after World War II than before or during it.

Education before the end of the war was closely linked to the war and the military, and was systematized and operated in a manner that made military education an inseparable part of academic education. Military education, national service, and training through military organizations had various effects on the economy. As previously discussed, military technologies were applied in the public sector, thus contributing to economic growth. Furthermore, contact between individuals with differing social backgrounds strongly stimulated self-improvement, which contributed to the competitive nature of postwar Japanese society. The moral and "spiritual" education that people encountered in military academies and during service likely

---

25. Koike (1976). See Iwai (2014) for statistical testing of the "contact effect" theory.

had significant socio-economic effects as well. Overseas military service broadens perspectives, in some cases encouraging not only those serving but also their children to relocate to other countries.

In previous research, I used primary documents to investigate how the dissolution of the military affected Japan's social economy in terms of both education and human resources development. While the small sample sizes make it impossible to draw general conclusions about changes in the labor life of Japanese citizens resulting from demilitarization, this research provides a glimpse into how the labor force worked at the time.[26]

The main document I used for this research was the "Student Association Roster for the 51st Graduating Class of the Army Academy." Published in October 1979, the roster lists the birthdate, prefecture of origin, graduated middle school, detailed military (war) experience, postwar work experience (company name, position, and date of entry), name and birthdate of spouse, number of children, and even recent hobbies for each of the 313 association members.

My primary interest was in the number of association members who entered the Japan Self-Defense Forces, the number who immediately enrolled in higher education (universities) after the war, whether they chose completely new careers, any relation between the industries they entered immediately (or following any periods of self-employment, agricultural work, or unemployment) and later on, and the educational and employment characteristics of their children. The following is an overview of my findings.

Over 500 students were enrolled in the 51st class of the Army Academy, and of the 313 who survived World War II and were listed in the roster, 116 later joined the Japan Self-Defense Forces (or its earlier incarnations, the National Police Reserve and the Police Reserve Force). Of these, 63 worked at private firms before returning to military service, 18 worked in agriculture, and 12 were self-employed. Thus, over half of those who found employment at private firms quit their jobs to return to service.

Others returned to university and began new careers. In many cases, these were individuals who, as part of their military service during the war, had been non-enrolled students with research experience in science or engineering departments at Imperial Universities. Following the war, they returned to university as normal students. Others took university entrance examinations for the first time and following graduation entered professions such as medicine, law, or engineering.

The information provided in the roster also allows for an investigation

---

26. Inoki (2004).

into the careers pursued by the children of career soldiers with overseas experience. Notably, many of these children travelled overseas themselves. This suggests that overseas military experience affects the educational and career choices of one's children, perhaps because overseas experience tends to broaden one's perspective.

Coeducation immediately following World War II. (Photo: Jiji Press)

CHAPTER 4

POSTWAR SCHOOLS AND EDUCATIONAL INVESTMENT

Japan's most disastrous war came to an end on 15 August 1945. According to a census study conducted by the Department of Statistics in preparation for the House of Representatives election, as of November of that year the population of Japan had declined to just under 72 million people. The national census of 1947 found a working population of 33.3 million, of which approximately 16.6 million (49.8%) were engaged in agriculture. Nearly half of all workers were thus farmers.

Approximately 10 million persons were demobilized from the military or recalled from overseas posts, creating a labor glut. Even so, unemployment rates at the time are estimated to have been around just 2%, largely because underemployment and latent unemployment absorbed much of the labor force. The agricultural sector absorbed the largest number of workers (5.4 million), followed by manufacturing (1.4 million).[1] Many people who were demobilized, recalled, or released from work at military factories found partial employment in agriculture.

According to the 1950 National Census, a postwar baby boom increased Japan's population by more than 10 million, to 83.2 million, in the five years following the end of the war. The number of employed persons increased to 35.6 million, of whom 16.1 million (over 45%) were still engaged in agriculture. Japan's ensuing period of rapid economic expansion was thus an era of mass migration to cities: the agricultural labor force today is under 4%, indicating the scope of change in Japan's working and living environments over the past 70 years.[2]

Alongside these changes in population and labor, political, economic, and social systems were also reshaped in rapid succession during the period immediately following World War II. Japan's constitution and laws were rewritten, and social systems and customs gradually adapted. Changes occurred in education as well, including the introduction of coeducation and the standardization of public school systems. High schools belonging to the old system vanished, and new institutions for higher learning appeared at an extraordinary rate — so much so that Ōya Sōichi once jested that there seemed to be a new university at every major train station. This of course led to a remarkable increase in rates of advancement to high school

---

1. Figures are from Ishizaki (1957, pp. 626–629). Materials related to demobilized and recalled persons are from Ministry of Health and Welfare reports, with labor force figures estimated from the 1950 National Census. Figures for numbers of persons released from military factories are from the National Census and industrial statistics tables. See chapter 2, section 2 in Umemura (1964) regarding increases in the agricultural worker population.
2. See chapter 2, section 2 in Umemura (1964) for a detailed description of the structural characteristics of Japan's prewar and postwar labor force.

and university studies.

This chapter begins with a description of the fundamental effects of changes in Japan's educational system implemented after the war, and concludes with a discussion of economic decision-making processes influencing postwar educational trends.

1. The occupation and educational reform

Educational reform directives from the GHQ

In the first few months after taking charge of the occupation of Japan, the General Headquarters of the Supreme Commander for the Allied Powers (GHQ/SCAP) issued to the Japanese government a number of directives related to educational policy. They are generally referred to as the "Big Four" directives for educational reform.

The first of the Big Four was officially titled "Administration of the Educational System of Japan," and gave broad instructions regarding reconsiderations and revisions to the educational content taught in schools. It also established education as one facet of Japan's occupation, requiring the Ministry of Education to report to the GHQ through a liaison office created by the directive. The second directive ("Investigation, Screening, and Certification of Teachers and Educational Officials"), issued in October 1945, called for a purge of educators who held militaristic or ultra-nationalistic views. The following month, Tokyo Imperial University's School of Economics restored the positions of seven professors (including Ōuchi Hyōe, Yanaihara Tadao, and Yamada Moritarō) who had been relieved of duties during the war, and expelled five others (including Hashizume Akio and Naniwada Haruo). As a result of this directive, educator review panels were established in 1946, and over 5,300 teachers were fired (2,623 through reviews and 2,717 by other means). The third directive, "Abolition of Governmental Sponsorship, Support, Perpetuation, Control, and Dissemination of State Shinto," abolished Shinto as a state religion, ensured freedom of religion, made provisions for the separation of religion and governance, and removed Shinto education from schools. The fourth directive, "Suspension of Courses in Morals, Japanese History, and Geography," was intended to revise previous educational content based on ultra-nationalist thought, and ordered that all related textbooks and teacher's guides be recalled. All shrines, religious objects, and monuments dedicated to the emperor were also removed from schools.

Moral education had been a core subject in all schools since 1881, with the aim of cultivating student virtue. The Imperial Rescript on Education of

1890 positioned loyalty, patriotism, and filial piety as the cornerstones of moral education.

The Civil Information and Educational Section of the GHQ recruited a panel of U.S. education specialists — called the United States Education Mission to Japan — to report on the reconstruction of Japanese education. The Mission came to Japan twice, in March 1946 and August 1950. The first visit included 27 educators and was led by G. D. Stoddard. Their report focused on equalization of educational opportunities through freedom of education, elimination of nationally uniform education, and respect for autonomy. It furthermore recommended the adoption of a "6-3-3" educational system (six years of elementary school, three years of junior high school, and three years of senior high school) with the first nine years compulsory and free of charge, coeducation of boys and girls, and directly elected local boards of education.[3]

This report hugely affected Japanese postwar educational reform. By August 1946, however, Japan was already taking its own steps in that direction, through the formation of the Education Reform Committee (later, "Council") as a consulting organization under the prime minister. The Committee comprised approximately 50 Japanese education specialists who were required to cooperate with the U.S. Education Mission. It was headed by Committee Chair Abe Yoshishige and Co-chair Nanbara Shigeru, and its members included Takahashi Seiichirō, Kido Mantarō, Amano Teiyū, Mutai Risaku, and Morito Tatsuo. Under the Committee, the educational system established by the Imperial Rescript on Education was abolished and replaced by a system based on the newly enacted Fundamental Law of Education.

From the Imperial Rescript on Education to the Fundamental Law of Education

There are likely few people today who can recite the Imperial Rescript on Education, but memorizing it was a required task for the grandparents and great-grandparents of many modern-day Japanese: "Our Imperial Ancestors have founded Our Empire on a basis broad and everlasting and have deeply and firmly implanted virtue; Our subjects ever united in loyalty and filial piety have from generation to generation illustrated the beauty thereof. This is the glory of the fundamental character of Our Empire, and herein also lies the source of Our education..." The Meiji emperor issued the Rescript in October 1890 to provide basic guidelines for education in Japan.

---

3. Murai and U.S. Education Mission to Japan (1979).

It stated that the fundamentals of education originate in the state as formed by the Shinto goddess Amaterasu and other deities and emperors since, listed the virtues of filial piety, love of family, friendship, loyalty, and adherence to law, and declared the need for subjects to commit to the aid of the emperor in times of national crisis. It also emphasized that such an educational policy was timeless, universal, and valid according to natural law.

In the January after the Rescript was issued, Uchimura Kanzō, an employee at the First Higher School, was forced to resign for "disrespect" after refusing to bow before a copy of the document.[4] Following this incident, Uchimura — who had studied in the U.S. — was branded a blasphemous traitor. He found himself unemployable, and to make matters worse, his wife, one of his few supporters, died suddenly. He spent several homeless years wandering among Osaka, Kumamoto, Kyoto, and Nagoya before finally finding employment writing an English column for the *Yorozu Chōhō* newspaper.

Following Japan's defeat in World War II and the enactment of its new constitution in 1946 and Fundamental Law of Education in 1947, contradictions arose between the new ideals of basic individual rights and the Rescript's old ideals of imperial sovereignty and a mythological national polity. As a result, the Japanese House of Representatives abolished the education Rescript (along with the Imperial Rescript to Soldiers and Sailors) in June 1948, and the House of Councilors later confirmed its revocation. This signaled the end of moral education centered on the Rescript.

In the spirit of the new Constitution of Japan, the preface to the Fundamental Law of Education described the goals of education and presented the law as the foundation for establishing a new system of Japanese education. The new law extensively incorporated ideals of pacifism and democracy, stated that the goal of education was to perfect the character of every citizen, established nine years of compulsory education, and promoted coeducation and social education. The law also forbade certain religious activities in national and public schools and set forth principles for the proposal of educational laws (rather than imperial edicts).

The School Education Law, enacted on the same day as the Fundamental Law of Education, further systematized the reformed school system established by its partner law. It established a system of six years of elementary school, three years of junior high school, three years of senior high school, and four years of college. The United States heavily influenced the enactment of both laws, and both reflect the educational theories and methods of

---

4. See Ozawa (2004) for details on the Uchimura incident.

that country. Even so, both were voluntarily adopted, notably through the efforts of Tanaka Kōtarō and other Japanese proponents.[5]

Another major postwar reform was the Board of Education Law of 1948. This law established offices and directors of education and education boards comprising five committee members (three for rural towns and villages). As of 1948, education board members were publicly elected, but starting in 1956 they were appointed, as dictated by the Revised Board of Education Law (the Act on the Organization and Operation of Local Educational Administration).

Demise of the old school system

While it may seem strange to the youth of today, some prewar high school students considered it trendy to dress in rough, shabby attire. The picture of students on their way to becoming the cultural elite singing "dormitory songs" while wearing threadbare clothing and ripped hats is indeed an odd image.

However, the lyrics to those songs express something of a yearning for common life, even while frankly acknowledging their status as the elite. See, for example, a school song of the First Higher School, *"Aa gyokuhai ni hana ukete"* (Flowers in a Jade Cup): "Look down at the prosperous masses, lost in their dreams... If we but rise together, we can accomplish great things... We must save our nation's people, adrift upon a murky sea."

The songs originated in the dormitories housing high school students under the old school system, and were sung by a select male elite in the process of developing their sense of social mission and mettle. Other well-known school songs included the Third Higher School's *"Kurenai moyuru oka no hana"* (Flowers Shining Red on the Hill) and Hokkaido University's *"Miyako zo yayoi"* (Spring in the Capital) (from the time when it was the Agricultural College of Tohoku Imperial University). Such songs have largely vanished from modern university life. Even if they are heard, it is for nostalgia's sake only; the only songs students today sing with enthusiasm are pop songs at karaoke.

The old high school system began in 1894 with the establishment of five high schools in Tokyo (the First Higher School), Sendai (Second), Kyoto (Third), Kanazawa (Fourth), and Kumamoto (Fifth), each of which had previously been a junior high school. Nearly all graduates went on to study at

---

5. Whether the "red purge" of "communist" university faculty from 1948 through 1950 was a Japanese initiative or the result of U.S. occupational policy is a separate issue. See Krämer (2005).

the Imperial University, so the Higher Schools in effect played the role of college preparatory schools. After 1900, the Sixth through Eighth Higher Schools were established in Okayama, Kagoshima, and Nagoya, completing what was referred to as the "number schools."

Between 1919 and 1925, new high schools were established in Niigata, Matsumoto, Yamaguchi, Matsuyama, Hirosaki, Yamagata, Mito, Matsue, Saga, Urawa, Fukuoka, Shizuoka, Osaka, Kōchi, Himeji, Hiroshima, Toyama, and Tokyo. In addition to these national schools, during the late Taishō period (1912–1926) private schools such as the Gakushuin, Musashi, Seikei, Seijo and Konan high schools were founded, and even overseas schools in Taipei and Lushun. Regional public schools including Naniwa High School and Tokyo Prefectural High School started appearing following the start of the Shōwa period (1926–1989).

Approximately one in two applicants passed the entrance exam for these high schools at the start of the twentieth century, but by around 1920 competition was extremely fierce, with only one in seven candidates succeeding. However, passing the test ensured a relatively smooth path to one of the Imperial Universities, if not necessarily the top pick of Tokyo Imperial University. High school life was relatively easy and free. This system of "hard to get in, easy to get out" institutions of higher education has persisted long after World War II.[6]

It is worth noting that the phenomenon of students entering a competitive university only to focus on social life, sports, and carousing is of course not limited to Japan, and — setting aside the question of how many students actually behaved in this way — seems to have been part and parcel of student life at the time. For example, in his autobiography, British historian A.J.P. Taylor recalls student life at Oriel College, Oxford in the mid-1920s as follows:

> Oxford was also a surprise to me academically. I had foolishly assumed that a university was a place devoted to the higher learning. Not so Oxford. Few of my College contemporaries were devoted to learning. They regarded Oxford as a place that would give them the necessary social stamp for well-paid jobs in the civil service.[7]

---

6. Takeuchi (2011) analyzes how the old-system high schools arose and how they affected Japanese prewar and postwar society through the "educational nobility" and cult of refinement. The final chapter, which addresses the deconstruction of the old system and the democratization of education by U.S. occupying forces, provides important insight into Japanese postwar society.

7. Taylor (1983, p. 87).

He later describes students there spending most of their time playing soccer and drinking beer.

Dormitories were the core of student life in the old Japanese high schools, and communal living likely had a powerful influence on students' personalities and attitudes toward knowledge. From their start, dormitories were run in a highly militaristic manner, with tight restrictions on outside activities and limited autonomy in daily life. Another effect of dormitories and their self-governance structures, however, was to form exclusive networks of male elites bonded through academic and social life. This eventually led to the creation of "academic cliques" based on alma mater.

Extension of education to women

As mentioned above, the Fundamental Law of Education advocated coeducation. This was in stark contrast to the Meiji-period Imperial Rescript on Education, which forbade coeducation. Japan was not alone in this policy, of course; separate education by gender remained a key feature of European schools throughout the nineteenth century, and coeducation at the college level generally did not begin until the end of the nineteenth or early twentieth century, likely due to concerns about differences in aptitude between men and women or disparities in their physical and psychological characteristics.

However, Japan faced its own historical context with regard to female education. Fukuzawa Yukichi's *Onna daigaku hyōron* (Critique on Greater Learning for Women), published in 1899, presents some of these factors. Fukuzawa targeted his critique at several popular primers for young women, particularly Kaibara Ekken's *Jyoshi ni oshiyuru hō* (Principles for the Instruction of Women) (volume 5 in his *Wazoku dōjikun* (Precepts for Children), published in 1710, but also the Kyōhō-period (1716–1736) *Onna daigaku takarabako* (Treasure Box of Greater Learning for Women) and the Meiji-period (1868–1912) *Shinsen onna daigaku* (Newly Selected Women's Learning). Fukuzawa decried these works as disparaging to women because they adhered to the "prejudiced theories of Confucian doctrine" and taught women "lessons for slaves," namely, that "the life of a woman is one of subordination to others." This type of textbook had long been used in Edo-period *terakoya* schools and Meiji-period finishing schools, where they formed the core of female moral education and refinement. Fukuzawa, however, considered these works to contain "all manner of immorality." He makes this point in the *Critique on Greater Learning for Women*:

Even setting aside tales of heroines from ancient times, our nation's history includes many great women of letters. The nations of the West see the value in teaching women physics, literature, economics, and other subjects, and are home to many women who have made a name for themselves in those fields. Given their talents for careful thought, women have furthermore been employed as accountants at government offices. Some researchers have theorized that women are more suited to medicine and the healing arts than are men, and indeed report that today there are increasingly many female doctors. From any perspective, claims that women are ignorant by nature are nothing but the mumblings of certain authors of texts for women.[8]

Note that the Confucian morality presented in these texts is fundamentally the same as that underlying the theories of female education in Jean-Jacques Rousseau's *Emile*, which emphasizes the importance of teaching girls housework, childrearing, and hygiene. While philosophers such as the Marquis de Condorcet and Robert Owen later influenced the development of more progressive theories, coeducation did not become the norm in Europe until the end of the nineteenth century.

In Japan, the establishment of schools for girls and women was long delayed, with only normal schools providing the equivalent of a junior high school education to girls. The first relevant law was the Regulations Concerning Girls' High School Organization and Facilities, issued in February 1899. The course of study at normal schools generally lasted for four years, and admission required the equivalent of two years of study at the upper elementary level. However, the curriculum included less than half the amount of time spent at boys' schools on mathematics, science, and foreign language, instead emphasizing needlework, morality, and Japanese studies. Until the postwar reforms, the core of junior high school education for women thus focused on housekeeping and other "womanly virtues," with the aim of training "good wives and wise mothers."

Tsuda Umeko's Women's Institute for English Studies and the Tokyo Women's Medical University were established in 1900, and the Japan Women's University in 1901. All of these, however, were educational institutions

---

8. Fukuzawa (1981). Ishikawa (1977), an anthology of primers for young women from Kaibara to Fukuzawa, is a valuable resource for examining the lineage of these texts. Fukuzawa developed his theories on the education of women in *Gakumon no susume* (An Encouragement of Learning), and fully addressed them in *Nihon fujin ron* (On Japanese Women), *Shin onna daigaku* (New Essential Learning for Women), and *Critique on Greater Learning for Women*.

established under the Vocational School Order of 1899, and so did not allow for coeducation. While the movement for coeducation and the certification of universities for women grew in the mid-1920s, historical biases regarding the social roles of men and women prevented government action. Shortly before the start of the Pacific War, plans emerged to establish a university for women under the University Regulations of 1919, and to restructure the Tokyo Women's Normal School as a university, but the war prevented this from happening. Coeducation and the admission of women to the Imperial University were also delayed until the postwar educational reforms.[9]

In 1948, these reforms brought about a new university system, and 27 schools for women that were previously classified as vocational schools — including the Japan Women's University, Tsuda College, Tokyo Woman's Christian University, University of the Sacred Heart, and Kobe College — were restructured as universities. Following this change, the ratio of women advancing to high schools and universities rapidly increased, and in recent years combined enrollments in universities and junior colleges have exceeded those of men at each grade level.

The status of female laborers has also changed. Production in modern Japan's textile and home appliance industries is predominantly supported by the labor of young women. The labor force participation rate of women has always been high, and even higher than in the United States at many points. While the U.S. is considered an "advanced" nation in terms of female social participation, it only caught up to Japan in terms of labor force participation following the 1973 oil crisis. In 1945, the ratio of labor participation by married women in the U.S. was around 20%, and this did not exceed 50% until the 1980s. However, the ratio of women in management positions in Japan has remained lower than in the West. Even so, progress is being made: of Japan's recent national civil service hires, over 30% of those in career-path management positions have been women.[10]

Along with expanded employment opportunities for women in all fields, wage disparity has also continued to decrease. This trend became particularly noticeable during Japan's period of rapid economic development in the 1960s, and since the 1980s the wage gap has shrunk further for employees in their thirties and forties. The primary reason for this is the lowered rate

---

9. See sections 2 and 6 in volume 1, chapter 4 of Amano (2013).
10. Wakisaka (1993) analyzes female labor from the perspective of career formation with a focus on workplace type and employment management by career path. Koike and Tomita (1988) is a collection of papers providing empirical research on female labor in Japan before and after enactment of the Equal Employment Opportunity Law in 1986. See Nakamura (1994) regarding the progress of women in managerial positions.

of career interruption due to marriage, childbirth, and childcare. Women in Japan are getting married later, leading to more years of uninterrupted employment, so there are increasingly fewer differences between men and women in terms of educational background and experience. A narrowing wage gap between men and women is another factor.[11]

2. A validation of human capital theory

The phenomenal rise in school advancement rates

To illustrate how school enrollment changed following the systematic transformation of Japan's postwar school system, Table 11 presents a rough overview of academic advancement rates, and Table 12 shows the proportion of new graduates finding employment between 1955 and 2000. The figures in these tables show the progress of higher educational attainment (in other words, increases in the purchase level of educational services as consumption) accompanying improving income standards. The rate of this change is noteworthy. In particular, during the fifteen years from 1960 to 1975, the number of persons employed following graduation from junior high school fell from 680,000 to just 90,000. Conversely, the number of college and junior college graduates hired jumped from 120,000 to 350,000. The number of high school graduate hires peaked in 1970, and starting in the mid-1980s over 40% of new graduate hires came from colleges and junior colleges. While junior high school graduates filled two out of three positions in 1955, by the end of the twentieth century two out of three hires were college graduates.

Such figures provide a simple picture of how educational attainment advanced during Japan's period of rapid economic growth, but they do not necessarily indicate a direct connection between the increase in general educational standards and the improvement in worker productivity in Japanese industries at the time. Considering that in many fields it takes decades to accumulate the experience needed for a labor force to contribute to increased productivity, during this period it was primarily junior high school graduates (and to some extent high school and vocational school graduates) that supported Japan's rapid economic development.

This point relates to questions such as the extent to which formal education actually contributes to labor productivity and the selection of qualified personnel. While direct answers are difficult to obtain, the issue can be peripherally observed, as we will do in the following sections.

---

11. Chūma and Ōishi (1997).

Table 11. Changes in school advancement rates, 1955–2000

	High school			Two-year college			Four-year college			Graduate school		
	Total	Men	Women	Total	Men	Women	Total	Men	Women	Total	Men	Women
1950	42.5	48.0	36.7									
1960	57.7	59.6	55.9	2.1	1.2	3.0	8.2	13.7	2.5			
1970	82.1	81.6	82.7	6.5	2.0	11.2	17.1	27.3	6.5	4.4	5.1	1.5
1980	94.2	93.1	95.4	11.3	2.0	21.0	26.1	39.3	12.3	3.9	4.7	1.6
1990	94.4	93.2	95.6	11.7	1.7	22.2	24.6	33.4	15.2	6.4	7.7	3.1
2000	95.9	95.0	96.8	9.4	1.9	17.2	39.7	47.5	31.5	10.3	12.8	6.3

Source: MEXT (various issues).

Table 12. Proportion of new graduates finding employment, 1955–2000

Unit: 10,000 persons (%)

	Total hires	Jr. high school	Sr. high school	College	Jr. college	Graduate school
1955	112.3 (100)	69.8 (62.2)	34.0 (30.3)	7.0 (6.2)	1.5 (1.3)	–
1960	137.3 (100)	68.3 (49.7)	57.2 (41.7)	10.0 (7.3)	1.8 (1.3)	–
1965	149.9 (100)	62.4 (41.6)	70.0 (46.7)	13.5 (9.0)	3.6 (2.4)	0.4
1970	137.0 (100)	27.1 (19.8)	81.7 (59.6)	18.8 (13.7)	8.7 (6.4)	0.7
1975	103.8 (100)	9.3 (9.0)	59.1 (57.0)	23.3 (22.4)	11.1 (10.7)	1.0
1980	110.0 (100)	6.7 (6.1)	60.0 (54.4)	28.5 (26.0)	13.6 (12.4)	1.2
1985	108.6 (100)	7.0 (6.4)	56.4 (52.0)	28.8 (26.5)	14.8 (13.6)	1.6
1990	121.2 (100)	5.4 (4.5)	62.2 (51.3)	32.4 (26.7)	18.9 (15.6)	2.3
1995	96.1 (100)	2.5 (2.6)	40.8 (42.5)	33.1 (34.5)	16.9 (17.6)	2.8
2000	71.0 (100)	1.5 (2.1)	24.7 (35.1)	30.1 (42.8)	10.5 (14.8)	4.2

Source: MEXT (1950–2000).
Notes: Values are for March graduates. Total number of high schools includes full-time and part-time courses at national, public, and private schools. Post-1965 junior college graduates include those from higher education vocational schools. Percentages for graduate schools are omitted.

Education as investment and consumption

Employers desire certain outcomes from college education, including basic academic ability, a sense of ethics, and a capacity for perseverance, cooperation, and empathy. There is not a particularly strong correlation between one's grades in college and performance after joining a company, which naturally leads to the question of why higher education is desirable in the first place. Why are parents willing to make such economic and other sacrifices to send their children to college? Human capital theory presents one possibility, namely that formal education increases skills and knowledge, which increase productivity, thus leading to an increase in future income.[12]

The value of formal education is, of course, multifaceted. One significant

---

12. A plethora of research related to human capital theory has been published in recent years, making a comprehensive listing impossible, but see Ashenfelter and Rouse (2000) for one empirical test of its assertions.

value lies in its contribution to an individual's satisfaction with the present, for example through socializing with friends or acquiring new knowledge. Another value is its potential contribution to deeper satisfaction in the future, for example through attaining the ability to read books in a foreign language or to enjoy philosophical works. From an economics perspective, this represents two types of consumption: consumption in the present and contribution to consumption in the future. In addition, however, formal education is also an investment in skills and knowledge, which raises future income for the investor.

Considering that formal education increases students' future incomes, it is indeed an investment, and this allows us to define individuals as produced means of production. This is a fundamental concept in human capital theory, but applying traditional investment theory to human beings as produced means of production requires some key refinements, as pioneers in this area of study such as University of Chicago economists Theodore Schultz and Gary Becker clearly recognized.[13]

Other questions that arise with regard to the value of formal education are whether students are the only beneficiaries of formal education, whether the full cost of formal education can be considered an investment cost, and just what components comprise the cost of formal education. Individual income is determined by many factors, including not only home environment and innate abilities, but also, for example, gender, region, and age. We must therefore determine how to differentiate between income resulting from such factors and that resulting from education. These questions have not yet been sufficiently investigated, but there have been many attempts to analyze the rate of return on investment in education. The following section presents one example, which demonstrates the assumptions in such calculations as well as several interesting results.

Return on investment in college education

The Japanese Ministry of Health, Labour and Welfare's 1982 White Paper on the Labour Economy examined reductions in the college wage premium from several angles, reflecting increased researcher interest in the economic

---

13. Elements of human capital theory can be detected in the writing of Smith and Marx, but Alfred Marshall was the first to clearly demonstrate their importance. Schultz, Becker, and others in the Chicago school of economics contributed to the revival of human capital theory within the framework of neoclassical economics developed following World War II. One motivation for this was the desire to help the US catch up with Soviet education and research following the Sputnik Crisis in the Cold War era. See Schultz (1981) and Becker (1993) for the most creative formulations and commentaries on human resource theory.

Table 13. Earnings ratios from college education for men in the manufacturing industry   (%)

Company size	1966	1970	1976	1978	1980
All sizes	8.2	7.5	6.4	5.7	5.2
1,000+ employees	9.0	7.9	6.5	5.7	5.1
100–999 employees	5.0	5.9	4.9	4.4	4.0
10–99 employees	4.5	4.9	4.6	4.3	3.9

Notes: Costs for college education are calculated as the per-student tuition for daytime attendance at national, public, and private colleges, plus the weighted average of enrollment fees, facilities, and equipment costs (using MEXT figures). Earnings ratio γ is determined so that it satisfies

$$\sum_{n=22}^{54} \frac{Y_n - X_n}{(1+\gamma)^{n-18}} = \sum_{n=18}^{21} \frac{X_n}{(1+\gamma)^{n-18}} + \sum_{n=18}^{21} \frac{C_n}{(1+\gamma)^{n-18}}$$

where X_n, Y_n are the respective annual incomes of age n high school and college graduates, and C_n is the cost of college education at age n.

Source: Ministry of Health, Labour and Welfare (1982).

effects of higher education based on human capital theory. The white paper found a trend of decreasing differences between the initial salaries of college and high school graduates in both clerical and technical positions. Industry statistics (excluding service industries) also show a continued trend of reduced disparity in the fixed portion of salaries between male college and high school graduates. This paper also reported reduced differences in lifetime wages from employment to retirement due to educational background. Taking college graduate values as 100, these figures show incomes for high school graduate males in the manufacturing industry of 70.0 in 1965, 73.8 in 1970, 77.5 in 1975, and 81.6 in 1981. The note in Table 13 addresses the rate of return for college education, which is our primary concern. The theory of human capital provides the basis for the method of calculation used here.

Roughly speaking, labor economics provides two main answers to why higher education is desirable. As indicated above, one is that higher education is an investment that increases productivity, and people decide whether to pursue higher education according to the difference in rate of return on investment in education versus the return from interest income from monetary investment (without education). The other answer focuses not on the effects of increased productivity resulting from higher education itself, but rather on individuals' demonstration of their abilities (productivity) resulting from revealing to the market the information that they have received education. The former is called human capital theory, while the latter is called signal theory and emphasizes innate ability. Both are theoretical models, so neither is "correct" — theories are no more than simplifications that aim to elucidate the core structure of ideas.

There are two types of educational cost in human investment theory: direct costs such as those for tuition and textbooks, and indirect (opportunity) costs, calculated as lost wages due to the time spent receiving education. The following equation can be used to find the discount rate obtained by setting equal 1) the present value of the direct costs of college education and foregone income that would have been received through employment immediately following high school graduation, and 2) the present value of profit from college graduation (the difference between high school and college graduates in lifetime earnings from age 23 to retirement):

Total investment = Present value of earnings discounted at the market interest rate.

The discount rate that establishes this equation is called the internal rate of return (IRR). Comparing the IRR with the rate of return from financial assets (to simplify, the market interest rate) allows one to decide whether it is advantageous to advance to higher learning.

Note that as education-related expenses (tuition, increased high school graduate incomes) increase, the IRR decreases. Conversely, the IRR increases with a larger disparity between high school and college graduate wages, and with longer terms of employment (through delayed retirement, etc.).

Table 13 shows earnings ratios calculated in this manner, which enable a comparison between Japan's period of rapid economic development and more stable periods. It shows a large decrease for men in the manufacturing industry, from 8.2% in 1966 to 5.2% in 1980.

So long as we restrict our inquiry to average income, there is of course a significant difference between high school and college graduates. Yet it is interesting to consider whether this relationship between educational background and income always holds true. Estimating variations in earnings ratios from income for various industries at different company scales reveals significant differences even among employees with similar educational backgrounds. For example, the ratios are noticeably lower in the transportation and communications industries, and higher in the finance and insurance industries. It is also clear, however, that differences between companies of different scales are overall larger than those between industries.

Individual income data is not available, but by using data on the number of employees at workplaces in various industries and at various company scales to calculate the number of workers at various earnings ratios, we can attempt to estimate an approximate distribution. The results suggest large differences in earnings ratios between high school and college graduates. In particular, while college graduates can expect a relatively stable earnings ratio, the ratio from investment in high school is unstable and features large variations. Put another way, there is extreme variety in the quality of high school education, and the shape of the distribution shows a bipolar decomposition. Conceivably, high-school graduates with high ability are evaluated accordingly.[14]

Lost income during education

The above calculations of earnings ratios view humans as "produced means of production," but they are inherently limited in that they ignore the issue of present consumption and investment in future consumption. Rather, the most noteworthy aspect of the ideas behind human capital theory is the cost concept.

The extent of lost (foregone) income due to school attendance far exceeds the overall direct public and private costs of formal education, so whether to consider foregone income a part of educational costs is a significant issue.

Opportunity costs (the inclusion of forgone income) were long ignored for a number of reasons. One is that in western European countries, high school education was historically considered preparation for advancement to college for a small number of students, and the most important function of college was to teach these students their role as social elites. Colleges were thus training grounds where the youth of the affluent classes (who had no need of scholarships) obtained what they needed to maintain their future position and prestige. Clearly, there is no need to apply concepts of "foregone income" to such students.

However, the modern-day expansion of junior and senior high school education (particularly in Japan, the United States, and the former Soviet Union) dramatically altered this situation, in that the time students dedicated to their studies had value. The concepts of time value and forgone income were found to provide systematic explanations for a number of "mysteries" surrounding education, including:[15]

1. Why the children from farm homes attended school for fewer days than the children of non-farmers,
2. Why the children from low-income homes in developing nations did not take advantage of increased opportunities for education, even when tuition was free or scholarships were available, and

---

14. Yano (2007) provides a clear interpretation of education from an economic perspective through calculation of internal earnings ratios under various conditions.
15. Schultz (1963, pp. 30–31).

3. Why an extremely low proportion of children completed primary education in low-income countries.

Each of the above can be largely explained by the concept of foregone income; in each case, children had no choice but to work to help support their impoverished households.

In this way, human capital theory allows us to calculate actual earnings ratios, but also makes great contributions toward the task of refining cost concepts as applied to education. Even so, significant questions related to education costs remain unresolved. One in particular is the issue of discerning between areas of consumption and areas of investment in increased income.

3. Actual movements

To what extent do changes in demand for higher education actually fulfill the predictions of human capital theory? It is generally observed that rates of advancement to colleges and other institutions of higher learning in postwar Japan decreased somewhat between the mid-1970s and the 1980s, but overall, demand has increased. However, the internal earnings ratio for investment in higher education as calculated from the above equation shows a steady decline, although it never falls significantly below the earnings ratio for financial assets. The cause for this seeming contradiction is that demand for higher education derives not simply from investment, but also has high consumption features. Higher wages, of course, increased the demand for education as consumption.

Another important factor is that when predicting our own future income, we tend to optimistically consider only the most successful case. The difference in X and Y values in the note to Table 13 is not a definite value at the time of investing in education, but simply a predicted value. However, this value reflects the productivity effect of education, and thus varies with individual ability. Humans have only incomplete information regarding their potential abilities, and so often make optimistic predictions. This can result in overestimates of the internal earnings ratio for investment in higher education, thereby leading to excessive investment.

Investment in education therefore varies with personal qualities, capabilities, as well as rate of time preference (how future uncertainty regarding economic value is evaluated) and expectations of one's future ability. For example, even assuming two individuals have the same time rate preferences, the marginal rate of return on education resulting from an additional year of education will vary according to their quality as students. Wage disparity by educational background is thus expanded not only through the number of years of education, but also by differences in ability. This leads to an ability bias in which those with higher ability inaccurately predict a higher earnings ratio for themselves (one that exceeds simple educational effects).

Selection mechanisms

In a departure from human capital theory, some believe that higher education plays no particular role in increasing productivity in economic activity. According to these theorists, a diploma from an institute of higher education is not a certificate of the skills and knowledge obtained through education, but merely an incomplete measure of aptitude and potential capacity for professional life. In human capital theory, higher education raises the market value of one's labor by increasing individual productivity. In screening theory, by contrast, education is not viewed as a necessary condition for increased productivity.

According to this theory, higher education is a mechanism that screens (selects) individuals with differing talents, thereby providing the purchasers of labor (firms) with information related to skills. Screening theory is not diametrically opposed to human capital theory, but it portrays education as simply a decision-making tool that employers use for their own benefit, and therefore views the social returns from education as practically zero.

Of course, screening theory alone insufficiently describes the functions of higher education. It can even be considered something of a caricature. In the case of Japan, it implies that the best strategy for students who pass a difficult university entrance exam is to immediately seek employment. After all, what would be the point of wasting four years at a university, if their studies are not expected to improve their productivity as workers?

In any case, screening theory alone cannot fully explain the increasing levels of education in Japan. Without question, higher education both directly improves students' abilities and serves as a selection mechanism by measuring their potential abilities.

When viewing formal education as an investment, however, we must take note of the large decrease in the earnings ratio of higher education during Japan's period of rapid economic development. In the years since 1965 in particular, these values have been at or below the earnings ratio of general financial assets, implying that purchasing some form of financial asset would have produced greater returns than advancing from high school to college. If lifetime wages reflect labor productivity, then these low earnings ratios are evidence that increases in years of education did not significantly contribute to increases in productivity. In other words, the consumption aspects of formal education — as opposed to the investment aspects — have been fortified, and higher income standards have led to increased purchasing of educational services.

The value of formal education

Most researchers take for granted the functional value (economic effect) of education, assuming that it promotes economic growth by increasing productivity and income, but in recent years a large number of studies have questioned the nature of this causal relation.[16] The stylized fact that those with more education receive higher salaries is not in question. However, there are two opposing theories regarding this proposition.

Human capital theory poses that formal education imparts skills and knowledge that improve individual productivity. This theory presumes that productivity is reflected in wages, and so asserts that education is an important factor for social mobility that brings about higher earnings. The other view, signal theory, emphasizes innate ability and poses that there is no causal relation between more years of formal education and higher wages. Following this line of thought, education does not increase income, but rather those with high abilities simply receive both more education and higher salaries. In other words, both education and wages stand upon the common foundation of individual ability, so of course a positive correlation will exist between the two.[17]

The opposition between these two views became increasingly clear in the early 1970s with the emergence of screening theory, which emphasized education's impact on human resources selection. In the U.S., income inequality attracted increasing attention as a social issue in the late 1980s, leading to renewed interest in this topic as a research theme. In particular, the question of whether wage gaps could be reduced through educational policy took on a highly political nature.[18] Proponents of human capital theory called for an expansion of government programs for education, asserting the need to provide an environment in which the low-income population could invest in education. Proponents of innate ability theory insisted that the poor do not benefit from additional education to the extent that the wealthy do, so expanded support for education would not raise their income. Figure 1

---

16. Note that here I will not address issues related to the intrinsic value of education, in terms of its tangible and intangible contributions to quality of life.
17. See Herrnstein and Murray (1994) for a representative example of this view.
18. Inoki (2008).

1. Human capital theory

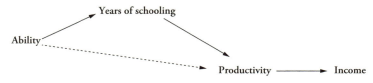

2. Innate ability theory (Signal theory)

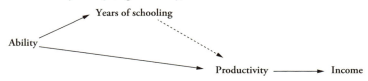

Figure 1. Differences in human capital theory and innate ability theory.

depicts the differences between these two viewpoints.

This naturally led to the question of whether the validity of these differing views could be tested. For example, one could design an experiment that controls for education by randomly selecting a group of youth without regard to ability or background, presenting them with differing levels of education, and tracking their income over a number of years. Such an experiment would be ethically unacceptable, however, so two alternate methods for measuring educational effects while removing ability bias were proposed:

1. Consider a group with similar genetics and family circumstances but differing educational backgrounds, and extract any relation between the number of years of formal schooling and income level. This could first be performed between parents and children, then among siblings. Conclusive research would come from a study of identical twins.

2. Search for variables that are not determining factors for income but are determining factors for education, and use those variables to investigate the effect of number of years of education (the instrumental variable method).

A twins study performed by two U.S. labor economists is representative of the first approach.[19] The researchers in this study collected a large amount of data at the Twins Days Festival in Twinsburg, Ohio to estimate the earnings ratio of formal education (the increase in income resulting from an additional year of education). They examined twins with identical genetics (and thus the same inherent abilities) who were raised in the same

---

19. Ashenfelter and Rouse (1998).

household environment, which allowed them to measure differences in income where years of education differed. Any differences in income would then likely be related to differences in education. (The study ignored various contingencies, such as individual emotional and motivational differences among twins.) The tentative conclusions from this study indicated that each additional year of education led to an income increase of 8 to 9%, suggesting that additional education increased wages. This result supported the predictions of human capital theory.

In any case, it is impossible to deny the effects of four years of college study on post-graduation careers. Many recent studies have supported the proposition that one's academic major, club activities, grades, and other factors have an effect on later vocational life.[20]

At what stage does education raise productivity?

In recent years, labor economists have become increasingly interested in determining the developmental stage at which education has the strongest effect on improving skills and income. In the course of previous research, I had the interesting experience of investigating the educational background of workers in Thailand's process industry. As of 1983, nearly 90% of workers in that industry had only completed four years of elementary education, yet were engaged in work using advanced control panels.[21] All education and training following employment came in the form of on-the-job training. In other words, fundamental linguistic and mathematical literacy combined with quality education and training after employment appeared sufficient for skill development. Many researchers have begun investigating this point using larger datasets.

Their work has led in a number of interesting directions. One study presents a theoretical model for observing the effects of childhood education on skill development, and attempts to verify these effects.[22] This research applies concepts of self-productivity and complementarity in human capital investment, and focuses on the lifecycle process of skill development from the womb throughout life. The findings indicate that the home plays a far greater role in skill formation than does formal schooling. Human ability is shaped by both genetic and acquired factors, but this study does not employ the oppositional analytic framework of nature versus nurture. Rather, it views investment in human capital in relation to both self-

---

20. For research from the field of educational sociology, see Takeuchi (1995). From the perspective of labor economics, see Matsushige (2004).

21. See Koike and Inoki (1991), particularly chapter 5 and table 6-2 in chapter 6.

22. Cunha, Heckman, Lochner and Masterov (2005).

productivity and complementarity. Here, self-productivity refers to how skills acquired in one lifecycle stage boost the attainment level of skills at subsequent stages, while complementarity describes how early investment facilitates the productivity of later investment. Put another way, early investment cannot fully promote productivity in the absence of later invest-ment. From this reasoning, the authors derive the proposition that "the returns to investing early in the life cycle are high." Self-productivity and complementarity thus make recovery from insufficient childhood educa-tion difficult and costly.

Using this theoretical framework, the authors examine how special edu-cational programs for children aged three and four affect the grades of the same children in high school and college, and find evidence to support their hypothesis. While not specifying a theoretical framework, Fryer and Levitt come to a similar conclusion.[23]

Curiously, such research serves to validate the following quote from Marshall's *Principles of Economics*, penned over a century ago: "The most valuable of all capital is that invested in human beings; and of that capital the most precious part is the result of the care and influence of the mother."[24]

Vocational education as an element of higher education

Finally, to touch on the relation between academic and vocational educa-tion, I would like to address the recent trend in Japan toward a growing emphasis on vocational skills in higher education. The Japanese Ministry of Education, Culture, Sports, Science and Technology (MEXT) has formed an advisory council related to this issue, and seems to be moving in the direction of policies advocating increased vocational education. MEXT's basic line of thought is this: As the hiring environment changes, demand for personnel increases, and workplaces become increasingly diverse, there arises both a corresponding need for a framework for practical vocational education and heightened expectations for the role of vocational education in higher education. Four related points have been raised:

1. The importance of providing an education that, to the extent possible, grasps and is responsive to economic and industrial trends and demands for human resources.
2. The need to support both lifelong learning activities and vocational life.
3. The importance of ensuring educational quality.

---

23. Fryer Jr. and Levitt (2004).
24. Marshall (1890) volume 6, chapter 4.

4. The need for expanded educational choice and appropriate evaluation of practical vocational education.

These points — in particular the first — give the impression that industry is demanding that schools serve as part vocational training institution and part staffing company. Indeed, some vocational schools and colleges seem to be heading in this direction, providing training in specialized professions and offering bachelor's-equivalent degrees aimed at fostering the specialized skills needed to become, say, a chef or a caregiver.

One might wonder, however, to what extent students at these vocational schools desire the new degrees on offer. Students in recent years have increasingly questioned the value of obtaining a college degree in the first place, as evidenced by the current plateau in college advancement rates. It seems likely that many youth today might prefer a no-frills education with an advanced vocational curriculum, spending far less than four years on classroom studies but more time acquiring work experience that gives them advanced skills, thereby becoming exceptional workers. In many competitive fields, having a degree is often said to signify nothing. There is thus a danger that the concept behind these "new" forms of college is not based on sufficient market research regarding needs on the demand side.

The MEXT document asserts the need for an educational system that "grasps and is responsive to economic and industrial trends and demands for human resources," but employment trends in various industries and occupations can only be determined through market-based adjustment functions. Determining rates of change and diversity is extremely difficult, even if one takes into account the predictions of company managers, government officials, and researchers. Gaining insight into which fields vocational colleges should invest in over the long term is therefore impossible, and this is exactly why formal education imparts principles that form the foundation of abilities that can adapt to change. The tasks performed at actual worksites are more complex and advanced than either the uninitiated or elite business managers imagine, and they require diverse and extensive competencies. Most of these competencies are obtained through on-the-job training, and we cannot ignore the fact that systems for developing skills and knowledge have long existed and functioned well in Japanese workplaces.

There is only weak evidence for the idea that public investment in vocational education improves skills and leads to increased economic activity and productivity. As I will argue in the next chapter, the skills needed for production activity are developed through actually performing the work, and classes, training, and vocational education can only supplement this on-the-job training. This important point was pithily expressed 2,400 years ago by Aristotle in his *Nicomachean Ethics*: "What we can only do by practicing, we practice only by doing. We become carpenters by building houses, and lyrists by playing the lyre."

When considering the process by which workers transition from higher education to industry, it is important to keep in mind the career path leading to the skills and experience needed for the position and rank in question. Without addressing issues such as the strengths and weaknesses of Japanese employment and educational systems, how they should be improved, and how such improvements as social givens address problems with the formal education system, we are only engaging in idle speculation.

This point has implications for MEXT's recommended review of liberal arts departments for potential restructuring or abolishment. For example, most Japanese liberal arts majors have found work after graduation in the offices of both large and small companies. While nearly all middle managers in Japan have bachelor's degrees, by global standards an unusually low number have graduate degrees.

Another characteristic of Japan is the weak correspondence between the skillset of those in management positions and their college majors. Most college graduate white-collar workers in Japan majored in law, commerce, business administration, or economics, but few actually use these skills in their day-to-day work activities. For example, in one study that I was involved in, approximately 30% of accounting department managers had majored in economics and another 30% in commerce and management, but an additional 14% had majored in law. Approximately one in three of those using sales-related skills had majored in engineering or law. This shows the extent to which on-the-job training is effective in Japanese workplaces. In a questionnaire that inquired whether the educational content of the last degree received was useful, respondents in the U.S. emphasized the pragmatism of some institutions of higher learning, but those in Japan and Germany indicated a low level of practicality, particularly in professional education.[25]

The same study also produced interesting results regarding skill certifications. Only 28.7% of Japanese respondents agreed with the statement "There are useful certifications available." Among the available certifications, those viewed as most important were "labor and social security attorney" in the human resources field (cited as important by 65% of respondents), and certified public accountant (30%) and certified tax accountant (20%) in accounting. No other certifications were considered particularly important.

---

25. Koike and Inoki (2002).

Furthermore, these certifications were not considered vital to finding employment or being promoted. This is a key point for predicting how companies would evaluate degrees from new forms of vocational college as a signal of ability. Even if vocational colleges are created in response to industry demands, they will be detrimental to the careers of many young people if industry does not trust the degrees they offer.

Notably, while only 28.1% of German respondents reported the availability of useful job certifications — a similar ratio to that seen in Japan — 38.7% said that certifications were vital to finding a job, and 39.8% considered them useful for promotions. Both of these values are much higher than those in Japan.

These studies show that discrepancies exist between countries, and these discrepancies are determined by whether industry (the labor demand side) considers educational background and certification necessary conditions for hiring and promotion. While certifications serve as a powerful signal of labor quality in the U.S. labor market, this is not the case in Japan (with the exception of the special cases mentioned above), despite a period in which certification was considered useful for changing careers. Individual labor market characteristics are thus an important determining factor in human resources selection. Without sufficient identification of the extent to which professional degrees and certifications serve as signals to industry, degrees from new forms of vocational colleges may even become stigmas for job-seeking graduates.

To consider this issue, we must thoroughly investigate where and how the skills required by industry are obtained. This will be the theme of the next chapter.

Honda Motor Co.'s Suzuka Factory. (Photo: Jiji Press)

CHAPTER 5

HUMAN RESOURCE DEVELOPMENT IN FACTORIES

This chapter focuses on how skills and knowledge are formed in economic systems, and how they are mobilized in industrial workplaces. The structures and functions behind systems for fostering, allocating, and rewarding human resources determine a country's economic strength. Human resources are particularly important in Japan, given the relative lack of natural resources. In the end it is people — and only people — who determine a country's level of economic development.

Even in countries with abundant natural resources, however, prosperity cannot be maintained without adding new value to those resources or developing systems for their renewal. Natural resources acquire new value through human labor, technologies produced through knowledge, and skills for supporting those technologies. However, institutions and practices that improve the quality of human labor develop slowly. The knowledge and techniques contained within people are called human capital, and human capital is fostered and allocated through human resource development. I begin this chapter with a discussion of blue-collar workers, with the goal of laying out the fundamental structures of human resource development that determine economic productivity.

1. Education and training for blue-collar workers

The relation between labor and productivity

Differences in productivity originate in differences in the skills and mastery level of workers — in other words, their stock of knowledge. A study that I engaged in from 1984 to 1986, which investigated the productivity of workers in cement factories in Japan, Thailand, and Malaysia, illustrates this point.[1] The Malaysian factory used the newest machinery, while the Japanese factory used vintage equipment with the lowest level of automation. The machinery in Thailand was somewhere between these two extremes. However, the Japanese factory had the highest labor productivity (defined as the number of millions of tons of annual cement production per worker), which by even the most conservative estimates was three times that of the Malaysian factory. Since the Japanese machinery had the lowest level of automation, these values do not overestimate productivity in Japan; if anything, they underestimate it. This indicates that the quality of a labor force plays a deterministic role in worker productivity, with the breadth, depth, and amount of work and skills all affecting productivity. Previous interviews and detailed workplace observations have shown that Japanese

---

1. Koike and Inoki (1991).

workers have much greater experience, breadth of work, and ability to respond to irregularities in tasks such as machine operation and making rounds than do workers in either Malaysia or Thailand.[2] However, previous research examined the nature of this "quality" only in extremely abstract terms.

A highly detailed understanding of the quality and quantity of formal, standardized education among workers can be attained through school records, such as curricula and class schedules. It is more difficult, however, to grasp the details of informal on-site training, since the content of this type of training is typically not written down. Several considerations must be kept in mind when discussing informal education and training.

The first is that while technological innovation certainly provides opportunities for increased productivity, it is not a *necessary* condition; even given a fixed set of equipment, improvements in how work is performed will continuously improve productivity. Furthermore, human labor and experience are key to realizing potentials for increased productivity through technological innovation. In other words, technological innovation is not a *sufficient* condition for increased productivity, either. A variety of case studies related to the so-called "Horndahl effect" have investigated the fact that productivity can increase even with a fixed set of capital equipment.[3] Recent microstudies based on interview surveys indicate that this effect arises both through the process of workers becoming accustomed to equipment, and because the manner in which workplace education and training are provided strongly determines the extent of learning that results.

Another important point is that even when formal technical knowledge (the content of inventions) enters a given country, its potential is frequently not realized until required equipment and experienced personnel also become available. Furthermore, low-cost propagation of these technologies and skills (or, in some cases, the very possibility of such propagation) requires highly similar economic standards between the giving and receiving countries. Supporting social and economic conditions (educational standards, related peripheral technologies, etc.) must be in place for new technologies to take root and flourish.

For instance, Thomas Newcomen succeeded in the first commercial application of an atmospheric steam engine in Worcester, England in 1712, but it took decades for similar engines to appear in Hungary, France,

---

2. Koike and Inoki (1991), chapter 5.

3. See chapter 3 of Koike and Inoki (1991) for theoretical and empirical research related to the Horndahl effect.

Belgium, Austria, and Germany, despite extensive international sharing of scientific knowledge during that period. The technology only spread after British engineers visited similar factories in these continental European countries to assemble engines there. In other words, transfer of the mechanical, operational, and maintenance skills to support the new technology became viable only with the transfer of engineers well-versed in the required techniques.[4]

Even in modern cases of direct investment, Japanese production managers frequently travel to overseas plants to supervise the introduction of new technologies, and conversely, foreign supervisors visit Japanese workplaces similar to their own. Whether it is more efficient to send people in one direction or the other depends on the situation at hand (starting a new factory, replacing out-of-date machinery, studying the situation at other workplaces, etc.), but modern cases nonetheless clearly demonstrate the effectiveness of individual, specific on-site education and training.

Forms of education and training

Education and training after employment generally take the form of on-the-job training conducted during work and off-the-job training conducted away from the workplace. This section surveys systems for human resource development in Japanese factories with a focus on the concepts of on- and off-the-job training.[5]

The stereotypical view of how Japanese companies train their employees is that most small and medium-sized companies do not have any particular training program in place, while large companies train employees for several months after hiring and then again in intensive courses just before or after promotions; in other words, they provide on-the-job training (this excludes specific knowledge and skills acquisition related to new products and technologies). On closer examination, however, we find that the supposed lack of special programs for education and training at smaller firms only applies to formal training. In actuality, these firms conduct highly informal on-the-job training that does not include classwork or long stays at training facilities external to the company.

Of course, on-the-job training alone is insufficient for human resource development, and training requires a foundation to take root. Even so, it plays a central role in skill development at modern Japanese factories. Training

---

4. Mathias (1979, p. 30).

5. Odaka (1993b) presents detailed cases of in-house training in Japanese organizations during the prewar era and period of rapid economic advancement.

systems that emphasize on-the-job training furthermore form the basis of Japan's history of highly efficient education and human resource allocation.

On-the-job training is most effective when combined with post-hiring off-the-job training that supplements some degree of formal learning. The required extent of formal learning — whether knowledge equivalent to, say, a junior high school education versus a vocational school degree is needed — depends on the content of the work involved. In most Japanese offices and production sites, completion of the nine years of compulsory education provides a sufficient foundation for further gradual learning through on-the-job training. Note that this is also a testament to the high level of the content of Japan's compulsory education.

Training programs are not always popular with employees, however, as Tayama Katai's 1909 novel *Inaka kyoshi* (Country Teacher) aptly demonstrates. In one scene, the teacher referenced in the title is attending a Saturday lecture not long after his appointment. This takes place in a large lecture hall, where a group of elementary school principals and instructors are listening to a discourse on basic child psychology delivered by a fat, bow-tied teacher from a normal school in Urawa. Everyone is sitting in rows, listening intently. Next up is an education official, who delivers his opinions on teaching methodology and lessons for instructors. After the lectures the crowd adjourns to a banquet at a nearby inn, where a principal — his tongue loosened by alcohol — enlivens the group with a comment about the uselessness of lectures like those they have just listened to. In modern terms, we would call this a criticism of off-the-job training. The scene is immediately followed by further opprobrium directed at elementary schools and pay scales based on length of service, making this work from over a century ago feel remarkably modern.

Focus on on-the-job training

Education is of course a shared task between teacher and student. Generally, an experienced instructor presents a model to learners, who attempt to copy it. Since students can only imperfectly mimic their instructors, the teacher points out deficiencies and areas for improvement. The repetition of this cycle of instruction and imitation is the very essence of on-the-job training.[6]

This feedback process generally continues as a one-on-one relationship

---

6. Since the techniques presented by instructors generally cannot be passed on through words and symbols, propagation of such skills is generally accomplished through demonstration. See chapter 4 in Polanyi (1958).

in which training is specific and individualized, and the task performed creates real products, not practice works. Put another way, the work is the training. The lack of separation between the two explains why on-the-job training is often not recognized as education or training, or at least is difficult to observe.

As the following case studies illustrate, on-the-job education and training is extensive at many small and medium-sized companies. They describe education and training methods adopted by four companies in Tokushima prefecture from the late 1970s through the early 1980s, during which time the companies introduced new technologies, particularly computer numeric controlled (CNC) machine tooling.[7]

Company A

Company A, established in 1963, was primarily a manufacturer of labor-saving devices. The 140-odd employees included 60 engineers engaged in development, design, mechanics, and electronics, another 60 performing machining on the factory floor, 13 process managers, and 5 or 6 office clerks.

In a typical year, the company hired 15 or 16 new employees and lost 4 or 5. Hires came in approximately equal numbers from engineering and electronics colleges and vocational high schools.

New hires were taught basic information about the company (activities within its organizational structure, guiding principles, etc.) before receiving technical training. Because education at colleges and industrial high schools covers only basic knowledge and principles, graduates from those schools cannot be expected to immediately operate equipment. The core of education for new hires was therefore on-the-job training under the supervision of a superior. Classroom learning occurred irregularly, as the need arose.

One example of classroom learning occurred upon introduction of CNC machine tooling, when instructors from device manufacturers were invited to teach basic computer usage, and employees spent up to a week studying at the manufacturer. The company was responsible for travel costs, but the manufacturer provided training tuition-free. Such training services will not and cannot be purchased if they are not offered by the manufacturer, so most offer them free of charge.

CNC machine tool operators at this company had a very high skill level. Eight operators specialized in CNC milling, all of whom were college or vocational school graduates with knowledge of automation programming.

---

7. Kansai Economic Research Center (1984). The cases presented here are from investigations conducted in 1983 by the author along with Tomita Yasunobu and Matsushige Hisakazu.

At the time of our investigation, the company's first CNC milling operator had become a 31-year-old team leader, and the youngest operator was a 22-year-old new graduate who had just joined the company. General training by manufacturers is effective, but specific finishing procedures can only be learned on the job. For example, there are always equipment-specific peculiarities, such as the "G01" machine command that moves the tool to the right in some devices, but to the left in others. On-the-job training is therefore extremely important.

Training by third parties, on the other hand, is both costly and of questionable effectiveness. Another uncertainty is the extent to which persons with the ability to teach needed skills are present at third-party educational institutions.

While CNC milling relies on off-the-job training more than conventional equipment does, on-the-job training was vital at Company A because, as mentioned above, machine operation varies among manufacturers. College-educated design and development employees attended conferences related to precision machining, where they obtained knowledge that is helpful when purchasing new equipment.

The company hopes to implement a system for in-house certifications in the near future. National and industrial certifications certainly have their place, and the company will likely continue to use them for some jobs. However, these examinations only provide a rough indication of worker ability. They are designed to apply to any company in a given field, and so inherently cannot address company-specific abilities. In-house certification systems are needed to address such shortcomings.

Company B

Company B designed and manufactured molds for plastic products. It was a subsidiary of a medium-sized company in a neighboring prefecture, and was capitalized at forty million yen. The parent company made parts and molds for diesel engines, but Company B was formed in 1972 to specialize in the manufacture of molds using CNC machinery. It had outgrown its current lot, and therefore was considering locations for expansion.

The company had around 110 employees, and hired around 10 new employees each year. It had plans to eventually employ around 200. Vocational high school graduates accounted for 80% of new hires, with the remainder coming from colleges and junior colleges. One hire had graduated from a public vocational training center. Several years prior to our study, the company tried to recruit from the machining programs of training centers, but found no suitable candidates and so no longer recruited from those facilities. The average employee age was 25, and retention rates were extremely high; in the previous five or six years, the company had lost only one employee.

Most education was provided via on-the-job training. While the company occasionally provided classroom courses for skills certification tests, they were the exception. During the first few weeks after new employees joined the company, they were provided with several hours per day of instruction focused on safety, regulations, and clerical procedures.

When new CNC machines were introduced, employees were sent to device manufacturers for training. The company had separate positions for machine operators and programmers. Operators did not need any specialized programming skills, and tasks were allocated so that new employees had ample work. At the time of our investigation, there were six dedicated programmers. When the company was first established, the programming team leader, a thirty-year-old high school graduate, spent around one year at the parent company studying programming. Since then, he had been teaching programming to new employees.

New hires spent one to three years as machine operators. Work assignments were based to some extent on aptitude, but most employees spent their first six to twelve months operating general-purpose devices. Following that, they studied programming. The use of general-purpose machines was learned solely through on-the-job training. Employees started with these machines because without experience with blades and milled materials, they would not have been able to create good programs.

College graduates spent one year learning CNC operations, then moved on to positions as designers, developers, or programmers. At the time of our investigation, the company was researching ways to implement computer-aided design and manufacture and office automation related to process management. Mold manufacture was increasingly becoming an equipment-based industry in which only the best-equipped companies would survive, so constant research on new tools was vital.

Company C

Company C had a number of factories, including one that began operations in 1944, which we visited. This factory mainly manufactured small bearings, of which it produced around 10 million per month. Around 41% of these were for automotive applications, and a major automobile manufacturer was both the company's largest customer and a shareholder. Around 21% of products were exported. Approximately 100 million bearings of this type were produced each month in Japan, and Company C's factories collectively accounted for 35% of them.

The factory had 1,260 employees, 900 of whom worked in production divisions and the rest in clerical, technical, and management divisions. Most technical division employees were engineers engaged in production technology development and process streamlining. There were 164 female employees, 30 in clerical positions and the rest in production divisions. The average employee age was 35.9, and the average employment period was 12.4 years.

From 1975 until the time of our investigation in 1983, the factory that we studied did not hire any new employees. This was because production during that time increased by less than 10%, a level that was accommodated through streamlining. Starting in 1982 the company progressively raised its retirement age over the course of four years from 56 to 60, so no employees retired during that time. The factory had a good retention rate, on average losing less than 1% of employees per year, including retirees.

Prior to 1975, the factory hired approximately half of its high-school-graduate employees from vocational high schools and half from traditional high schools and trade schools. All college graduates were hired by Company C headquarters. Due to expansions starting around 1970, the factory hired around 500 mid-career employees via personal connections and public employment agencies, peaking with a workforce of around 2,400. The number later fell, in part due to the transfer of 400 employees to a new factory in a neighboring prefecture. In 1978 Company C was designated as belonging to a depressed industry, which qualified it for employment adjustment subsidies. The company implemented a three-month career-change assistance system, and induced 200 early retirements through allowance benefits.

Grinding is the primary technique used to manufacture bearings, along with heat treatment and lathing. Technological progress related to bearing manufacture is extremely slow, and because they are mass-produced, transfer machines are more efficient than CNC equipment. Bearings compete based on quality, but because there are no model updates, the fundamental technologies required for their manufacture do not change.

Most in-house education at Company C occurred through on-the-job training, mainly conducted by supervisors and section chiefs. Automation had alleviated the need for highly experienced operators, whose tasks became limited mainly to quality inspections, periodic blade replacements, and product insertion and removal. A division of one hundred employees would typically include around five specialized engineers who performed retooling. These engineers were trained mainly on the job, but the company occasionally conducted in-house workshops intended to reduce retooling times.

With regards to production processes, the supervisor's ability to keep a line running smoothly is more important than the skill of its operators. During the year of our study, twenty to thirty candidates for supervisory positions started a skills training course geared toward in-house certification. This off-the-job training consisted of 150 hours of classwork about hydraulics, electrics, measurement, drafting, and bearings.

Employees actively sought skills certifications, and many were certified in lathing, heat processing, machinery maintenance, and jig tools. Third-party training institutions were not commonly used, but external instructors for topics such as arc welding and forklift operation had been utilized in the past. Employees had also been sent to public vocational training schools to improve their skills related to electrical and gas facilities.

Since 1977 the factory had fully transitioned to a *kanban* inventory control system, in which components are produced as needed in a system that includes a production logistics framework. The factory introduced the new system through group and on-the-job group training. This highly responsive inventory system reduced work-in-process stock from one day's worth of inventory to three hours' worth, enabling more rapid response to demand.

Company D

Company D was founded in 1949, and in 1966 became a subcontractor for a major shipbuilder. The company produced industrial machinery castings, primarily for marine equipment. At the time of our investigation, it had 195 million yen in capital and 125 employees, of whom 20 were design engineers, 80 were general engineers, and 25 clerical and sales staff. Eighteen of these employees were in management positions. There were 3 female employees in clerical positions, and 4 on the factory floor.

In 1982, the year prior to our study, the company hired 1 college graduate, 1 vocational high school graduate, and 4 standard high school graduates (3 men and 1 woman). They also hired 1 mid-career employee with a graduate degree and 7 patternmakers who had retired from a major shipbuilder with whom the company had business dealings.

This company was notable for its many mid-career hires, which are much less common in Japan than in the West. Most of these hires came via public job-placement agencies, but in some cases via personal introductions and connections, or by direct contact from applicants.

As of July 1983, the average employee age was 40. While worker retention for those over age 30 was very good, many younger educated employees left the company two or three years after being hired. Among the 7 high school graduates and 2 vocational training school graduates hired in a previous year, only 2 of the former and 1 of the latter remained at the time of our investigation.

There were few differences in the skill sets of vocational training school graduates and industrial high school graduates at the time of hire, but vocational school graduates did not have the knowledge base to perform complex tasks that required consulting blueprints, which limited the work they could engage in to some extent.

New employees were trained in groups for approximately one week after hiring. During this time they learned about the corporation, prepared for job duties, and learned safety precautions. High school graduates hired from within the prefecture began training in March, immediately following graduation, but college graduates from outside the prefecture began work in April. Orientation was thus performed separately for these groups. New employees then engaged in field training for approximately six months, during which time they learned processes ranging from welding to molding. This broad training was provided for various reasons, including because it allowed workers to understand all the processes the company engaged in, improved their work flexibility, and made future reassignments easier. The aptitude of high school graduates was evaluated during this time for future position assignments.

After positions were assigned, training proceeded primarily on the job. The company manufactured a wide variety of products in small lots, so knowledge accumulated through experience was important. For safety purposes, some experience was also necessary before taking on tasks such as using grinders for finishing.

At the time of our survey, the company faced two main problems related to on-the-job training. One was that employees were very busy, so applied knowledge tended to be emphasized over basics, making it difficult to develop effective human resources over the long term. The other issue was that due to a previous temporary hiring freeze, there were no third- or fourth-year employees. This was problematic because it limited the number of young employees that new hires were able to look to as role models; for some time, mid-level managers had to provide instruction and training.

Company D relied much less on third-party training facilities than on-the-job training. When launching new products or projects in the past, the company dispatched employees to trade-partner shipbuilding plants, and it also sent employees to safety seminars conducted by the local occupational safety association. The company was considering hiring three college graduates to expand its design technology division. It did not send employees for further college studies, but was considering dispatching employees to an industrial laboratory.

Four employees had recently received high-level skills certifications. The company did not provide test preparation courses, so each prepared at the factory on weekends. The examinations were held in a neighboring prefecture, so the company covered travel expenses and test fees. Employees who obtained certification receive salary benefits. Certification was not a specific requirement for promotion, but it was taken into consideration.

2. Why on-the-job training is effective

Passing on "living knowledge"
The four case studies summarized above demonstrate that when new equipment is introduced, equipment managers typically provide special training sessions, but after it is in use, training occurs on the job. Furthermore, at all four companies off-the-job training occurs irregularly, such as when employees are hired or promoted, or when they are preparing for certifications.

In general, then, companies educate employees through on-the-job training. There are several likely reasons why this is the case.

While outsiders often assume that simple labor does not require experience, close observation of worksite tasks shows that laborers constantly face uncertainty and unpredictable events. Machine operation is thus not as simple as it appears. Machines inevitably perform routine tasks; the operator's job is to reduce production processes to steps simple enough for the machine to handle. One example is retooling. Retooling tasks are always required, regardless of automation; indeed, the more automation permeates a factory, the more important and difficult these tasks become.[8]

Frank Knight made the interesting point that while the operator's job can never become completely routine due to mechanical conditions, events prior to production processes, and lack of uniformity in raw materials, the operator's capacity for responding to such unpredictability can be determined with some certainty.[9] Selection and evaluation of operators is therefore the responsibility of their supervisor (foreperson, etc.). The supervisor's task of evaluating operators is in turn reduced to routine, and any exceptional contingencies must be passed up to a superior. It is important to note here that the knowledge needed by supervisors in higher positions is not specific knowledge regarding production site problems, but rather

---

8. Inoki (1991, pp. 276–315).
9. Knight (1964).

knowledge concerning employees' ability to address problems. To summarize Knight's assertion, the most important decision is the selection of the person who will make decisions; other decisions and judgments are automatically reduced to routine. Put another way, true uncertainty lies in estimating the level of uncertainty with regard to human capability, and the ability to make such estimation measures potential for dealing with other types of uncertainty.

Change is a constant in any economy. One significant concern for those who engage in daily economic activity is how to reduce costs based on individualized, specific knowledge. In an idealized society in which all activity is performed in response to past events, new decision-making is unnecessary, and therefore there are no economic problems in the true sense of the term. There is also no need for new planning. In a real-world economy where change is constant, however, the ability to respond to change greatly affects workplace productivity.[10] But to what extent does the stock of empirical knowledge necessary for an effective response come from formal education or group training, and to what extent does it arise organically?

Operators working on the production floor do not clearly recognize the details of their work as knowledge; they simply go about performing tasks that require a high degree of experience. This is not due to a lack of perception, but rather because their skills cannot be clearly expressed in words.

Because the details of such skills cannot be clearly articulated by those teaching them, let alone in a manual, they can only be passed on by example. As learners watch teachers perform a task and do their best to copy them, they unconsciously internalize the rules behind the techniques. The existence of indefinable knowledge at production sites suggests that wholly managing and transmitting skills in isolation from worksite machines and tools is very difficult.[11] Therein lies the strength of on-the-job training for transferring this type of "tacit knowledge" — a strength which the managers of Japanese production sites realized from an early date.

In addition, each worksite has its own peculiarities that arise from differences in machinery and personality. This too creates minor (yet marginally important) characteristics that are difficult to learn as general principles in a classroom setting. Thus while on-the-job training is extremely effective for passing on tacit knowledge, it is also a highly efficient and democratic component of human resource selection and allocation. Japan

---

10. Friedrich Hayek developed an important comparative system regarding this point. Hayek (1945) in particular describes uncertainty and incomplete knowledge in the context of the efficiency of economic activity.

11. Polanyi (1958), chapter 4.

has traditionally placed a much greater emphasis on on-the-job training than other countries have. Below I discuss Koike's theoretical model as it relates to the economic and democratic features of on-the-job training.[12]

Improving skills at low cost

When workers learn particular tasks through on-the-job training, they both broaden and deepen their skills. Exactly how that occurs varies with the type of work and the skills involved. Taking lathing operations in metal machining as an example, workers first learn how to produce simple forms, then tackle more complex blueprints. As the blueprints become increasingly complex, specifying the production of more advanced forms, learners turn to senior workers for advice, thereby improving their skills while receiving instruction related to a specific blueprint. (Of course, regardless of whether an individual is explicitly designated as an "instructor," the extent of that person's dedication to education and training strongly influences the results.) Skill development for tasks with strong artisanal characteristics — machining, for example — does not necessarily lead to varied experience within the company that forms a career. Those who are highly skilled and demonstrate teaching and decision-making abilities when in supervisory positions are promoted from group leader to foreperson. At the same time, however, finishing with lathes and milling machines is highly uniform (setting aside mechanical peculiarities and the characteristics of the machined material), so movement between companies does not devaluate the worker's skills. There is therefore little chance that such movement will negatively impact a worker.

However, in modern industrial society these types of jobs have gradually lost their value. In large, modern companies in particular, capital equipment allows further subdivision of work, so more workers are able to learn various jobs, thereby expanding the breadth of their work and deepening their knowledge of overall production activity. This is true of the steelmaking, petrochemical, and other heavy chemical industries, as well as some tertiary industries such as banking and large-scale retail.

Companies in these industries tend to finely divide tasks and rank them according to difficulty. New employees first engage in the simplest tasks, and after they have gained some experience move on to more complex but related tasks. This "relatedness" is important: there is no economic benefit in randomly transferring workers among tasks or assigning them to jobs completely unrelated to what they did before. When workers engage in

---

12. Koike (1966); Koike (1977).

tasks that are slightly more complex than prior tasks but related in terms of knowledge and skills, the monetary and time costs of learning are significantly reduced as compared with the costs of learning a completely new task. Progressive job movement within the company or workplace is therefore the best way to form a career path.

Democratic methods for personnel selection

When job vacancies are filled with employees hired from other companies or industries, productivity usually falls. A primary reason for this is that career paths differ in minor ways between companies, even within the same industry. The longer a career path (in other words, the more jobs a worker experiences during his or her career), the higher the variation between companies in the order in which jobs are learned, and the larger company-specific differences become. This prevents workers who transfer between companies from immediately applying the skills they have accumulated in the past. Increasing worker retention (the number of years employees spend at a company) therefore has an extremely important impact on productivity. The relatively high retention rates of blue-collar workers in postwar Japan have for this reason benefited human resource development and skill formation.

Another reason for the drop in productivity when workers are hired from outside the company relates to employee motivation to do good work. This happens because it is difficult for managers to oversee workers performing tasks that they themselves have never performed — particularly if they are in on-site supervisory positions, such as group or section leader, or are involved in worker training. Furthermore, when workers are managed by someone who was promoted to their supervisory position, they have greater hope for their own future promotion. Workplaces that customarily fill supervisory positions with externally hired, highly educated employees are bringing in people who (despite their extensive education) have little experience with workplace tasks, and are thus unable to lead effectively. This problem demonstrates that workplace-specific skills obtained through on-the-job training are separate from and at times more important than those obtained through formal education and other types of off-the-job training.

For both of these reasons, in-house career path development plays an important role in skill and knowledge formation. In-house career development implies phased skill formation through on-the-job training and internal promotion. In other words, in-house career development essentially occurs through on-the-job training in which workers start with simple tasks and gradually proceed to more complex ones, thereby greatly contributing to the efficiency and economy of education and training.

In-house career development also gives workers a sense that opportunities are equal and fairly allocated. As workers perform tasks at various complexity levels, they are both trained and screened, and because many workers are able to participate in this screening process, it supports equality of opportunity. Filling middle-management positions through in-house screenings that evaluate how well work is done is clearly more democratic than hiring someone from outside of the company.

Despite the democracy of these systems, however, they pose several drawbacks for workers. Namely, when many workers gain experience in related tasks, the result is increased competition and substitutability. When workers obtain skills with low substitutability, they no longer compete amongst each other. Therefore, while increased worker substitutability is beneficial in terms of increased flexibility in allocations of human resources, it increases competition between workers. If labor unions do not appropriately control competition, it can weaken worker voice and bargaining power.

In any case, the fairness of evaluations is a core issue in human resource systems.[13] Fair performance assessments encourage workers to do better. Fulfillment of the company's potential as an organization — and even its very existence — depends upon both a democratic system of career development that provides opportunities for engaging in a broad range of work, and fair evaluations of performance, preferably by multiple parties. The timespan that evaluations cover is also an important consideration. Whether the company relies on short-term results or long-term observations and data when evaluating employees greatly affects the nature and consequences of competition within the enterprise.[14]

3. Lessons from developing countries

In this section I will examine the role that human resources play in skill formation and economic development in developing countries, in light of the discussion above. I assume the validity of several generally accepted suppositions. One is that employees are provided, through higher education, with sufficient knowledge of science and technology from advanced

---

13. Performance assessments (evaluations) of even blue-collar workers is characteristic of Japanese companies. See Fujimura (1989) for an international comparison.
14. See Nakajima et al. (2013) for a discussion of various issues related to personnel evaluation.

countries, and are able to adjust and adapt that technology to the developing country. The second is that elementary education imparts a certain mentality for establishing an industrialized society, particularly an emphasis on punctuality and a willingness to work in groups under the instructions of a supervisor. Presuming both these conditions are met, on-the-job training can develop human resources and enhance skills. This raises some important points regarding the connection between formal education and income.

First, formal education does not immediately and directly increase income. According to one meticulous comparison of Japan and the United States, attainment of similar educational standards in Japan far preceded attainment of similar income standards.[15] The study provides a factual basis for discussing the relation between education and economic development, and supports the theories of human capital discussed in the previous chapter. Similar comparisons have been made between Japan, South Korea, and the United States.[16] Other discussions of the relation between education and income (productivity), while generally only considering formal education, have made the following points:

1. Formal junior and senior high school education has not been particularly important for initial industrial development in developing countries,[17] including in East Asian nations such as Taiwan and China.[18]

2. During Japan's period of rapid economic development, formal junior high school education became important when technological standards started to increase and imitation (introduction) of modern technologies began in earnest.[19] More broadly, the importance of formal education increases in tandem with technological innovation and competition in marketing.[20]

3. Education plays a small role in agricultural productivity, but an important role in nonagricultural productivity.[21]

Furthermore, the economic effects of education are not limited to the productivity of the workers who receive that education. The more education a head of household receives, the higher that household's resilience to income variation. The higher the education level of a parent — the mother in

---

15. Gōdo and Hayami (2002, pp. 961–978).
16. Gōdo (2003).
17. Koike and Inoki (1987).
18. Ōtsuka and Sonobe (2003).
19. Ueshima, Funaba, and Inoki (2006, pp. 50–76).
20. Ōtsuka and Sonobe (2003).
21. Kurosaki (2003a).

particular —— the larger the impact on the child's education and on-the-job training.[22] It is particularly interesting that the lower the educational level of the parent, the higher the earnings ratio of the child's education (note that this is the earnings *ratio*, not absolute earnings).[23]

Future research in this field will likely focus on questions such as how education relates to economic development during each stage of industrialization (initiation, quantitative expansion, and qualitative improvement) and how educational effects vary with the attributes of those receiving education.

4. Japan's period of rapid economic development

I will next consider the impacts of formal education, particularly in the context of technological innovation during Japan's period of rapid economic development. During the 1960s, Japan made significant capital investment in new technologies, but this investment led to improvements in productivity only because the new equipment was paired with a high-quality labor force.[24]

Adapting to a new technological environment without replacing existing staff requires significant time and monetary investment in retraining. Indeed, the adoption of new production technologies forced many organizations to restructure their labor force. The introduction of new technologies often has characteristics of skill-biased technological change (SBTC), which shifts labor demand in the direction of those with relatively high educational backgrounds. This occurs because resolving the various issues that initially arise in new production processes requires scientific knowledge and logical cognitive skills like those obtained in formal education.[25]

Research from the U.S. examining the long-term effects of technical innovation on labor demand have also shown that the introduction of new production methods shift demand toward more educated workers. During the electric revolution that transformed the U.S. manufacturing sector in the early twentieth century, for example, mechanization of transport and assembly tasks advanced particularly quickly in fields that purchased energy from power plants, and the ratio of high-school graduates in the labor force increased.[26]

Data from the 1960s through the 1980s show that industries with newer

22. Kurosaki (2003b).
23. Ashenfelter and Rouse (2000).
24. The following description is based on Ueshima, Funaba, and Inoki (2006). See Mitani (2003) for an overview of labor, employment, wages, and labor relations in postwar Japan.
25. Bartel and Lichtenberg (1987).
26. Goldin and Katz (1998, pp. 693–732).

capital stock have relatively high demand for college graduates.[27] These finding suggest that new technologies are generally complementary with a highly educated labor force. New technologies do not dismantle skills; to the contrary, they require more advanced skills.

By separating the process of adopting new production technologies into stages of introduction and mastery, we can examine how existing research uses the theory of SBTC to explain why labor demand shifts toward workers with more education. Below I describe two effects of technology introduction in order to assess biases for educational background.

Responses to uncertainty, change, and irregularities

A workplace in the process of introducing new technology faces various uncertainties. The precise production methods that will improve efficiency remain unclear, and workers must understand production processes and the mechanisms of machinery and equipment to determine the most inexpensive solutions to problems that arise. Logical reasoning like that developed through formal education is indispensable to these ends. By the time new technologies reach the mastery phase, however, basic troubleshooting has generally been codified in manuals, and solutions to problems can be learned through on-site experience.

Hazama Hiroshi has examined the distinction between the introduction and mastery of new technology in the petrochemical industry.[28] When Hazama carried out his investigation in 1959 at a chemical plant established in Iwakuni in 1955, most manufacturing processes with the exception of some batch systems (terephthalate manufacturing equipment, etc.) had recently been thoroughly automated. As a result, the factory only hired high school (not junior high school) graduates as operators, and recruited over a broad geographic area, utilizing difficult qualification exams and school recommendations of exceptional students. The number of employees was drastically reduced, and frontline supervisors (a managerial engineer position) were eliminated.

When Hazama revisited the factory in 1962, the company was coping with the sudden introduction ("transplantation") of technology by allocating "young, highly flexible high school graduates" with knowledge and skills as operators, and college graduates as on-site managers. He notes that in plants that had entered the mastery phase, daily task routines had been standardized, and frontline supervisors were not college graduates, but rather

---

27. Bartel and Lichtenberg (1987).
28. Hazama (1963, pp. 21–32).

those with extensive experience as factory operators. Furthermore, hiring of high school graduates by mastery-stage factories was restricted to the local area, and did not focus on exceptional students. This illustrates the clear difference in educational background required for workers in the introduction and mastery stages of technology introduction.

Sophistication of capital equipment

Another important point is that newly introduced equipment typically has more complex internal structures and functions than the equipment it replaces. More advanced scientific knowledge is therefore required to understand how to operate and maintain the new equipment, as well as to understand the production processes preceding and following its use.

Process industries provide a notable illustration. For example, workers at prewar chemical companies relied on intuition regarding the appropriate conditions for chemical reactions while they monitored thermometers and flow meters and skillfully operated valves. The transition to automated systems starting in 1955 necessitated the ability to understand chemical reaction equations while monitoring instruments for automatic adjustments, and perform preventive maintenance against abnormal situations. The introduction of computer-based process control in 1969 further increased the demand for knowledge, which now had to encompass systemic knowledge of computers and overall processes.[29]

Orii Hyūga provides interesting observations about the relation between technological innovation and labor force composition in the steel industry.[30] At strip mill plants, automation enabled workers to control all metal transport, from the furnace through rolling and cutting, by pressing buttons. Rolling steel was no longer the hot, labor-intensive task that it once was, and instead "called for knowledge of metallurgy, electronics, and machinery, which was provided by young high school graduates; laborers who had previously relied on intuition-based skills were thus driven out of these areas."

The automation of machine finishing worksites also led to the hiring of workers with higher educational backgrounds. CNC machining tools, which were broadly introduced in the 1970s, are one example of technological innovation in machine finishing. CNC tools enable computer-based numeric control of traditional metalworking devices such as lathes, mills, and machining centers, and their operation requires knowledge of both

---

29. Yamamoto (1994), chapter 4.
30. Orii (1961, pp. 21–24).

mechanics and electronics. To study how the introduction of CNC tools changed the qualitative makeup of labor forces, I observed 75 employees at small and medium-sized companies and found that these tools were used in an iterative process by highly experienced machine-tool operators and technicians who had received formal electronics training, generally at the college level. They worked together to develop and continually correct and refine computer programs for product creation.[31] Engineers with experience using general-purpose (non-CNC) machining tools had to be involved, because the development process required knowledge related to retooling and the creation of jigs and tools, while the extent of involvement by young technicians varied with the precision that the product demanded and the difficulty of the finishing techniques employed. In general, the move to CNC machining calls for a combined understanding of both machinery and electronics, which increases workplace requirements for advanced scientific knowledge.

Expansion of back-office departments

While the introduction of new capital reduces demand for manufacturing-division staff, in many cases it increases demand for maintenance section engineers. This in turn increases the demand for highly educated workers, leading to SBTC. Automation substitutes investment in capital equipment for investment in manufacturing division engineers, while simultaneously requiring expanded maintenance divisions to ensure the continued operation of capital. This increases capital coefficients, labor–equipment ratios, and the proportion of highly educated workers. While equipment may at first be prone to breakdowns, maintenance and continued improvements ensures smooth operation of equipment in the mastery phase. At this point, one can expect further reductions to maintenance staff.[32]

Matsushima Shizuo proposes that with extensive capital investment, "the more technological innovation proceeds, the more complex machinery and equipment becomes and the more important their maintenance, forcing a gradually increasing emphasis on maintenance division personnel (indirect labor)." He notes that one steel mill he investigated increased its operator staff by 30% between 1951 and 1957, but increased indirect laborers by 70% over the same period.[33]

The situation is somewhat different in the assembly industry, where

---

31. Inoki (1988, pp. 375–460); Inoki (1991, pp. 276–315).
32. Bright (1958) provides a similar hypothesis regarding the effects of automation on the demand for direct and indirect labor (particularly in maintenance sections).
33. Matsushima (1962, pp. 438–444).

mechanization of individual manufacturing processes is possible, and so the cost of introducing new equipment is measured against the resulting wage savings. Thus, in situations where the future of the product market is uncertain and a low-cost labor force exists, multi-talented engineers are employed to perform minor repairs, and most are hired as temporary or part-time workers who perform simple, repetitive tasks. Even so, such workers are replaced by machinery as the market expands.

In the automotive industry, the introduction of rotary transfer machines (metalworking devices with automatic transport) separated blade sharpening, attachment, and repair tasks from assembly line tasks. Research and development was conducted in the late 1970s in response to tightened restrictions on emissions and noise, and automobile manufacturers adopted multi-product strategies to increase market share. The introduction of new production technologies (CNC for machining equipment, welding robots for automobile assembly, etc.) further shifted employment policies toward an emphasis on increased education.

Statistical analysis of the empirical cases presented above yields the following conclusions.[34] Industries making the largest investment in new equipment during Japan's period of rapid economic development hired the most new graduates with advanced educational backgrounds, and during the period from 1963 through 1970, the labor demand for high school and college graduates versus junior high school graduates increased annually by more than 1.0 and 1.2 points respectively. In other words, the introduction of new technologies required a more highly educated work force. Wage disparity based on educational attainment did not grow during this time because education was expanding on the labor supply side.[35]

Of course, the conclusion that new technologies require skills obtained through advanced education does not refute the importance of skills obtained through on- and off-the-job training. Indeed, applied training in new technologies presumes advanced education in order to function well. In on-the-job training, experience is presented in manuals and embedded in machines and equipment. The introduction of new production technologies creates new skill hierarchies. As previously discussed, irregularities and change are constant in mechanized workplaces, and their effects on production efficiency depend on how well they are handled. As capital equipment becomes larger and more complex, the skill with which it is handled strongly impacts productivity.

---

34. Ueshima, Funaba and Inoki (2006).
35. See Sugayama (2000, pp. 193–264) for an analysis of this point.

Focusing solely on manual-based knowledge does not improve the organization's ability to cope with change, and instead reduces education and training to the accumulation of dead fragments of knowledge. Because it is difficult to document skills for dealing with change, workers must accumulate on-the-job training by combining objective knowledge and intellectual ability.[36] More research is needed to understand to what extent formal education can foster the ability to cope with change by job type, or whether this ability can only be obtained through on-site training.

5. Are "Japanese employment practices" unique to Japan?

Long-term employment and seniority wages

As mentioned above, career development through on-the-job training relies on internal promotions. Of course, internal promotions also increase the length of worker service. When employees can expect to advance through promotion routes (career paths) after spending a certain number of years performing a particular job, they are more likely to stay in positions for the length of time required for promotion. In addition, when mid-level supervisory positions are filled from within the company rather than by external hires, this, too, extends the number of years these employees spend with the company. The democratic and efficient aspects of on-the-job training thus result in career development within the organization, and systems which encourage internal promotion also lengthen employee service.

This point relates to the most important reason that wages increase with seniority. Namely, when on-the-job training expands skills from simple tasks to difficult ones, and increased wages are viewed as compensation for heightened skill, wages naturally increase with years of service (and, when employees stay for many years, with age). This is why years of service remains an important measure of ability and wage profiles unavoidably improve with age, no matter how much human resource divisions and company executives wish to emphasize ability over seniority when determining wages. Labor is allocated internally and wages are determined based on the organization's systems and practices. The "internal labor market" is shaped through mutually dependent factors including length of employment, limited hiring outside of entry positions, internal promotion, internal career paths, and the organization's wage systems.

The correspondence between wages and length of service is inextricably linked to skill improvement through on-the-job training. These wage curves

---

36. See, for example, Koike and Inoki (1987), Yamamoto (1994), and Odaka (1993b).

exist among white-collar workers in countries throughout the world, as the next chapter demonstrates. In Japan, however, similar wage systems also exist among blue-collar workers, who benefit from a fairly wide range of raises based on performance reviews.[37]

Neoclassical economics explains the upward-right curve of wage profiles as a form of labor incentives. There is an implicit contract for wages below productivity levels in the first half of employment, in exchange for wages exceeding productivity levels in the latter half. This improves worker retention and motivation.[38] However, while these incentives cannot be ignored, they do not account for improved productivity through increased skills. Over the course of my research, I have frequently observed that Japanese workers in production divisions are highly capable of adapting to change and uncertainty. Common theories overlook this fact.

Arguments promoting the vague concept of "lifetime employment" often note the high level of retention among Japanese laborers. High worker retention does not appear to be unique to Japan, however.

A 1993 OECD report on patterns of worker retention and length of service among European laborers found a remarkably similar pattern to that of Japan.[39] Anglo-Saxon countries settled through immigration, such as the United States, Australia, and Canada, occupied one end of the spectrum, while Japan and continental European countries like France and Germany occupied the other. The report argues that because Japan and the U.S. are at opposite extremes, comparisons between these two countries represent a comparison of extremes. It is therefore dangerous to assume that differences between Japan and the U.S. hold true between Japan and other countries. Below, I consider this issue quantitatively.

Figure 2 shows average lengths of service by age and sex. Solid lines represent data from the United States, while dotted and dashed lines represent data from Germany and Japan respectively. As the graph shows, American men under age 60 have much shorter average lengths of service than do men in Japan and Germany. There is not much difference between Japanese and German men through their mid-fifties, but following that, length of service for Japanese men drops rapidly. This is likely because many older employees in Japan are permanently relocated to group companies, which in the data set is viewed as starting over at a new company with zero years of prior experience. In fact, this type of movement between companies is a

---

37. Koike Kazuo has long emphasized this fact. See, in particular, Koike (1966), Koike (1981), and Koike (2005). See Inoki (2009) for an analysis of research by Umemura Mataji.
38. See for example Borjas (2007).
39. OECD (1993).

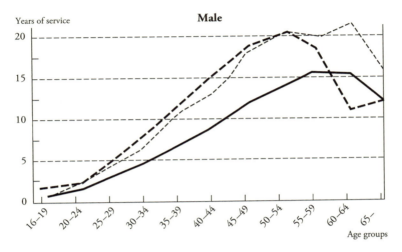

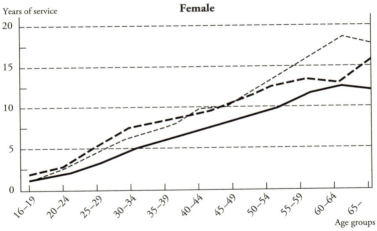

Source: OECD (1993, p.124).

Figure 2. Average years of service by age and sex

common feature at both the early and final stages of careers in Japan, a fact that should be kept in mind.

Long-term employment at large companies

The Labour Center Office of the Japanese Ministry of Health, Labour, and Welfare has used employment insurance data to calculate the number of new-graduate hires who quit their first job within three years. Approximately 65% of male and female junior high school graduates, 40% of high school graduates, 20% of male college graduates, and 40% of female college graduates fit this criteria. These figures rise and fall to some extent with the economy, but are largely stable. As this data shows, theories of lifetime employment in Japan do not reflect the actual state of affairs. The young labor force is put through a few years of trial-and-error reshuffling before being assigned to longer-term positions, and many workers will change jobs during this period.

Figure 3 shows the relation between short- and long-term job turnover by country in 1985 and 1991. In the graph, the horizontal axis represents the average number of years of service, and the vertical axis represents the rate of job departure within one year of employment. (Note that units on the horizontal axis are presented in the reverse of the normal order.) Countries in the first quadrant (upper right) have low average lengths of service and high short-term turnover. Those in the third quadrant have long service lengths and low turnover. Worker retention is thus low in the first quadrant, and high in the third. As mentioned above, the United States was far to the right in both 1985 and 1991. In contrast, Germany, Japan, and France were in the third quadrant. Worker retention in Japan improved somewhat during that period, moving it deeper into the third quadrant. This is a significant difference between Japan and the continental European countries.

Nevertheless, Japanese systems for long-term employment are not unique to Japan, nor do they reflect a continuation of employment practices from before World War II. The Japanese Department of the Interior provides statistics on the movement of blue-collar workers in the 1920s and 1930s in its "Shokkō idō shirabe" (Investigation on Factory Worker Transfers).[40] According to those statistics, worker relocation rates were very high in the 1920s, when experienced workers were in extremely short supply. On average over 70% of workers changed jobs each year in the first half of the 1920s, but this fell to around 40% between the late 1920s and the mid-1930s. The decline began in a period that coincides with the adoption of seniority

---

40. Sawai (2012b).

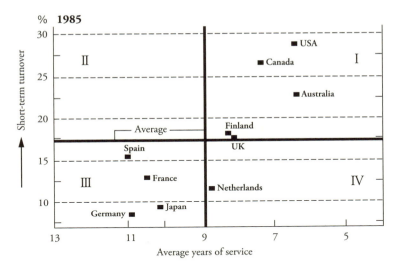

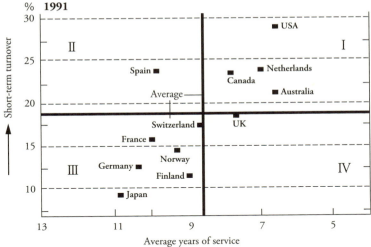

Source: OECD (1993, p.133).

Figure 3. Short-term turnover and average years of service in 1985 and 1991

wage systems at factories.[41] As mentioned above, while seniority wages for white-collar workers exist in many countries, the application of this system to blue-collar workers is somewhat unique to large Japanese companies.[42]

Job turnover was much higher during Japan's postwar period of rapid

---

41. Chūma (1987, pp. 307–320).

development than it is today. Even among regular employees (not part-time or temporary workers), around 17% of men and 30% of women left their jobs annually. These numbers fell after the first oil shock, and settled at around 10% and 20% respectively. The so-called "Japanese" practice of long-term or lifetime employment is, in actuality, restricted mainly to certain labor segments at large companies, which account for less than 20% of all employed workers.

From the viewpoint of labor economics, the economic rationale for long-term employment can be summarized as follows. First, there are two types of skill: general skills that once acquired can be applied at any company (for example, foreign language ability or basic computer skills), and enterprise-specific skills that only increase productivity if the employee stays at the company where they were obtained (for example, knowledge of the organization, its career paths, and the characteristics of its workers). Enterprise-specific skills are largely invalidated when workers change jobs, and it is rational from both the perspective of the worker and the organization that the costs of recovering these skills be shared by both parties. Because both the worker and the organization share in the long-term return on investing in this type of training, it is furthermore rational for both to strive toward maintaining a long employment relationship.

It is impossible for employers to fully grasp the abilities (productivity) of workers at the time of hiring. The best strategy for the employer, therefore, is to be highly selective in hiring, to evaluate worker abilities through long-term observation of work performance, and to accumulate this observational information. It is vital that job satisfaction be maintained through equitable evaluation systems based on long-term observation. In this respect, too, long-term employment — specifically, employment that involves selection based on length of service over a long career within the organization — has a significant positive impact on productivity.

Koike Kazuo classifies skills and their development processes into four categories according to skill level and time required for acquisition.[43] His system is important because it does not simply classify skills as belonging to high- or low-skilled labor, but rather emphasizes the realities of modern industrial society, in which worker ability rises with experience.

Koike proposes the following skill categories: Type A skills are high and unchanging, and commonly associated with skilled labor. These skills

---

42. See Koike (1981) for a comprehensive analysis from EC data. Umemura (1967, 1971) provides international comparisons of how wages are both determined and increased.

43. Koike (1977), chapter 7.

improve through focused training under an apprentice system, and are retained once mastered. Type B skills are low and unchanging, and are commonly associated with low-skilled labor. Type C skills are developed over a long time through systems for internal promotion. Type D skills can be obtained over a relatively short period, and are associated with semiskilled labor.

Among these, Type C skills spread as the heavy chemicals industry expanded, particularly through long-term in-house training of semiskilled workers at large corporations, indicating organizational recognition of the rationality of such skills. Because training occurs over a long time, interruptions increase training costs. The work itself therefore becomes the training, simultaneously providing worker education for future expected tasks. On-the-job training is thus efficient and rational, although skills must be associated with both the present job and the next in the organizational career path. For internal promotion systems based on experiencing sequential related jobs to function as intended, the organization must be of sufficient scale and provide a logical progression of learning tasks to form specific career paths. Of course, even if career paths are largely similar among firms within a given industry, they are not identical. Workers must therefore develop some enterprise-specific skills.

These observations suggest that career paths based on on-the-job training exist in many large companies, and form the basis for long-term employment in Japan.

A long-term look at employment practices

I will close this chapter with a discussion of recent changes in hiring and skill-development practices in Japan, in particular with regard to skills that are formed over the long term through internal promotion systems.

Of the 1.12 million new graduates who entered the Japanese labor market in 1955, 62.2% — nearly two out of three — had a junior high education.[44] Only 6.2% of new workers had graduated from a four-year college. The number of newly graduated job applicants peaked in the late 1960s, and gradually fell after 1970. By the mid-1990s this number had fallen to 600,000, less than half of peak values. Educational backgrounds also changed significantly during this period, with college graduates (including those from junior college and graduate schools) making up over 40% of new job seekers in the late 1990s, and junior high school graduates falling to just over 1%.

Japanese firms placed these young workers into systems that improved

---

44. MEXT (1955–2000).

their skills, largely through on-site tasks and — in the case of large companies — in-house and third-party institutions for secondary education. These systems also improved skills through long-term evaluations of worker quality and achievements. While each company had its own rules for allocating work based on education or promotion, as late as the 1980s many exceptional workers in Japan's manufacturing industry occupied supervisory and team leader positions despite having only a junior high school education. These were employees with high latent potential who were unable to attend high school or college due to family economic circumstances.

Such workers supported production during Japan's period of rapid economic development. Superior production-site managers arose from the ranks of junior-high educated job applicants who made up two-thirds of new hires, and were promoted to positions as educators, managers, and supervisors in the sites where they worked. In order to build labor forces capable of significantly contributing to productivity, most Japanese manufacturing-sector companies implement long-term selection and promotion processes characterized by harsh internal competition. The influential individuals who emerged from these processes comprise one of the most important features of the postwar Japanese economy, in that their enhanced skills contributed to improved workplace productivity and order. Meritocracy likely existed in prewar times as well, but human resource systems relied more on educational background; individuals with more education received preferential treatment in employment and job selection, and rules for promotion clearly differentiated between workers in clerical and labor positions.

Today, over 50% of youth advance to college, far more than advanced even to junior high in prewar Japan. Systems for human resource development and selection at postwar production sites underwent a "contact effect" similar to that described in chapter 3, becoming environments of harsh competition that many employees engaged in. As opportunities for competition expanded, skill formation and human resource development improved. This is the environment in which the high productivity of Japanese production sites formed.

However, Japan's shift to a postindustrial society has led to a climate of neglect for manufacturing industries, and skill improvement through internal promotion rooted in long-term perspectives has gradually faded. Indeed, by the mid-1990s less than 20% of the workforce is employed in manufacturing. However, from an inter-industry perspective, manufacturing remains important since its products (for example, highly efficient machinery and equipment) enable the development of many jobs in tertiary industries. Neglect of the manufacturing sector thereby equates to ignoring the fact that productivity in the service and public sectors relies on technological innovation that arises from manufacturing.

Rush hour at Tokyo's Yaesu train station. (Photo: Jiji Press)

CHAPTER 6

WHITE-COLLAR WORKERS

Employees engaged in product creation at production sites are generally called "blue-collar" workers, while those who wear suits and work in offices are called "white-collar" workers. While this distinction is convenient when compiling statistics, a growing number of positions blur such clear-cut classifications. For example, some managers support the production or distribution of goods, and some engineers supervise and train workers at production sites. Increased recognition of the intellectual tasks involved in many production-site jobs, and the prevalence of simple, routine tasks in many office positions, has diminished the common association of white-collar jobs with brains and blue-collar jobs with brawn.

Historically, many white-collar positions were in the commercial and finance industries, and in government. As corporations in the manufacturing industry increased in size with industrialization, the number of managerial positions in this industry grew as well.

Chapter 1 gave an overview of the apprentice systems of Edo-period merchants. These practices changed in interesting ways during the transformation of social systems that occurred in the Meiji Restoration. One notable change was that as companies transitioned from apprenticeship to employment systems, workers went from being live-in, uniformed servants to commuting employees who were paid wages. This brought an end to education and training in the employer's household; instead, human resources were selected through academic tests that measured mastery of the "three Rs."

By the end of the nineteenth century, however, some industries needed employees who had received higher education and could oversee modern banking services. The basis for hiring this type of worker shifted from test results or other demonstrations of academic ability to the schools attended and the experienced garnered since graduation.[1] This change took time, however, because those who were educated at the Imperial University and similar institutions traditionally went on to positions in government, education, or law; few took jobs at private firms.

Nakamigawa Hikojirō, who in 1891 left his position as president of Sanyo Electric Railway Co. to become executive director of Mitsui Bank, advanced policies for hiring the academic elite into private companies. Nakamigawa significantly raised bank employee salaries, thereby making private employment much more appealing, and implemented meritocratic policies that rewarded achievement with promotions. Mitsui Bank developed human resource policies that treated employees as two distinct groups: an elite who

---

1. Chimoto (1989, 1994).

had received higher education, and the mass of general workers, who had not. Following reorganization of the school system in 1920, hiring and worker allocation based on academic background became the predominant system for education and training.[2]

1. White-collar workers before and after World War II

Prewar trends

The June 1930 "Report on education among company and factory workers" provides information related to the academic background of white-collar workers in prewar Japan.[3] This report concerns a survey investigating the relation between academic history and position attained in various industries. From among the eighteen industries covered, I will discuss the banking and insurance industries and department stores as representative examples of white-collar employment.

The report provides statistical data for 48 banks, including Nippon Kangyo Bank, Daiichi Bank, Yasuda Bank, Mitsui Bank, and Mitsubishi Bank. Of the 32,627 office employees working at these banks, 10.5% (3,438) had graduated from a four-year university or college, 9.6% (3,122) from vocational colleges or the equivalent, 27.0% (8,798) from vocational high schools such as industrial or commercial schools or the equivalent, 13.8% (4,501) from standard junior high schools (including girls' schools), 2.8% (925) from vocational junior high schools, and 35.8% (11,683) from standard elementary schools. (Note that school types with very low values are omitted here and below.)

The relation between academic achievement and job position is particularly noteworthy. Of the 107 employees at the department manager level or above, 31.7% had graduated from university, 22.4% from vocational colleges, 13.1% from vocational high schools, 17.8% from standard junior high schools, and 12.1% from standard elementary schools. While the ratio of university graduates is high, the number of junior high and even elementary school graduates is also significant. Of the 401 employees in section management positions, 26.8% held only an elementary school diploma. These figures demonstrate that during this era a lack of higher education did not rule out opportunities for advancement.

At the 33 insurance companies examined, which together employed

---

2. Using human resource strategies at Mitsui & Co. as a case study, Wakabayashi (2007) attributes the rise of the modern Japanese "salaryman" to changes in education and infrastructure such as the telegraph, the telephone, and modern transportation.

3. Research Office of the Bureau of Practical Education, Ministry of Education (1930).

10,927 workers, the distribution of academic achievement was much more even: 15.1% of employees had graduated from university, 16.4% from vocational colleges, 15.5% from vocational high schools, 12.9% from standard junior high schools, 11.1% from schools for girls, and 15.0% from elementary schools. The bias in distribution among job types, however, was greater at insurance companies than at banks: 34.2% of department managers and above had graduated from university, 43.0% from vocational colleges, 11.4% from vocational high schools, and 10.1% from junior high schools. Elementary-school graduates became section managers at best (9.0% of the total).

The report covered eleven department stores, including Shirokiya, Matsuzakaya, Daimaru, and Takashimaya, and collected data for 17,579 employees. Among these, 2.4% had graduated from a university, 3.4% from vocational college, 9.9% from vocational high school, 4.9% from junior high school, 12.9% from a school for girls, 49.7% from upper elementary school, and 11.6% from lower elementary school. Over 60% of employees thus had no education beyond elementary school.

Department managers in department stores were considered company executives rather than employees. Looking instead at the educational backgrounds of section managers, we find that 13.0% had graduated from a university, 7.7% from vocational college, 10.1% from vocational high school, 10.1% from junior high school, 48.6% from elementary school, and 8.7% from lower elementary school. Again, nearly 60% had only an elementary school education.

It is clear from this data that different industries had different compositions of educational attainment among their office workers. Even so, at this time even white-collar workers with only an elementary school education had sufficient opportunity for career advancement.

Postwar trends

Following World War II, the service industry expanded as a percentage of the labor force, while the manufacturing industries declined. A remarkable trend toward hiring more white-collar workers also emerged. Indeed, college-educated white-collar workers took a leading role in the labor market. As mentioned above, however, the concept of the "white collar" worker is difficult to clearly define. For expediency, I will equate white-collar workers with prewar "office workers," and blue-collar workers with prewar "factory workers."

While the number of white-collar workers clearly increased, attaining precise data on this trend remains challenging. The Ministry of Health, Labour and Welfare's highly respected *Basic Survey on Wage Structure* compiles statistics using two categories of workers: production and supervisory, clerical, and technical. Production (blue-collar) workers are defined as "persons who engage in work at the production site of goods or construction sites, etc." Specific job examples by industry provided in the report include the following:

1. Mining and quarrying of stone and gravel: Workers engaged in tasks related to coal mining, mineral mining, excavation, mine transport, shaft struts, shaft repair, hoisting, ventilation, drainage, blasting, grinding, coal preparation, mineral processing, transportation, maintenance, general repairs, etc.
2. Construction: Workers directly engaged in construction work at construction sites.
3. Manufacturing: Workers engaged in manufacturing, processing, assembly, inspection, calibration, transportation, legal affairs, maintenance, repair, etc.
4. Port transport: Workers onboard ships engaged in coastal cargo handling, etc.

The report defines "supervisory, clerical, and technical workers" as "persons who are not production workers."[4] However, workers in production divisions who are primarily engaged in clerical, technical, or supervisory tasks such as group and section leaders are generally considered white-collar workers.

In recent years, the gray zone between production and non-production tasks has expanded, making it increasingly difficult to categorize all employees in a binary fashion. This is due to an increase in the "technical" class, namely workers who perform monitoring tasks and operate advanced equipment. Similarly, advances in office automation increased the number of office workers with jobs involving machine operation tasks. While I recognize the uncertainty surrounding these concepts, in the following section I use several definitions of white-collar workers to quantitatively describe their increasing prevalence during Japan's period of rapid economic development.

Education and company size

Table 14 shows decadal changes from 1960 through 1990 in the occupational composition ratio of workers according to National Census

---

4. Major classifications follow the Japan Standard Occupational Classification used in the National Census. The *Labour Force Survey* by the Ministry of Internal Affairs and Communications uses twelve categories of occupation types, from "A" (administrative and managerial workers) through "L" (workers not classifiable by occupation).

Table 14. Changes in employment ratios among major job categories   (%)

Job category	1960	1970	1980	1990
A. Specialized and technical workers	5.0	6.6	8.7	12.0
B. Administrative and managerial workers	2.2	3.9	4.7	4.4
C. Clerical workers	10.2	14.0	16.5	19.4
D. Sales workers	10.8	12.0	14.6	14.1
E. Service workers	5.2	6.1	6.9	7.2
F. Security workers	1.1	1.2	1.4	1.4
G. Agriculture forestry and fishery workers	32.5	19.2	10.8	7.0
H. Transport and communication workers	3.4	4.5	4.3	3.8
I. Production process and related workers	29.5	32.4	32.1	30.1
J. Workers not classifiable by occupation	0.0	0.0	0.1	0.6
White-collar ratio 1 (A + B + C + D + E)	33.4	42.6	51.2	57.1
White-collar ratio 2 (A + B + C + D)	28.2	36.5	44.3	49.9
White-collar ratio 3 (A + B + C)	17.4	24.5	29.8	35.9
Blue-collar ratio (H + I)	32.9	36.9	36.4	33.9

Source: Statistics Bureau, Ministry of Internal Affairs and Communications (National Census,
       various issues).

classifications. The "white-collar ratio 1" category in this table uses the broadest definition, that of "non-manual" workers, as in EU statistics. In contrast, the "white-collar ratio 3" category uses the narrowest definition. The "white-collar ratio 2" category follows what is likely the most common definition, and shows white-collar workers making up half of all employed persons.

While each definition yields somewhat different values, all clearly show that the proportion of white-collar workers nearly doubled over the thirty years covered. Conversely, when blue-collar workers are defined as "transport and communication workers" and "production process and related workers," their percentage holds largely constant at around 35% over these thirty years.

Table 15 shows manufacturing industry labor compositions by occupation, based on the *Basic Survey on Wage Structure* for 1992. Looking at male workers, there is a clear trend for the proportion of white-collar workers to increase with increased company size. Two points are clear with regards to educational attainment. First, while approximately 50% of clerical and technical workers were college graduates and 50% high school graduates, around 60% of production workers were high school graduates and 30% junior high school graduates. In other words, there is a clear difference in educational background between white- and blue-collar workers. The second point is to some extent a rewording of the first: higher levels of educational attainment imply a higher likelihood of obtaining a white-collar position. For example, while only 16% of men with a junior high school education became white-collar workers, over 90% of male college graduates did. This can also be seen by comparing ratios of white-collar to blue-collar

Table 15. Manufacturing industry workforce composition by job type (1992)　(%)

		Clerical & Technical	Production Workers	White-collar Ratios
Company size (male employees)	1,000+	46.6	30.7	53.8
	100–999	33.9	33.2	44.0
	10–99	19.8	36.1	29.4
Education (males)	Junior high school	8.1	32.6	16.0
	High school	43.1	61.8	34.9
	Junior college	6.4	2.4	67.7
	College	42.4	3.3	90.8

Note: White-collar ratios are the number of white-collar workers by company size and educational background as a proportion of all employees.
Source: Ministry of Labor (1992).

workers in different age categories, which shows a trend toward higher percentages of white-collar workers among younger, more highly educated age groups.

These points can be generalized as follows. The proportion of white-collar workers increases with company size, because larger companies have a larger proportion of managerial positions. Furthermore, workers with more education are more likely to find white-collar jobs. While no numerical data is presented here, white-collar workers also dominate workplaces in large cities, because cities attract managerial work.

Postwar Marxism among upper management

This section touches on one unusual characteristic of upper management in Japanese companies prior to the 1990s. While the postwar purge of business leaders by U.S. occupying forces unquestionably rejuvenated Japanese management, triggering a wave of innovation during Japan's period of rapid economic development,[5] the influence of Marxism in the Japanese industrial world was also notable. For example, many recollections by former business leaders published in the *Nihon Keizai Shimbun* newspaper's *Watashi no rirekisho* (My Resume) column, particularly those from the 1970s and 80s, describe attending lectures on Marxist economics while they were students at major universities in the prewar years. Perhaps this is not surprising, considering the powerful influence of Marxist theories in the economics departments of Imperial University schools. These columns often go further, however, and mention the influence of Marxist scholars like Kawakami Hajime or relate stories of participating in social

---

5. Okazaki, Sugayama, Nishizawa, and Yonekura (1996, p. 25) describe the age structure of the Japan Association of Corporate Executives during its early days just after World War II, showing that 56% of members were in their forties, and over 90% were in their late thirties through early fifties.

movements and study groups concerned with issues of the underclass. Some of these authors later went on to corporate jobs and advanced through the ranks to become leaders of human resource divisions.

There are many examples of such leaders taking part in labor–management conflicts and negotiating in language shared by both sides. While the existence of a business elite sympathetic to Marxist philosophy might seem odd — particularly from a Western European perspective — considering the character of labor–management issues arising at worksites, one can imagine that the presence of individuals capable of negotiating within a common intellectual framework made a significant positive difference.[6]

Other data shows that those with experience as labor union executives in postwar Japan became corporate executives at higher rates than in other countries. According to a 1978 report by the Japan Federation of Employers' Associations described in an article in the *Nikkeiren Times*, of the 352 organizations responding to a survey, 235 (66.8%) had at least one executive with experience in labor union leadership. Of the 6,457 executives at these companies, 1,012 (15.7%) had served as labor union executives.[7] These figures show that there was a career path to upper management for former labor union executives, who likely provided some degree of stability to corporate governance. In any case they suggest that the diffusion of Marxist thought among the highly educated does not necessarily have a negative impact on the business community.

The *Nikkeiren Times* article interprets this difference between Japan and Western European countries as follows. Western European labor participation in management generally involves union leaders joining the company's board of directors or supervisory board. In the case of Japan, however, participation often takes the form of labor–management joint consultation systems at all levels of the company, from the production site up. Company executives attain their position by being promoted from general staff to corporate officer, so union leaders are more likely to take a stance that considers the future of the company that they may one day lead, rather than standing in opposition to it.

This may not describe all Japanese companies, but it shows that Japan's history of fierce disputes between labor and management and its cadre of corporate leaders who studied Marxism as students does not pose a contradiction.

---

6. Inoki (1991).

7. Shirai (1992, p. 79). The newspaper presented these results on its front page, under the headline "Executives at two in three companies were union leaders."

2. "Japanese employment practices" and white-collar workers

This section summarizes characteristics and changing trends related to managers, clerical workers, and laborers since the 1973 oil crisis.[8]

Lifetime employment and seniority systems

The 1990s are often considered the final days of lifetime employment in Japan. I would therefore like to consider how the proportion of long-time male employees (namely, those aged 45 to 49 who have worked for at least twenty years at the same company) at manufacturing firms with over 1,000 employees changed in the last two decades of the twentieth century.

Immediately preceding the oil crisis, 76.4% of college graduates and 86.0% of high school graduates were long-time employees as defined above. Twenty years later, in 1993, these numbers had risen to 90.4% of college graduates and 94.0% of high school graduates.[9]

Hiring in the 1990s was predominantly focused on males graduating from college, and only around a third of companies hired mid-career workers with specialized skills. Of course, not every male hired by a large company straight out of college spent his entire career there; on average, nearly 20% left their jobs for new ones. Even so, as mentioned in the previous chapter, this phenomenon was largely limited to men in their twenties and fifties, with company reassignments being the norm in the latter case.

The salaries and promotion of Japanese white-collar workers were commonly assumed to be determined on the basis of factors such as years of continued service, educational background, and age, with meritocracy playing only a small role. The data contradicts such assertions, however. It is true that a given cohort of workers with similar educational backgrounds could expect uniform promotions and wages over the first six or seven years of employment. However, these workers were evaluated from the day they joined the company, even if such assessments were not apparent to them, and during later phases of employment promotions depended more heavily on merit. One report showed that on average only around 60% of a given cohort were promoted to section chief or the equivalent, suggesting intense competition among workers.[10]

---

8. Much of the following data was obtained from Ministry of Labor, Secretariat for Policy Research (1995).

9. Ministry of Labor (1994).

10. Yashiro (1995) provides a detailed analysis. See Koike and Inoki (2002) for a comparison of white-collar workers in Japan, the U.K., and the U.S.

If we look only at averages, salaries did appear to increase with age and number of years of employment. It would be an error, however, to conclude from this that wages were determined according to seniority, not by merit. First, there was a lower rate of wage increase by age between 1983 and 1993. Second, disparity in wages increased as workers aged, suggesting that salary differences reflected variations in worker performance. These points can be quantified using values from the *Basic Survey on Wage Structure*.

Looking at male, college-graduate, white-collar (managerial, clerical, and technical) workers at manufacturing industry companies with over 1,000 employees, we find the following. Setting fixed salaries of employees aged 20–24 as 100, wages for the 45 to 49 age group were 303.9 in 1983 and 271.0 in 1993. To create an index of individual fixed wage disparity, we can use the difference between the ninth and first decile, taking the median value as 100. Doing so for 1993, we get an increasing index of 33.7 for 30-year-olds, 45.8 for 40-year-olds, and 49.3 for 50-year-olds. In other words, wage disparity increases with age, as differences in ability become more evident.

This analysis shows that there is no basis for claims that Japanese wage systems are based on seniority rather than merit. To the contrary, the facts show that Japanese salaries are meritocratic, and thus appear to be based on seniority when averages are considered.[11]

Meritocracy and evaluation systems
As white-collar workers became more educated, college-educated white-collar employees lost their status as elites. Instead, many became specialized staff that took on front-line operational duties. At the same time, the presence of so many college graduates meant a broader range of disparity in individual abilities. Against this background, some began to argue that previous systems for determining wages based on professional credentials were unsuited to the times. Such systems were advantageous because they provided long-term measures of latent worker abilities, thereby stimulating skill development while reflecting the results through salaries. However, latent worker abilities do not necessarily improve company profitability in the short term. In addition, disparity in latent worker ability was increasing, and it had become clear that uniform management was not possible with wage systems that adhere to a single rule. These points led to inquiries into how the system could be reformed to better evaluate and reward the abilities of college educated white-collar workers.

---

11. See Mitani (1997) for an analysis of wage structures in Japanese companies and an interesting comparative analysis of Japan and France.

Since the end of World War II, arguments have occasionally been put forth for introducing meritocratic systems that reward employees for improving company performance, regardless of age or years of service. These arguments tend to arise during economic downturns, and the current period is no exception. Several companies have attempted to apply such systems not only to specialized positions and contract workers, but even to mid-level management. Performance-based salary systems are one example of shifting the emphasis of wage management from seniority to performance. There is indeed a certain logic to the idea that if evaluations can be performed fairly, then those receiving the best evaluations should receive the highest salaries.

Implementing these ideas, however, presents some challenges. What does a "fair evaluation" encompass? By what rules or calculations should wages be allocated to those evaluated? There are various reasons for not adopting performance-based wage systems, but two of the most common are the difficulty of including qualitative data in performance standards, and the barriers posed by tax, pension, and insurance law. The former in particular is problematic, although arguments for performance-based annual wage systems addressed these issues.

Performance-based annual salaries have become more popular, particularly for management positions, but much room for debate remains regarding how to accurately evaluate such systems and to what job types they should be applied. The following section discusses these issues in the broader context of white-collar human resource management, with which they are linked. I first describe a questionnaire survey of existing performance-based wage systems that investigated topics including the necessity of quantified evaluations, connections with management by objectives (MBO), job types to which these systems are applied, whether evaluations can result in lowered salaries, and the breadth to which assessments are performed. Following that, I present several cases that draw on my research in Japan and the United States.

3. Forms of Remuneration

The three types of performance-based wages

Piece rates and time rates are fundamental types of remuneration, and chapter 3 described some of the problems related to these and to bonus systems. An additional issue not discussed there is how often wages should be adjusted, since they can be paid hourly, daily, weekly, monthly, or yearly.

Wage revisions in unionized business sectors generally occur annually, as in Japan, or every three years, as in the United States. (Note, however, that semiannual negotiations are increasingly popular.) In actuality, however, some union contracts call for shorter-term adjustments, occurring more frequently than once per year. In the U.S., "escalator clauses" are often included that call for quarterly adjustments according to changes in wages and prices.

There is of course the theoretic possibility of a system in which wages are not increased periodically but instead only when employee merit is recognized. However, such methods do not consider trends and changes in the external labor market. In order to successfully determine wages based on merit only, there must be no change in the conditions of external labor markets, and there must be some way to objectively measure merit (this will be described in more detail below). When shocks such as supply-and-demand imbalances occur in the external labor market — for example, a critical shortage of R&D technicians — companies must somehow respond through wage revisions. Methods that only consider performance within each division also lack fairness if there are inter-division performance gaps in the organization.

Nonetheless, performance-based systems remain attractive. One reason for this is that wages can be tied to division- or workplace-specific results, making objectives management at the workplace level easier. Associating division results with individual results furthermore contributes to a sense among employees of a personal connection with the organization. Of course, the magnitude of monetary rewards also affects labor.

Classifying performance-based wage systems into several general categories simplifies discussion of them. The following three categories consider factors such as guaranteed base salaries, the relation between these base salaries and market wages, the proportion of wages determined by performance, the amount of and payment period for performance rewards, and the extent of variable elements in the overall payment.

Type 1 systems for performance-based wages retain the essence of traditional wage systems, in that average market rates are assured regardless of performance, but there are provisions for some small portion of additional payment based on results. In this case, evaluations cover only limited areas of performance, so additional payments are extremely small compared to the guaranteed portion of the salary. This method is characterized by the payment of relatively small performance bonuses, so base wages are not recalculated from zero.

Type 1 systems retain the core of professional-qualifications-based systems

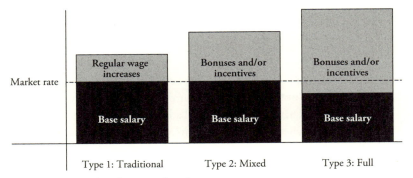

Figure 4. Types of performance-based wages

seen in large Japanese companies, while adding just a touch of salary management. They therefore may not adhere to strict definitions of performance-based wages, because they simply incorporate some form of performance calculation; they do not use negotiable considerations to directly determine wages themselves.

Type 2 systems determine core wages in accordance with the market rate, like Type 1 systems, but add incentives as well as bonuses. Here, "incentives" refers to payments made when workers meet previously specified goals, while "bonuses" are based on ex post evaluations of overall company and personal performance. Bonuses provide some level of worker stimulus, but only indirectly and not to the extent of incentives. Incentives are generally capped, but they make Type 2 systems more stimulating than in Type 1 systems. Incentives are furthermore paid for specific periods, so they cannot be accumulated in the same way as Type 1 raises and base-salary increases.

Type 2 systems add bonuses and incentives to the market labor rate over a given period. It remains somewhat unclear whether bonuses should simply be considered a portioned-out part of fixed salaries, or whether they are truly reliant on company performance. Some research has shown a strong connection with average industry performance. It is clear, however, that their relation with individual performance is limited.

Some performance-based systems in Japan and the U.S. simply add a bonus portion to monthly wages, which is expected to provide a powerful worker stimulus. These systems serve to further differentiate between bonuses and evaluation-based incentives, but do not represent a wholesale replacement for traditional monthly salaries. While Type 2 systems in Japan may seem to be nothing more than a monthly portioning out of traditional biannual bonuses, they should instead be viewed as reallocations that provide a starker contrast between the ratios of bonus and incentive payments.

Type 3 systems include the possibility of paying below-market rates, but no clear cap on total wages. If objectives are met or exceeded, then wages exceeding the market rate are possible, but below-market rates also are possible if objectives are not met. This is the purest form of performance-based wages, and is characteristic of professional athletes such as baseball players. As we shall see below, however, these systems are only used in a narrow range of job types. In short, purely performance-based wages are suited to cases where performance in the wage period can be objectively measured, and where it is clear to all the extent to which employee performance matches established goals or contributes to company performance.

Performance-based wages in the workplace

Two relevant surveys were conducted in the early 1990s, when performance-based wages became a topic of discussion in Japan: the Japan Productivity Center's *Survey on Performance-based Wages*, conducted in October 1992, and the Institute of Labour Administration's *Focus on Performance-based Wages for Management Positions: Assessment by Recipients*, conducted between December 1993 and January 1994.

Japan Productivity Center survey

This study provided different surveys to companies that had implemented performance-based wage systems and those that had not, and was designed to highlight differences in the attitudes towards these systems. The survey received responses from 357 companies (for a recovery rate of 17.0%), around 10% of which had implemented performance-based wage systems and just under 30% of which were considering such systems.

At the implementing companies, performance-based wages were frequently used for management positions (83.3%) and irregular specialized and technical positions (100%), and only rarely applied to service (3.3%) or clerical positions (6.7%).

Three reasons for implementing performance-based systems accounted for nearly 80% of all reasons given: to clarify performance reviews, to create a greater sense of meritocracy, and to increase managers' sense of participating in company management by providing them the same salary structure as officers. "Previous-year results," "expectations," and "roles" were frequently cited as factors behind the decision to implement performance-based wages.

This study also included a survey of human resource representatives at both companies implementing performance-based wage systems and those that did not. Regular employees at implementing companies ranked these systems highly, and irregular employees even more so. The study particularly noted that performance evaluations became clearer, and companies found it easier to engage in recruiting activities for irregular employees. In contrast, employees at non-implementing companies had negative views of such systems, claiming that they placed a high burden on evaluators, made it more difficult to move between job types, and had an adverse effect on human relationships.

Institute of Labour Administration survey

This study mailed questionnaires to 1,684 managers receiving performance-based salaries at large companies, and received 367 responses (a recovery rate of 21.8%). Most of those receiving performance-based wages were salespersons or managers at the section leader level. Most had been receiving performance-based wages for only one to three years, suggesting some extent of prematurity for asking respondents to evaluate the system's merit. Nonetheless, I will summarize the survey's main findings.

Around 60% of those receiving performance-based wages found the system "good," but the remaining 40% remained unconvinced, selecting "not very good" or "unsure." Salespersons were most likely to respond "good," followed by clerical workers. Those in technical and R&D positions gave the most negative reviews, suggesting a clear correlation between job type and the ease of evaluating performance. Sales performance is easy to quantify over short terms, so in many cases evaluations were clearly justified. For technical positions, on the other hand, results are difficult to measure over the course of just one year, and objective evaluations of individual performance and contributions are less clear-cut.

"Increased meritocracy," "increased feelings of participation in management," and "improved morale" were given as positive aspects of performance-based systems, while "increased difficulty of work," "increased uncertainty about the future," and "longer work hours" were listed as negative aspects. Those in sales positions tended to emphasize positive aspects, while those in technical positions emphasized negative aspects (particularly "longer work hours").

This study also presents responses related to the standards used to determine performance-based wages. Around half of respondents expressed satisfaction with the standards, agreeing that received wages "largely match my performance and abilities," while over 40% responded that their wages were "somewhat low" or "very low," indicating a clear split in employee opinions. Dissatisfaction was somewhat stronger among technicians, R&D positions, and managers in deputy group leader positions and below. Employer standards for setting wages included not only "performance" (89.0%) and "ability" (66.5%) but also "market price and wage increase amounts" (43.5%), "credentials" (36.4%), and "age" (35.4%).

Some respondents reported increased uncertainty in life planning when a large portion of wages were determined according to evaluations, but many responses from employees in technical and R&D positions and from section leaders indicated that this was not a problem. Those who had received performance-based wages for three years or more, however, tended to express somewhat negative opinions. Overall, over half of responses indicated a preference for evaluations determining at most a 20% increase over base wages and a 10% decrease. In terms of absolute amounts, the plurality opinion was that evaluations should increase or decrease wages by at most one million yen in either direction.

The overall conclusions we may draw from this study are that performance-based wages can be applied effectively to only certain positions, that more than half of those receiving performance-based wages prefer them, that evaluations should increase or decrease wages by around 10% at most, and that — with the exception of contract employees with specific skills — traditional wage models based on professional qualifications with a fixed schedule of raises remain the most common.

4. Japan and the United States

To examine differences in white-collar salaries and promotions between Japan and the United States, this section presents several case studies from comparative research by Koike[12] and interview surveys that I conducted in the U.S.[13]

Company A

Company A produces information and communications equipment in Japan. In April 1993, this company adopted an MBO system for managerial positions. Review items included guidance of subordinates and cooperation with other departments. There were initially five evaluation rankings, but a sixth was later added so that those showing improved performance

12. Koike (1993).
13. Nippon Institute for Research Advancement (1994). Note that I was the principal investigator in this study, but because its conclusions contradicted generally accepted theory, it remains an unpublished, internal document.

over the previous evaluation period could be assigned one of the upper three ranks. MBO uses absolute evaluation standards determined through discussions between superiors and subordinates, and human resource divisions transform these into relative evaluations. MBO also requires direct feedback to those being evaluated.

The wage system at Company A was called a performance-based system, but according to the classifications presented above it was a Type 1 system, with limited salary management and base salaries determined according to professional qualifications. Specifically, wages varied somewhat due to bonuses applied atop a traditional system of additive wages. Projected winter bonuses were determined in the spring and revised when the winter bonus was actually calculated, thereby tying them to evaluations related to current objectives.

The company cited unresolved difficulties related to linking retirement bonuses and pensions to the current wage system as a reason for not moving to a full performance-based salary system. Overall, the company's wage system was in transition, and while management was interested in "performance-based wages," it remained uncertain as to exactly what changes to make.

Company B

Company B is a Japanese automobile manufacturer. This company underwent major organizational changes in 1990, moving from product-specific divisions and a regional structure to a headquarters-based system with three primary divisions: automobiles, motorcycles, and general-purpose products. As a result of this reorganization, performance-based wages were introduced for approximately 4,500 managers (around 10% of employees).

According to the new system, superiors and subordinates consulted on an individual level to establish work objectives, deciding on up to five important objectives for the year. After a year passed, the degree to which the employee had met those goals was evaluated. The first step in this evaluation was a self-appraisal, followed by evaluations by the employee's superior and persons in leadership positions in related divisions. The process concluded with feedback to the employee.

The company took several measures to avoid extreme salary fluctuations. First, it retained a traditional salary-plus-bonuses system, with the bonus portion determined according to performance in the relevant period. Monthly salaries were kept the same, with bonuses awarded twice per year. In theory, a forty-year-old employee could see a salary variation of around 2 million yen per year, but the actual variation was limited to around 1.2

million yen. Second, starting in 1992, the company increased the weight of evaluations in determining monthly salaries. Pay grades were broadened by decreasing the number of grades from seven to five, and the number of evaluation rankings was increased from six to eight to provide more finely gradated evaluations.

As a result, employees were assigned lower evaluation scores to prevent excessively high salaries through performance bonuses. The new system made it theoretically possible to enter the management ranks two years earlier than before, but in reality the conditions for doing so were so strict that no noticeable cadre of rapidly advancing employees was seen.

The third step would be a transition to a fully performance-based system, but the company expected that to take a minimum of four to five years.

Company C

Company C primarily develops and sells novel agricultural chemicals in the United States. Manufacturing was delegated to subcontractors, so the company had only around 200 employees at the time of the study, mostly in white-collar and technical positions.

Employee credentials were evaluated in ten ranks for non-union employees and seven ranks for union employees. Individual employees provided a written description of their job duties at the start of each fiscal year, after which the employee's position and salary for the year were determined, taking into consideration scores on the previous year's evaluation, responsibilities and difficulty of job duties, and the division's budget.

Line managers determined employee credential ranks according to job duties. However, there were upper limits on the number of persons credentials could be assigned to, requiring inter-departmental negotiations between managers. The company had implemented an MBO system, so employees with the same credentials could still be differentiated to some extent through evaluations, and their salaries adjusted accordingly.

Evaluations were graded on a six-level scale, with highest (A) and lowest (F) grades resulting in a 20% increase or decrease in wages as compared with the mid-point. In other words, salaries varied over a 40% range. The average assessment was a C, and grades of F, which signaled grounds for dismissal, were only rarely assigned.

As in the case of credentials, line managers alone determined evaluations. The company reported that objective standards were largely maintained because a superior had oversight on the various line managers' evaluations of same-job positions. Evaluation results were given to subordinates as feedback, and acknowledged by an employee signature.

Salary standards for a given credential were determined according to market standards, and varied each year according to consumer price levels and company performance (which likely improved in most years). However, when evaluations considered performance in the same job as the previous year, salary was determined solely in relation to the previous evaluation, regardless of other factors. In other words, receiving a higher salary required either improvement over the previous year or obtaining a higher credential.

With the goal of improving organizational morale, in 1993 the company began issuing year-end bonuses predicated on improved corporate performance to supplement the performance bonuses described above. A fund was established that rose or fell according to company performance and linked individual salary bases with the MBO system. At the time of the study, however, individual bonus payouts were extremely low (less than 4% of annual salaries).

Taking 3% of annual salary as x, bonuses were x in fiscal years where pre-tax profits met management goals, $0.8x$ in years where goals were not met, and $1.2x$ when goals were exceeded. Because this was also linked with MBO evaluations, however, the full bonus could only be received when company-wide goals (30%), division goals (35%), and personal goals (35%) were met. For example, when company-wide and personal goals were met, but division goals were not, only 65% of the base payout could be received as that year's bonus.

Risk and departmental disparity

Several steps are involved in the introduction of performance-based wage systems. These include individual wage management to avoid increased labor costs due to workforce aging, addressing the loss of overtime wages when employees advance to management positions, and using higher wages to improve employee motivation and retention. It is particularly important to extend to managers the wage systems typically applied to company executives in order to heighten feelings of responsibility and increase their sense of participation in management. Put another way, providing managers and even technicians and salespersons with a performance-based wage can increase their willingness to take on risk.

This relates to the risk that upper-level management assumes when directing the actions of others within the organizational hierarchy. Workers who climb higher in the hierarchy must make increasingly subjective decisions, with an accompanying increase in risk. Taking a short-term view, there is thus a change in the manager's contribution, which can be considered as productivity (Fig. 5). Performance-based wage systems are designed to associate this change with wages. However, the manager's attitude toward risk determines how mid-level managers view such systems for sharing risk between oneself and the company. When managers are neutral toward risk and non-management workers are risk-averse, implicit contract theory infers that both would prefer a system of fixed wages.

The discussion thus far has considered changes in performance over time, but the way in which performance-based systems address disparity in cross-sectional, inter-departmental performance is also an important issue. In any large corporation, there will often be divisions experiencing rapid growth while others are in decline. Under fixed-wage systems, human resource reallocations between divisions with performance disparities are not problematic. When a performance-based wage system is introduced, however, being transferred to a lower-performing division is desirable neither for the employee nor the employee's superiors. This can hinder human resource development and allocation for the company overall. When considering performance-based wage systems, it is therefore important to develop strategies for overcoming limitations on human resource allocation between divisions with performance disparities.

Hiring and promotion in Japan and the United States

This section summarizes the findings of interview surveys that I conducted in July 1993 in New York, Washington D.C., San Francisco, and Dallas, with the goal of highlighting several differences between white-collar human resource systems in the U.S. and Japan.[14]

While Japanese companies utilize scheduled mass hiring of new college graduates, American companies hire throughout the year, focusing on mid-career workers. American firms use a variety of recruitment methods, but many large companies also hire new college graduates through campus recruitment activities aimed at mass hiring. As in Japan, young human resource representatives predominantly visit well-known schools, and applicants advance through a series of interviews until a final meeting with management that determines whether an offer will be made. Even so, some divisions (investment divisions at securities companies, for example) lose 60–70% of new-graduate hires in the first year, for reasons such as entering business school, so in some cases hiring takes completely different forms even within the same company.

In both Japan and the U.S., small to mid-sized companies are more likely

---

14. Nippon Institute for Research Advancement (1994). See also Koike (1993) for pioneering research.

Organizational hierarchy   **Risk**   **Wage type**

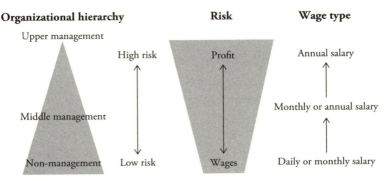

Figure 5. Relations between position, risk, and wages

to engage in year-round hiring of mid-career workers than mass recruitment. Headhunting for management positions occurs in the U.S., but quantitative data regarding this practice is lacking.

It is possible, however, to estimate to some extent the prevalence of internal promotions. Among established companies, internal promotion to management positions is clearly the norm, even in the U.S., and internal promotion focuses on those hired as new high school or college graduates. In some cases those with experience working at other companies in the same industry are accepted as mid-career hires as well.

At securities companies, employees only rarely move between departments, and promotions are generally internal. Investment divisions, which experience high turnover, are an exception, but investment divisions and traders at banks and securities companies are very special cases and cannot be used to illustrate the general situation in other industries or job types. Furthermore, while the number of these positions has increased in recent years, they remain only a small part of the overall job market.

There is disparity in the rate at which same-year hires are promoted in American firms. Some U.S. employees undergo "fast-track" promotions, having been selected after around ten years at a job as having the potential to join the elite, and thus are rotated among company divisions. The roster of such candidates is revised each year, with some employees being removed and others added. Japanese companies, in contrast, prefer to base promotions on long-term observation, so systems for fast-track promotions are rare in postwar Japan.

U.S. companies sometimes lay off white-collar workers. In unionized businesses decisions are based at least in part on seniority, while at non-unionized workplaces or for management positions decisions are sometimes based on performance evaluations. In the case of traders at banks and securities firms, two years of poor performance generally leads to dismissal.

Both Japanese and American firms emphasize on-the-job training for the internal education of white-collar workers. Excluding orientation for new hires, in both countries off-the-job training is provided only sporadically, such as following promotions. Training programs for newly hired college graduates are in general the same as in Japan; new employees are divided into groups and spend a month or two at various posts. Group instruction is provided before and after this, and the results are verified through testing.

While "fast-track" employees in the U.S. are rotated throughout the company, others are sometimes designated as specialists and assigned to fixed positions. In some systems, employees can opt to receive training at third-party human resource development companies.

In typical systems, at the start of the wage year annual or monthly salaries are set within a range that depends upon the job level but also reflects some form of evaluation. There are generally fewer than ten job rankings, which may vary depending on whether the company is unionized. Rank and start-of-year wages are set in consideration of the work content, evaluation scores, the difficulty of the job, and the hiring division's budget. Resource allocations are adjusted in meetings between line and division managers.

While the above represents a simplified wage model for college educated white-collar workers in the U.S., year-end performance bonuses are also awarded in some cases. The proportion of total wages that such bonuses account for varies by job type and industry. While such bonuses are generally lower than in Japan, they can be quite significant. Some jobs at banks and securities firms, for example, link bonuses directly to employee-attributable profits, which can result in large year-to-year variation. This type of job is particularly suited to performance-based wage systems.

5. A model for white-collar workers

Challenges of skills assessment

In order to determine whether internal processes for promoting and training white-collar workers should be fundamentally different from those used for blue-collar workers, we must first clarify several issues.[15] One issue related to selection is how the knowledge, skills, growth potential, and trainability of white-collar workers can be measured. Other important issues include what index to use for such measurements, and how and when

---

15. Inoki (2002a).

to apply such an index to promotions and wages. Also, should job assignments be made at an early stage, before many evaluations have been conducted, or is it better to wait until results are so clear that they are unlikely to change? Should evaluation results be directly reflected in large differences in wages, or used to gradually differentiate wages over the course of continued employment? Once such differences in promotions and wages have been established, should there be a system for undoing them? Each of these questions is also relevant for blue-collar workers, but the issue of measuring skills and growth potential is particularly difficult in the case of white-collar workers.

Another important question is how white-collar workers learn their jobs. Even if a worker is highly educated, he or she will not be able to do the same job as an experienced worker from the very start. Only through conscious and unconscious guidance from experienced co-workers and on-the-job training can he or she learn to do it well.

What kind of alternative or supplementary relation exists between formal education and on-the-job training? The jobs performed by blue-collar workers have been divided into various skill categories, such as those that can only be learned through extensive on-site experience, and those that require experience but presume previous formal education. Such differences affect the saturation point of skill levels and the rapidity with which workers can reach that point.[16] Is this also the case for white-collar workers?

Another important question is what kinds of patterns or principals lie behind jobs and the acquisition of skills they require. The process of accumulating knowledge and systematically instilling it within individuals necessarily requires some prioritization of learning, and the order in which things are learned is dictated by efficiency (in other words, effectiveness). This is similar to the case of mathematics, where it is impossible to understand a given theorem without first understanding the other theorems on which it relies. One cannot understand a given part of a systematized body of knowledge without a comprehensive understanding of the whole; in any corporate organization, there exist knowledge systems to which this principle applies.

Risk and responsibility
Generally speaking, there is a lack of constancy in the day-to-day work of white-collar positions that involve complex managerial tasks. In most cases, lower positions require the constant performance of routine tasks. As

---

16. Koike (1977).

one assumes higher positions, however, the formulaic aspects of one's duties are replaced by increasingly complex ones. At the highest levels of management, work primarily consists of external social interactions interspersed with occasional key decisions.

This relation can be generalized as follows. White-collar jobs involve greater responsibility as one moves up the hierarchy, increasing the risk associated with failure of judgement. In large Japanese organizations, those in higher positions tend to have spent more time at the company. This trend corresponds to the amount of remuneration, as follows: When highly experienced employees with many years of service at the company assume high-risk, upper level positions, the likelihood of failure is reduced. Such individuals are less likely to cause financial loss, and this savings can be passed on in the form of higher salaries. Differences in the risk associated with a job can thus explain differences in the salaries paid for that job, according to how years of continued service (as a proxy for breadth and depth of experience) influences risk.

This relation is also relevant to arguments concerning the possibility of early selection for high-level jobs. Consider an employee who has an MBA, but has no experience in production divisions and has only been with the company for a short period of time. Placing this person in a high-risk position entails a high possibility of failure, and the financial impact of such a possibility must be reflected in his or her salary. Hiring MBAs, paying them high starting salaries, and placing them in high-risk, high-responsibility positions will thus not fit the mid- to long-term financial calculations of many companies.

We can also consider likelihood of success or failure from the perspective of risk adversity. In many cases, jobs that are difficult and uncertain are also highly profitable in the long term. Avoiding such work can therefore lower corporate profitability. Losses can be particularly large when companies prevent employees who are capable of handling difficult tasks from tackling those tasks in the name of risk avoidance.

A political cartoon by Takamiya Takeo addressing revolving-door politics. The caption reads "No way I'm going to give this up easily." The cans from the vending machine (labeled "revolving-door politics") are labeled "concessions," "perquisites," and "corruption." (Source: 27 March 1980 morning edition of the Yomiuri Shimbun newspaper)

CHAPTER 7

THE PUBLIC SECTOR

In Japan, the general view of public servants is that they are promoted entirely according to seniority, and therefore no competition exists once one of these workers have been hired. Many assume that such injudicious equality in routine work leads to reduced efficiency when performing official duties.

This depiction, however, is not entirely accurate. As an example, consider the Tokyo municipal government's system of managing promotions through testing. This system limits promotions for employees unable to pass the requisite test, except in medical, research, and other specialized positions. Such tests add a competitive aspect to the promotion process.

One might argue that because these tests are limited to large cities like Tokyo and Osaka, they are exceptions to the rule. However, even disregarding these tests, there is sufficient evidence of quite intense competition for higher public posts. Given a pyramidal organization, in which the number of available positions declines the higher one goes, increased competition for the few uppermost seats is unavoidable. Unfairly assigning those positions without consideration for ability — through random selection or nepotistic favoritism, for example — lowers the motivation of those not selected, hindering their performance. Even so, the public consensus regarding selection and promotion of government employees is that a lack of competition between local governments prevents anyone from leaving their posts, and therein lies the core of workplace malaise.

However, competition does exist at both the local and national level. Not only is it untrue that local governments monopolistically provide public services, but local government bodies also compete with federal ones in many areas. It is thus an oversimplification to conclude that public offices and competition are mutually exclusive.

This chapter begins with a historical overview of systems for assigning public posts in Japan, and then considers several theories regarding personnel policies at large government institutions to correct some common misconceptions. This section focuses on the megalopolis of Tokyo because its long history as a regional government illustrates several approaches to a number of issues. The following section introduces the human resource systems used for Japanese public servants, taking up the problem of revolving-door politics and describing both the problems with and reasons behind this practice. The chapter closes with the quantitative issue of whether there are too many or too few government officials in Japan. Throughout, the descriptions relate primarily to human resource selection and promotion during and after Japan's period of rapid economic development, in order to demonstrate how hiring, promotion, and resignation have changed during that time.

1. Government Appointments

The Pendleton Civil Service Reform Act

From a modern perspective, selecting government officials through competitive testing seems obvious. Such systems have a very long history: China's old system of imperial examinations is well known, and in 1888 Japan began adapting Prussian systems for testing candidates for public office. One might assume, then, that this has long been the global norm.

Competitive selection of officials does not have a particularly long history in Europe or the United States, however. Despite the implementation of competitive systems in Prussia starting in the early eighteenth century, favoritism commonly determined public appointments in other European countries through the mid-nineteenth century. In the United States as well, open testing was not officially introduced until enactment of the Pendleton Civil Service Act in 1883. Before that, a "spoils system" existed in which the winning political party had free reign to fill public positions, leading to government corruption and inefficiency. Each change in president triggered a reshuffling of officials that promoted money politics and failed to ensure that the most qualified individuals filled government posts.[1] The Pendleton Act ended this by mandating a merit system. (Note, however, that even today a newly elected U.S. president can appoint many officials.)

The Pendleton Act established a bipartisan human resources committee, and instituted a test for many posts. Public officials were furthermore forbidden from making donations or engaging in other political activities. This act was reportedly influenced by civil service reforms in the United Kingdom, and in turn influenced the National Civil Service Law in postwar Japan.

Imperial officials

Under the Meiji constitution, a position as a public official did not involve an employment contract like those used in modern civil service systems, but rather was closer to a legally recognized relationship of ethical servitude to the emperor. Imperial officials were classified as senior or junior, with senior officials further divided into those appointed by general screening and those appointed by imperial decree. In the system established by

---

1. The Pendleton Civil Service Act was crafted in response to the 1881 assassination of President James Garfield by Charles Guiteau, who was angered because he felt owed a government post in exchange for his help in getting Garfield elected. The act was passed in 1883 by Garfield's vice president and successor, President Chester Arthur (Aruga, Ōshimo, Shimura, and Hirano 1993, pp. 52–54).

the Civil Servant Appointment Ordinance of 1893, all public posts except those filled by imperial decree required passing a civil service examination. The ordinance also removed testing exemptions for graduates of the law school at the Imperial University.

Even so, the scope of free imperial appointments and the degree of permissible limitations on them remained points of contention between parties and politicians. The political structure of Japan prior to World War II practically compelled a spoils system, and free appointments were not completely abolished until after the war ended.[2]

The civil service examination was conducted once per year in Tokyo, and was open to all men at least twenty years old. While its content varied somewhat over the years, it predominantly covered economics and constitutional, political, and civil law.

Due to this heavy emphasis on law, many of those who passed the exam were Imperial University graduates, and particularly graduates of the College of Law at Tokyo Imperial University. From the start, therefore, the examination contributed to the formation of academic cliques. Table 16 illustrates this point by showing the alma maters of those passing the administrative section of the test. Imperial University graduates were systematically groomed to take key government positions, which meant that these schools served as shortcuts to becoming an elite government official. However, an Imperial University education was not the only path to success. As Table 16 shows, not all appointments were given to Tokyo Imperial University graduates.

Postwar "fast-track" officials

While prewar officials owed fealty to the emperor, they occupied a privileged position with respect to the general populace. Some therefore occasionally failed to completely separate their public and private duties. There was also extreme discrimination between upper and lower officials, to the point that government offices had segregated cafeterias and washrooms.

Under the new postwar constitution, however, the civil services underwent sweeping reforms that repositioned government employees as servants of the people. In 1947, the prewar civil service exam was abolished, and in 1949 it was replaced with one that was more fair and open. Officials no longer enjoyed special status, and previous large gaps in wages were narrowed. The National Personnel Authority was formed as a central personnel

---

2. See National Personnel Authority (1975) regarding systems for appointment of civil servants since the Meiji period. Mizutani (1999) too provides insightful commentaries.

Table 16. Number of persons passing the administrative section of the civil service examination and number of test-takers from the Tokyo Imperial University School of Law (1895–1935).

Year	Total	School
Nov 1895	37	Tokyo Law: 25; Chuo: 4; Meiji: 2; Waseda: 2; Other: 4
Nov 1905	64	Tokyo Law: 39; Hosei: 7; Chuo: 3; Meiji: 3; Other: 12
Oct 1915	136	Tokyo Law: 110; Kyoto Law: 11; Tokyo Kosho: 4; Other: 11
Nov 1925	331	Tokyo Law: 181; Kyoto Law: 26; Kyoto Econ: 17; Tokyo Econ: 13; Other: 94
Oct 1935	295	Tokyo Law: 147; Kyoto Law: 13; Tokyo Econ: 9; Chuo Law: 8; Nihon Law: 7; Keijo Law: 6; Other: 105

Source: Hata (1981).

administration agency to ensure equal treatment of civil servants across ministries.[3]

Prewar differences in status did not completely disappear, however. Those who passed high-level examinations received jobs in principal ministries and thus became key "fast-track" officials. Compared to typical public servants, these individuals advanced among the ranks much more rapidly and attained much higher final posts. This has changed somewhat in recent years, likely because over 90% of those passing the intermediate-level exam are college graduates, which has improved their potential for advancement. With the exception of large cities such as Tokyo and Osaka, however, promotion through testing is not always available, so conversion from standard to fast-track status remains difficult for many.

Prefectural and municipal personnel commissions provide open testing similar to that used for central government employees, but in small local governments those with the power to make appointments directly hire staff according to personal recommendations or less impartial testing, so the potential for favoritism remains high.

In the regional civil service systems of the prewar era, control over human resources was strongly influenced by the Interior Minister. Prefectural governors were freely appointed by imperial edict and dispatched from the central government. Party influence was strong in the era of party

---

3. A historical perspective on institutions and practices related to wages is needed to fully understand human resource systems for government employees. Inatsugu (2005) summarizes development of the present-day system of National Personnel Authority advisories through the eras of Meiji-period imperial edicts related to public servant wages, Shōwa-period wage cuts for officials, and postwar collective bargaining. Nishimura (1999) describes government wage policy from a public administration perspective, providing analyses of four aspects: public–private balance through private sector compliance, internal balance in official duties, public-sector balance at the national and regional levels, and civil balance between regional governments and the general population.

cabinets (until 1932), so the ruling party largely determined the political leaning of appointed governors. During the prewar Shōwa period, prefectural governors were reassigned every 18 to 24 months.[4]

2. Human resource systems in the Metropolitan Tokyo Government

Chapter 8 of the Constitution of Japan guarantees the right to local self-governance, and the Local Public Service Law of 1950 clarifies four fundamental principles of public service:
1. To avoid domination of public service positions by a select group, these positions must be open to the general national population.
2. Hiring and promotions must be performed according to a merit system based on objective demonstrations of ability.
3. Those in public service must remain politically neutral and in service to the populace as a whole.
4. Efficiency must be maintained through the establishment of a dedicated and objective personnel administration.

To enable democratic and efficient operation of a public service system according to these principles, Congress and local heads of government established independent personnel commissions to determine personnel policy. The commission in Tokyo, comprising three members appointed to four-year terms by the governor with the consent of Congress, held its first meeting in June 1951. The commission enacted rules related to municipal human resources, and conducted reviews and rulings related to working conditions and other employment matters. It furthermore had broad authority to issue recommendations related to wages and working conditions. While specific positions were filled by nomination, hiring for municipal posts was generally determined according to competitive testing conducted by the personnel commission.

Features of the appointment system
The primary feature of Tokyo's system for appointing workers to various posts is that initial hiring is limited to the lowest positions, following which employees are promoted internally. As a specific example, Fig. 6 shows the appointment system for general administrative posts.

As of the 1990s, there were three primary entry points for positions in

---

4. Momose (1990).

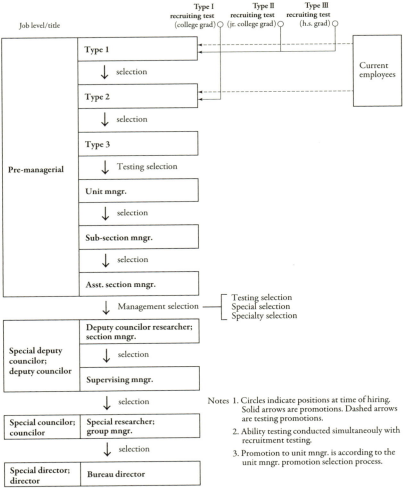

Source: Tokyo Metropolitan Government Personnel Commission (1992).

Figure 6. System chart for general administrative post appointments in Metropolitan Tokyo

the Tokyo bureaucracy. The Section I Recruitment Examination, available to college graduates or the equivalent aged 22 through 30 (or 28 for clerical, civil engineering, architecture, mechanical, and electrical positions), is required for "rank 2" positions. The Section II Recruitment Examination, available to junior college graduates or the equivalent aged 20 through 26, is required for "rank 1" positions. The Section III Recruitment Examination, available to high school graduates or the equivalent aged 18 through 22, is required for entry-level "rank 1" positions. The term "or the equivalent" is used because educational attainment is not an absolute requirement for eligibility. Age is the official determinant of eligibility, and the educational levels are provided simply as a measure of expected academic ability.

The number of candidates taking the exam as well as the number hired fluctuated significantly over time. Hiring increased overall in the early 1970s and peaked at 1,277 new employees in 1973. In 1975, hiring dramatically decreased to around 280 persons due to the economic downturn, which necessitated cost-cutting measures focused on personnel expenses.

Data show that competition within recruitment exam sections rises and falls with economic conditions. A strong economy increases demand for workers in the private sector, lowering competition for public jobs. Around 10% of college-educated applicants were hired for "college graduation or equivalent" (clerical) positions through 1975, but this fell to 2.1% as economic conditions worsened in 1976, then rebounded to 5.5% as the economy began to recover in 1979. The figure fell again to 2.5–3.3% following the 1979 energy crisis, then increased to 9% as the bubble economy began to heat up in the 1990s.

Trends related to the educational background of hires are clear. During the era of peak hiring from the mid-1960s to the mid-1970s, 200 to 300 college graduates and 500 to 600 high school graduates were hired each year on the basis of recruitment tests for clerical and technical positions. For municipal positions overall, on average around 1,800 high school graduates were hired each year. Hiring began to decline drastically in 1976, but the ratio of college graduate hires increased to half or more, reflecting the overall increase in educational attainment in Japan.

The Metropolitan Tokyo system

The Tokyo municipal government requires candidates for advancement to middle management positions to pass promotion tests. Among Japanese human resource systems for public servants, only Osaka uses a similar system. Many private companies promote workers using this method, however, and late Qing Dynasty China is a well-known historic example of government officials being selected under a qualification system. The following examines qualification systems and advancement testing, the most commonly used tools for promotion of public servants.

As shown in Fig. 6, civil servants in general administrative posts in Tokyo start at rank 1, 2, or 3 positions (with those passing the Section I exam entering at rank 2 positions and others at rank 1), after which they are promoted through a series of mid-level and upper-level management positions.

Along the way, they must pass two promotion exams. In this sense, promotions in Tokyo's municipal government are managed in a manner that supports meritocracy.

Unit managers

The Tokyo Metropolitan Government Personnel Commission describes selection of personnel for unit manager positions as follows.[5]

In the sixth through eighth year after those with a "college degree or equivalent" receive a position by passing the recruitment examination (otherwise, when promoted to a rank 3 position), passing the Management Selection Test A allows promotion to sub-section manager. Those who do not pass the test may in practice be promoted to sub-section manager after ten years in a rank 3 position. Promotion to section manager is based on sufficient experience of on-site job duties as a sub-section manager. Note that the Management Selection Test A is extremely difficult: of the 6,493 qualified recipients in 1983, 1,043 took the test and only 30 passed, for a success rate of 2.9%. Furthermore, while employees become qualified for promotion after ten years in a rank 3 position, the limited number of available posts means that promotions generally do not come until around the fourteenth year. Some concern has been raised that these factors may severely undermine worker morale. Looking at the staff structure in April 1984, 6.4% of workers were in management positions, 28.3% were sub-section managers, and 61.2% remained in rank 3 positions.

In an effort to raise morale, in a 1983 wages advisory the Personnel Commission proposed creating a new position between rank 3 positions and sub-section manager. This was the birth of the "unit manager" position.

Promotion to unit manager requires at least four years' experience in a rank 3 position. This would come at approximately age 27 for someone who was hired after passing the Section I Recruitment Examination and then worked as a public servant for 5 years. In reality unit managers are selected from among those with five to ten years' experience, based on performance evaluations and a written examination covering basic education, knowledge of metropolitan government, and awareness of current issues. Alternatively, unit managers can be selected on the basis of long-term service in the metropolitan government at a rank 3 position, with the written examination replaced by an essay and heavy emphasis on performance evaluations.

---

5. Tokyo Metropolitan Government Personnel Commission (1992).

Management selection

As described above, postwar metropolitan Tokyo's system for selecting managers — shown in simplified form in Fig. 7 — is so strict as to recall the civil service examinations of ancient China. This method of internal selection uses work experience within the metropolitan government as a qualification for testing. Those who make it past the initial recruitment examination face similar exams when advancing to higher positions. Workers become eligible for this test two years after being promoted to sub-section manager (which requires five years experience as a unit manager).

However, changes such as a reduction in the number of available posts resulted in an increased average age of workers, lower pass rates for the advancement examination, and reduced motivation for taking the examination in the first place. Furthermore, the creation of additional advancement examination levels (Examinations B and C, for example) undermined uniformity in the order in which promotions were awarded. The system was also damaging in that by offering three opportunities to take the test each year, the burden on employees was unnecessarily increased.

To address these issues, the system underwent comprehensive revisions in 1973 and 1985. The latter revision reevaluated the content of the A, B, and C examinations. The category A exam was rewritten for young employees, who after passing it would be systematically trained through a series of job rotations. The category B exam was oriented toward mid-level managers, who after passing it would undergo further training, and the category C exam was rewritten to verify the experience and depth of management ability in veteran employees.[6]

Under these three variations on the management selection method, approximately 8,500 candidates took the 32 tests conducted from their first offering in 1958 through 1991. Table 17 shows changes in the number of test takers from 1981 through 1991. Category A test takers declined steeply until 1987, after which the number held relatively steady. The decline was likely due primarily to limits placed on the number of new hires starting in 1974. Self-selection probably played a role as well, in that the test's difficulty likely made taking it seem like a waste of time to some workers. As the table shows, only 10–20% of qualified candidates actually took the test. The average age upon passing the test was 30 years old.

The number of persons eligible to take the category B exam increased until around 1985, but in 1987 eligibility requirements were revised so that

---

6. See Tokyo Metropolitan Government Personnel Commission (1992, pp. 68–77) for details of this selection method, and the written examination in particular.

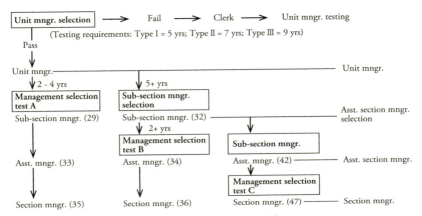

Figure 7. The promotion system in the Metropolitan Tokyo government

Table 17. Management selection in Metropolitan Tokyo.

	Year	1981	1983	1985	1987	1989	1991
Selection type A	a. Qualified (persons)	7,063	6,493	4,969	3,070	3,330	2,580
	b. Tested (persons)	1,304	1,043	552	379	492	313
	c. Passed (persons)	30	30	30	29	29	30
	Participation rate (b/a) (%)	18.5	16.1	11.2	12.3	14.8	12.1
	Pass rate (c/b) (%)	2.3	2.9	5.4	7.7	5.9	9.6
	Avg. age at passing (yrs)	31.3	30.8	30.7	30.7	30.6	30.9
Selection type B	a. Qualified (persons)	13,258	17,630	20,494	15,230	12,961	12,809
	b. Tested (persons)	2,986	3,000	2,668	1,909	1,380	1,325
	c. Passed (persons)	90	90	94	91	96	101
	Participation rate (b/a) (%)	22.5	17.5	13	12.5	10.6	10.3
	Pass rate (c/b) (%)	3.0	2.9	3.5	4.8	7.0	7.6
	Avg. age at passing (yrs)	39.1	39.7	39.8	40.0	41.6	42.1
Selection type C	a. Qualified (persons)	3,994	3,890	3,845	695	763	834
	b. Tested (persons)	769	892	990	314	381	444
	c. Passed (persons)	41	42	42	41	47	67
	Participation rate (b/a) (%)	19.3	22.9	25.7	45.2	49.9	53.2
	Pass rate (c/b) (%)	5.3	4.7	4.2	13.1	12.3	15.1
	Avg. age at passing (yrs)	49.7	49.5	50.5	49.6	49.8	50.6

Source: Tokyo Human Resource System Institute (1993).

only those at the sub-section manager level or above could take the test. This reduced the number of eligible candidates and significantly lowered the number of test takers. Before the revision, up to 100 persons passed the test each year, for around a 3% pass rate, but after the revision pass rates improved to around 6 or 7%. The average age upon passing the test was 39 in 1981 and 42 in 1991.

Many employees took the category C exam through 1985, and pass rates were just over 4%. The 1987 revision limited eligibility to assistant section managers and above, decreasing the number of test takers and raising the pass rate to 13%. The average age of successful candidates was around 50.

Screening for suitability through competitive principles

One particularly notable feature of the hiring and promotion systems implemented by the Metropolitan Tokyo government is that testing is used to screen promotions from a very early stage. Passing the unit manager exam provides opportunities for transfer to other departments, and promotion once there. Section managers who pass the management candidate exam are assigned as section managers in other organizations, then returned to their posts in central government offices. These methods of testing college graduates early in their careers and categorizing those who pass as candidates for executive positions represent another system of fast-track promotion.

Because employee career paths are not determined upon hiring, but rather some time after initial employment, differences in ability are evaluated over an extended period of time (although in the bigger picture of a career it may actually be relatively short). This type of system does have its critics, as the following quote by Sasaki illustrates:[7]

> From their late twenties, most workers in the Tokyo Metropolitan government spend their time studying for advancement tests with extremely low pass rates. This forces them to spend years cramming their heads with textbook knowledge. Can we really say that this kind of human resource management system leads to improved government for Tokyo residents?

If government employees are spending their late twenties through their late forties studying for tests, then it is indeed hard to imagine that their experience leads to the development of practical skills, or improved government services for the public. This is particularly true if the test content is aimed at evaluating skills unrelated to present job duties. A similar situation was seen in the Chinese civil service examinations.

However, others argue that test content can correlate positively with practical skills even if examinations do not cover practical skills directly, and therefore the exams function adequately as a selection mechanism. To give an example from ancient China, while academic knowledge of the writings of Confucius or Mencius may not in and of itself have been precisely associated with abilities as a public servant, if some positive correlation existed between ability and such knowledge, then following signal theory an examination testing such knowledge would have been a logical filter for human resource selection.

---

7. Sasaki (1991).

From this perspective, even if promotion testing does not directly improve "productivity" in a specific job, it may help select individuals with a diverse range of skills, and provide information about worker abilities. When objectively and accurately assessing individual worker performance requires tremendous cost, utilization of signals from promotion testing should greatly increase fairness compared to systems that use no signals, and allow for selection at lower cost. An important premise to such a system is that the cost of promotion testing is low for those undergoing it; those with high ability should spend a relatively small amount of time preparing for tests, and testing should be available early. The effectiveness of promotion testing is strongly dependent on whether this premise is fulfilled. If it is not, the system will produce only a small "testing elite" and many disgruntled workers.

3. Revolving-door politics

A certain portion of postwar Japan's academic "best and brightest" have consistently been absorbed as fast-track officials in the central government. This is not necessarily the case in other countries, and with the exception of France, Japan may indeed be unique. Salaries, however, are clearly not competitive with what could be expected at a large private company. Of course, it is inappropriate to directly compare the cash salaries of fast-track government officials with average salaries in the private sector. Upon graduating from college, most future fast-track officials likely considered positions at private firms, compared salaries in the private and public sectors, and realized that joining a large company and climbing the ranks to a high position there would no doubt result in a much larger salary than could be expected from a position in the national government. Salary alone thus poorly explains why some of the smartest people in Japan aim at government positions.

Naturally, human resource allocation in modern industrial society is not solely determined by economic rewards. In the case of fast-track government officials in particular, the greatest benefits derive from the prestige, sense of accomplishment, and political and economic influence such positions provide. However, arguments that officials select their careers based on these benefits at the expense of financial compensation ignore the potential economic effects that authority provides. High salaries are both a symbol of accomplishment in modern industrial society and a necessary condition for powerful authority, while low salaries are the reverse. Bureaucratic corruption where limited authority can be applied to receiving behind-the-scenes payments is somewhat widespread in Japan, suggesting the need to reconsider how our government officials are financially compensated.

This section describes the flow of personnel to public posts in postwar Japan from a labor economics perspective. I do not delve into how committed officials are to governance, however, or the extent of economic value associated with such authority. Rather, I limit the discussion to the reasons a high-quality segment of the Japanese workforce pursues careers in the public sector, despite the surface-level appearance of relatively low economic rewards for doing so. To that end, I focus on benefits other than salary, particularly the potential for government officials to access a "revolving door" to positions at government corporations (partially or wholly government-owned entities created to pursue commercial or industrial activities) at the end stages of their careers, and the role that this phenomenon plays in human resource allocation in Japan's bureaucratic structure. I will also consider whether government corporations should be viewed as external to that bureaucratic structure, or as substructures within it.

Revolving-door (*amakudari*) politics are neither peculiar to Japan nor new, having existed here since before World War II.[8] They are even mentioned in a 1902 short story by Uchida Roan, a literary figure in the late-Meiji and Taishō periods, to describe the hiring of former public officials by private companies. However, the systematic flow of public officials to government corporations seems to be a uniquely postwar phenomenon.

This practice is called *pantouflage* in France, where by some estimates it is ten times more common than in Japan. Furthermore, while most Japanese bureaucrats enter the revolving door in their forties or fifties, French *pantouflards* find new positions in their twenties or thirties, after just short stints as a public official.[9]

The three exits from Japan's revolving door

The revolving door in Japan generally leads to one of three destinations, each differing in political and economic characteristics: to an executive position at a private firm or industry group (including chambers of commerce, etc.), to an executive or mid-level manager position at a quasi-government corporation such as a public company or agency, or to an executive role in a regional government, dispatched from the central government.

The first type is strongly regulated. Item 2, article 103 of the National Public Service Act states (in a previous provision): "Officials shall not, for a period of two years after separation from the service, accept or assume a

---

8. See Muramatsu (1981) for quantitative measures of revolving-door politics in prewar Japan.
9. Inoki (1995).

position with a profit-making enterprise with a close connection to any agency of the State defined by rules of the National Personnel Authority, or any specified independent administrative institution with which such persons were formerly employed within five years prior to separation from the service." The following item 3, however, states that "the provisions of the preceding two paragraphs shall not apply to cases wherein approval is given by the National Personnel Authority on the offer from the head of the government agency employing that official, pursuant to the provision of rules of the National Personnel Authority," making the definition of "exclusion from private enterprise" that this section is named for not as restrictive as it first seems.[10] Three-year averages at 1970, 1980, and 1990 of the number of placements through this first type of revolving door (i.e., direct moves from a public post to a for-profit corporation) show not only an extreme upward trend in its frequency, but an overall acceleration of that trend.[11]

Officials from the Ministry of Finance frequently find positions in private financial institutions such as banks, insurance companies, and securities firms, and in large corporations from all corners of industry. However, many also move on to public service corporations and industry groups, such as the Japan Real Estate Institute or the Nippon Automated Cargo and Port Consolidated System.

The second type are former officials who take jobs at quasi-government corporations not covered by the National Public Service Act stipulations.[12] Movement of this type falls into two categories. The first includes those who leave ministry posts very early to take middle-management positions as department or section managers at quasi-government corporations. Among these, some will be promoted to executive positions, but the more common scenario involves returning to the ministry they hailed from after spending a few years at mid-level posts. Considering that quasi-government corporations operate under the jurisdiction of the ministry involved, these movements are very similar to transfers within an organization. The second category is made up of bureaucrats who are appointed to executive positions

---

10. Specific exemptions approved by the National Personnel Authority since 1963 are listed in the Authority's annual publication, "Eiri kigyō e no shūshoku no shōnin ni kansuru nenji hōkoku-sho" (Annual report on the approval of employment in commercial enterprises).

11. National Personnel Authority (1963–1991).

12. "Quasi-government corporations" are companies with a highly public nature that would likely find it difficult to operate under profit-based principles. Examples include public corporations, industry groups, special banks, credit unions, and public finance organizations. Many such organizations have been abolished, privatized, or converted to independent administrative agencies since financial reforms enacted in 2011 (the Basic Law for Special Public Corporations Reform).

at quasi-government corporations, most commonly after reaching fifty years of age as fast-track officials.

The third type of revolving-door movement involves appointment of central government officials in regional government offices. A typical scenario is reassignment of a Ministry of Home Affairs official as deputy governor in one of Japan's prefectures, a remnant of prewar human resource practices from the era of the old Home Ministry. By the late twentieth century, however, these reallocations were no longer limited to the Ministry of Home Affairs. For example, officials from the Ministry of Finance, the Ministry of International Trade and Industry, and the Ministry of Labour occupy somewhat "hereditary" executive posts in prefectural governments. In most cases, the bureaucrats assigned to these posts are still young, and can eventually return to their ministry of origin. This can undermine decentralization of power and central control of regional governments.

These three types of revolving doors are similar, but they can also lead to other types of movement.

For example, an initial move to a quasi-government corporation sometimes leads to a second move to some type of public benefit corporation. Secondary movement also occurs between or within the three types described above, in a pattern frequently compared to migrating birds. In this case, however, the move is to a different level, in that the destination is often a subsidiary organization beneath the quasi-government corporation, most commonly a public benefit corporations. Taking the Japan External Trade Organization — a governmental organization under the Ministry of Economy, Trade and Industry's Trade Bureau Division — as an example, subsidiary organizations include the Overseas Human Resources and Industry Development Association, the Japan–China Economic Association, the Interchange Association, Japan, and the Manufactured Imports and Investment Promotion Organization. These organizations receive many revolving-door assignments from their parent organization. This is sometimes recognized in criticisms as the so-called "reverse assignment" problem.

Another type of movement involves public officials from regional governments, such as the Tokyo metropolitan government, taking positions at public benefit corporations under local government jurisdiction. Since these movements are not regulated like those from public to private enterprises are, they are largely removed from the public eye.

The revolving door spins the other way as well, with private organizations assigning personnel to governmental organizations or to the central government for a fixed "study" period, often two years. This is another form of public–private hobnobbing that is frequently considered problematic, because it interferes with the confidentiality expected in official public duties. As many observers have noted, the movement of personnel from the private sector to government corporations or to the central government raises numerous issues, particularly when such personnel eventually wind up back in the private sector.

As mentioned above, not all of those moving to government corporations obtain executive posts. Officials around forty years old will often enter government corporations as mid-level managers, and later return to the central government. They may also be internally promoted to executive positions, or even remain in the mid-level position until retirement. Many patterns are possible.

Of course, the converse is also true: not all mid-level posts in government corporations are filled through the revolving door. Even in the case of "hereditary" posts, there is often flexibility regarding the career background of the official filling them. However, it is worth noting that mid-management positions have become embedded as part of the career path in all major ministries. Specifically, since government corporations provide bureaucrats with official duties as a labor service, these organizations can be considered part of the internal structure of central government ministries. Of particular interest is the career path in which bureaucrats temporarily leave for a position at a government corporation at around age forty, return to their ministry after a few years, stay there until their mid-fifties, and then after ministry retirement once again move to a government corporation, possibly the same one they worked at before. Indeed, every year when human resources are being reallocated, one of the jobs of the secretariat division in each ministry is the arduous task of figuring out how to reshuffle same-year cohorts of bureaucrats among the available posts within the ministry and at the government corporations under the ministry's purview. In this sense too, government corporations are in essence an internal structure of the Japanese bureaucracy.

Many government corporations can also be considered part of the bureaucracy from a management perspective, in terms of who is issuing paychecks. (This does not apply to public enterprises that are highly independent from an accounting perspective, particularly national corporations operating under special accounting rules like the old state-owned railway business, and government monopolies like those once used for tobacco sales and telephone companies.) The following section explores this point with a particular focus on bureaucrats who remain in a ministry until around age fifty and then move to a government corporation.[13]

---

13. The description below follows Inoki (1995).

The revolving door leading to government corporations

Opinions differ as to whether governmental organizations such as public corporations and industry groups are internal parts of central government ministries or external sub-organizations. Let us consider this in reference to Fig. 8. Generally speaking, same-year cohorts of fast-track bureaucrats constantly compete for promotions, and with each year of continued service some number of that cohort are squeezed out of the ministry's organizational pyramid. They end up at various external organizations, including private firms, but among their potential destinations government corporations are unique in two regards. One is that movement often occurs while the bureaucrat is in his or her forties, allowing time to return to the ministry of origin in a few years. In this respect, movement between the central government and government corporations is highly flexible. The other is that movement of personnel to government corporations as executives is in most cases at the discretion of the cabinet secretariat of the source ministry. The government corporation thus has a low degree of independence with respect to the middle managers and executives running it. This provides powerful evidence that ministries do not regard most government corporations as fully external to their organization.

The following description of promotions at the Ministry of Finance illustrates the principles of competition and exclusion that begin when a bureaucrat reaches his or her fifties.

The Ministry of Finance hires around twenty fast-track bureaucrats each year. The position at the top of its promotional pyramid is the administrative vice-minister, followed by the vice-minister of finance for international affairs, the commissioner of the National Tax Agency, and directors-general of the various bureaus. Officials can be promoted as directors or assistant directors after 14 years of employment, and this is when the first screening occurs. The second comes after 25 years of employment, and determines placement as a deputy vice-minister or other head manager. In many cases, this second screening results in a transfer to lead a regional finance, tax, or customs bureau. At around 30 years of employment, the period of general competition and exclusion ends, and competition becomes focused among the few who have made it this far. These individuals are assigned to key posts such as deputy vice-minister and director general, promoted from regional directors to deputies, or assigned to positions at agencies such as the Economic Planning Agency, the Defense Agency, or the Management and Coordination Agency.

Many fast-track officials in the Ministry of Finance transfer to government financial institutions like banks or credit unions, to public service

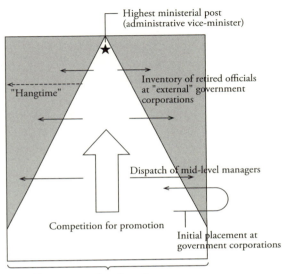

Figure 8. Bureaucratic hierarchy

corporations and industry groups, or to private firms, financial institutions, and securities companies. Compared to other ministries, the Ministry of Finance provides avenues to a wide variety of destinations. Most of these government corporations are operated under the Fiscal Investment and Loan Program or by subsidies, and the Ministry of Finance has broad authority over everything from budget planning to daily accounting.

The upward direction in Fig. 8 represents increased continual years of employment at the ministry. Areas outside the triangle show those in a given age cohort who have left the Ministry of Finance, while the interior area is the relative number of those remaining. The problem at hand is whether we should consider those outside the triangle who have moved on to government corporations as having left the ministry, or having been reassigned within it. The personal secretary to the finance minister determines how these reallocations of human resources will occur. Among the assigned posts are executive positions at government corporations controlled by the ministry. An important job of the secretary, therefore, is determining who in the ministry should be promoted to which position, while also considering who should become an executive at each particular government corporation.

The issue of whether government corporations lie inside or outside the bureaucratic organization is thus not only one of independence in personnel decisions, but is also a reflection of more fundamental organizational differences. The salaries of those within the triangle in Fig. 8 — in other words, those who have remained in the ministry and continue to compete there — are determined according to standard pay rates set by the National Personnel Authority, and are paid with tax money. In contrast, those transferred from the triangle to new positions at government corporations are sometimes paid in nearly the same manner as civil servants, but when assigned to an organization with independent accounting they are paid from the resources of that organization.

Criticisms of the revolving door

Revolving-door policies like those described above have been harshly criticized, particularly since the mid-1960s, by journalists as well as by the Labor Federation ("Council" until 1990) of Government Related Organizations, a union for workers at government corporations. Particular points of criticism include: closed-door practices in the controlling ministry's oversight of the government corporation, which inhibits autonomy and reduces fairness and efficiency; reduced motivation among the organization's regular employees due to posts being "claimed" by the controlling ministry; and preferential treatment of assigned executives that is incompatible with their job description.

In response to these criticisms, the Cabinet approved several notable measures related to executive selection at government corporations, including "On the Issue of Executive Selection at Public Corporations and Finance Corporations" (passed by verbal assent of the Cabinet on 14 May 1965), "On the Issue of Executive Personnel at Public Corporations" (passed by verbal assent of the Cabinet on 7 February 1967), and multiple measures on 23 December 1977. Specific approved restrictions included limiting executive tenures until age 65 (until age 70 for president-level positions in special situations) and limiting the duration of postings to six years (or eight years for governor and vice-governor positions). A cabinet meeting on 18 December 1979 established a target of no more than half of executive director positions at government corporations being directly filled by national government officials or the equivalent. It also specified that back-and-forth personnel allocations to government corporations should not be repeated, regardless of the reason, and reduced the number of executive postings by at least 10% at each ministry. Another cabinet meeting just ten days later adjusted the salaries and retirement allowances for government corporation executives.

These measures were followed by a series of cabinet decisions related to personnel management at government corporations in accordance with personnel reduction plans for the national civil service. Meetings on 29 December 1980 and 25 August 1981 reorganized government corporations, and one on 28 December 1989 addressed personnel management at government corporations. However, these cabinet meetings tended only to establish goals, and did little to actually correct problems regarding the extent of revolving-door practices, the rotation of personnel between various organizations, the duration of assignments, the age of assignees, or the number of executive staff.

The difficulty of attaining these cabinet goals is partially explained by the circumstances under which government corporations are established and the effects that their expansion and subsequent stagnation had on movement of human resources. Until Japan's period of rapid economic development got underway in the mid-1950s, many government corporations performed controlled-economy functions. Examples include the Foodstuffs Distribution Corporation (abolished in 1951), the Petroleum Distribution Corporation (abolished in 1948), and the Industrial Reconstruction Corporation (abolished in 1950). Many of the government corporations established after the war were financial institutions for supplying money to key industries, such as the National Finance Corporation (established in 1949), the Japan Export–Import Bank (1950), and the Development Bank of Japan (1951). These were intended to serve as institutions for restructuring and strengthening Japan's financial system under the Fiscal Investment and Loan Program. Many organizations were also established in the same period to funnel national subsidies to the coal, power, and petroleum industries. Examples include J-Power (1952), the Aichi Prefecture Water Corporation (established 1955, abolished 1968), the Coal Mining Development Agency (established 1955, renamed the Coal Mining Rationalization Agency in 1960, and abolished in 1980), and the Japan Petroleum Exploration Company (established 1955). The goal of each of these was to provide direct investment for postwar reconstruction.

Following 1955 — and particularly between 1955 and 1965, when Japan's period of rapid economic development accelerated — many government corporations financed by the Ministry of Finance Trust Fund Bureau were created. These served as instruments for large-scale public investment in industrial infrastructure development according to Fiscal Investment and Loan Program plans. Examples include the Japan Housing Corporation (1955), the Forest Development Corporation (1956), the Japan Highway Public Corporation (1956), and the Water Resources Development Public

Corporation (1962). This period saw remarkable technological innovation in various industrial fields, and increased exports. Examples of government corporations established to promote trade, research, and development include the Japan Atomic Energy Research Institute, RIKEN (which became a government corporation in 1958), the Japan External Trade Organization, the Overseas Economic Cooperation Fund, and the New Technology Development Agency.

Between this era and the 1973 oil crisis, organizations such as the National Education Center and the Social Security Institute were created, alongside many mutual aid associations, pension funds, government corporations for the support of agriculture and small businesses, and related public benefit corporations. After 1973, the number of new corporations fell dramatically, and many existing corporations were eliminated or consolidated. Nevertheless, their number swelled from 33 in 1955 to 92 in 1992, altogether employing 600,000 persons in that year — a remarkable expansion.

A hypothesis for the rationality of revolving-door politics

In contrast to the many criticisms leveled at Japan's revolving-door systems, some observers argue that they are, in a sense, rational. For example, it might be necessary in some cases to appoint executives if human resources at a government corporation are insufficient. Alternatively, a familiar face might facilitate procedures when government corporations require authorizations from their governing ministry, or when they undergo budget assessments from the Ministry of Finance. Government corporations generally do not have the authority to determine budgets or make appointments on their own, so some view personnel assignments from ministries simply as reallocations to subunits within the larger organization. If these corporations are viewed as being a part of the ministry, then such arguments of course make sense.

Revolving-door policies are also rational in terms of personnel management of civil servants. I would like to consider two hypotheses that support this assertion. One is that when employees leave their positions in their forties, before retirement, younger bureaucrats can be promoted more rapidly. In other words, authority is transferred to a younger cohort, which energizes bureaucratic organizations. The second is that passing through the revolving door to government corporations has characteristics of internal movement within the organization, and that patterns of selection and allocation as indicated by such movement is one way in which ministry employees are evaluated. The first hypothesis implies that expanding the scope of transfer to include government companies prevents stagnation within the central government and motivates young employees. The second suggests that revolving-door positions are a form of delayed compensation. From this perspective, the system can be considered a wage mechanism that increases competition in the bureaucracy's internal labor market, thereby increasing the efficiency of human resource allocation and retaining balance in allocations between the public and private sectors. As mentioned at the start of this chapter, the wages that can be expected from jobs in the bureaucracy are not particularly attractive to talented individuals, when compared with the wages they can expect to earn as elite businesspeople. Furthermore, wages are very similar at various ministries and even among positions within a given ministry. The theory is thus that revolving-door positions have persisted because they correct such disparities.

Several points must be considered in order to investigate these hypotheses. One is that transfer from the promotion path within the ministry to a government corporation comes at an advanced age, and that higher ministry posts imply higher positions and salaries at the government corporation. Promotion through the ranks at the ministry of origin and retirement from a high position mean continued progress despite long-term competition, so the financial rewards are high, and these rewards should be retained in the form of position and length of service at the government corporation. This will be the next topic of discussion, taking as its example a ministry employee over the age of fifty who moves permanently to a government corporation as a top-tier, fast-track official.

Length of service at government corporations

Many cases show that those who have extended their length of service in a ministry through successful competition for promotions receive higher positions and salaries when moving to government corporations. As I discuss in this section, those appointed to higher posts stay at government corporations longer. Specifically, I consider how much longer former ministry employees stays at their new positions after moving to a government corporation. This is equivalent to the "hangtime" concept illustrated in Fig. 8.

To precisely compare monetary rewards at early retirement and subsequent relocation, it is necessary to use large amounts of data to track each individual movement (including movement between government corporations and to private firms) and to calculate how much and for how long officials were paid following ministry retirement. Here I use a somewhat simplified approach, which considers only the average number of years that fast-track officials spent at government corporations following relocation, and does not consider back-and-forth transfer to other government corporations or reemployment at private firms.

As described above, cabinet decisions have officially limited executive appointments to around six years, or eight years for presidents and vice presidents. However, data from the *Amakudari hakusho* (White Paper on Revolving-Door Appointments)[14] show that these requirements are not always strictly followed, either in government corporations or in industry groups. Particularly through the early 1980s, in some years there were more than ten executives with appointments that had exceeded six years. Because this data is generally calculated as number of years at a particular job, the number of years spent at a given government corporation can be underreported; promotion to a higher position would mean that not all years of employment are accounted for.

Table 18 lists data collected from the Council of the Labor Federation of Government Related Organizations presented in the "White Paper on Revolving-Door Appointments." This table demonstrates three points: first, that the average duration of appointments at some government corporations (specifically at twelve companies, including Japan Tobacco Inc., the Electric Power Development Co., Ltd., the former Japanese National Railways, and the Nippon Telegraph and Telephone Corporation) was much longer than at others, both for president and vice president positions and for general executive positions; second, that presidents and vice presidents served longer than did directors on average; and third, that it was more common for presidents and vice presidents to serve for longer than six years than for directors to do so.

The same points hold true for age as well, because up until the point of passing through the revolving door, length of service and age are fully correlated. However, the age at appointment to president, vice president, and general officer is not particularly high as compared with the case of other government corporations — indeed, there is a trend toward younger appointments. The reason for this is clear: with the exception of the Kansai International Airport Co., Ltd., less than 20% of these roles are filled by appointment of central government officials, with promotions from within the government corporation comprising the remainder. Average lengths of service are therefore relatively long, but ages at appointment are not particularly high. This is a fundamental difference in human resource policy between government corporations and other quasi-governmental organizations and industry groups.

We have examined incentive structures that encourage movement of

---

14. National Personnel Authority (1963).

Table 18. Period of employment and average age of executives at government corporations

a. Period of employment

	Presidents, vice-presidents, etc.				Other officers		
	Number of companies	Persons	Avg. appoint-ment (months)	Executives appointed for 73+ months	Persons	Avg. appoint-ment (months)	Executives appointed for 73+ months
Public company	13	25 (25)	32	1	80 (92)	28	
Industry group	17	28 (28)	36	1	79 (92)	30	
Finance corp.	9	15 (15)	39	1	43 (45)	24	
Credit union	3	6 (6)	35		19 (24)	24	
Special bank	—	— (—)	—	—	— (—)	—	—
Authority	1	2 (2)	59	1	6 (11)	24	
Special corp.	12	20 (33)	69	8	35 (195)	42	
Other	37	40 (45)	45	4	113 (164)	31	3
Total	92	136 (154)	44	16	375 (623)	30	3

b. Average age

	Presidents, vice-presidents, etc.				Other officers		
	Number of companies	Persons	Avg. age	Executives 70+ yrs old	Persons	Avg. age	Executives 70+ yrs old
Public company	13	25 (25)	60.2		92 (92)	56.1	1
Industry group	17	28 (28)	61.5		92 (92)	57.3	2
Finance corp.	9	15 (15)	61.7	1	45 (45)	56.3	1
Credit union	3	6 (6)	63.0		24 (24)	56.5	
Special bank	—	— (—)	—	—	— (—)	—	—
Authority	1	2 (2)	63.5		11 (11)	56.9	
Special corp.	12	33 (33)	58.1	7	182 (195)	55.1	9
Other	37	43 (45)	62.9	2	146 (164)	57.5	4
Total	92	152 (154)	61.0	10	592 (623)	56.4	16

Note: Figures in parentheses are totals.
Source: Council of the Labor Federation of Government Related Organizations (1992).

retiring fast-track bureaucrats to government corporations in postwar Japan. This discussion was prompted by the question of how the Japanese bureaucracy has continually managed to attract a portion of high-quality college-educated workers, and of whether government corporations are internal or external organizations with regard to the bureaucratic structure of the central government. Another point of interest was how relatively early retirement (as compared with the private sector) and subsequent movement to government corporations relates to human resource development and allocation in the bureaucracy.

Recall the two hypotheses described above. One is that early retirements increase promotions of younger workers, potentially motivating them. The other is that passing through the revolving door is considered movement within the organization, and the inherent selection and allocation patterns include evaluations of performance during tenure in the ministry. This implies that assignment to a governmental corporation is a form of delayed compensation. Presuming that both of these hypotheses are correct, it should be possible to determine their prerequisites from data. Data related to both salaries after movement to government corporations and years of service support the idea that revolving-door practices stimulate competition within the bureaucracy.

As previously described, however, revolving-door practices have many negative aspects. As critics have frequently pointed out, these practices can breed corruption. Regulations and the extent and depth of their implementation of course play a role here. In addition, from the perspective of government corporations that systematically accept officials from the bureaucracy, those officers and mid-level managers are coming from outside, which can easily dampen staff motivation. In light of these points, it is clear that the issues addressed in this chapter constitute just one part of the full discussion. Nevertheless, the fact remains that revolving-door policies function as a human resource allocation mechanism, and they have allowed Japan's bureaucracy to continuously attract high-quality workers.

Quantitative issues related to public officials

The media frequently claims that Japan has too many public officials, but this is not true in an international context.[15] While some sectors of public service are indeed top-heavy, others, like the judiciary, the police force, education, financial oversight, tax collection, and immigration control face severe worker shortages. There is thus an aggregate problem related to allocation between sectors.

The scale of government expenditures provides insight into this issue. The Organisation for Economic Co-operation and Development (OECD) provides an index that summarizes the ratio of total expenditures on general government (including central and regional governments and social security funds, but excluding public companies) and current expenditure of goods and services to average gross domestic product (GDP) over the past twenty years.[16] In northern European countries like Sweden and Denmark, government expenditures (specifically, the sum of final consumption expenditures

---

15. Inoki (2002b).
16. Since 1995, the OECD has provided graphical comparisons of GDP-related statistics of its member nations in its *National Accounts at a Glance* publication.

by government, public debt interest payments, subsidies and social security transfers, gross capital formation by government, and land and tangible fixed assets purchases) have reached 60% of GDP. In comparison, Japanese expenditures are among the lowest for OECD nations — just over 30%, lower than even the United States and Australia. Notably, Japan's ratio of social security benefits to GDP is higher than in the U.S., Canada, and Australia, but lower than in France, Germany, and Italy.

This raises the question of what the ratio of public sector workers to total workers has been throughout history and in different countries. In recent OECD statistics, the worker population in the Japanese public sector is the lowest among member nations. Of course, defining "public workers" in a way that allows for international comparison is difficult; one must consider, for example, whether employees at government corporations or certain authorized corporations and public benefit corporations should be included. Regardless of definitions, however, Japan remains in the lowest rankings of public sector employment.

Another World Bank and OECD publication presents overall employment ratios in the non-military public sectors of OECD member nations.[17] According to that publication, the ratio is highest in northern Europe, as represented by Sweden, where 33.3% of the worker population is employed in the public sector. Switzerland and Belgium follow at over 20%. It is perhaps not surprising to see higher ratios in smaller countries. Among other industrialized nations, the figure is 17.8% in France, 16.7% in the U.K., 15.0% in Italy, and 13.8% in the United States. Germany is notable for its low value of 9.5%. Japan, however, is far removed from even this, with the lowest value of just 6.5%. The order of ranking remains unchanged when considered by number of workers per 1,000 population. Indeed, the gap between Germany (77) and Japan (39) widens.

The scale and effect of government is defined by its budget. So while laws generally describe their principles and goals in their preamble, it is impossible to discuss the actual costs and benefits of economic and public policy without first obtaining a quantitative grasp of budgets and human resources, especially the number of public employees. No researcher takes the simplistic view that the intent of policy always equates to its results. However, even if the discussion is limited to postwar Japan, I believe historic international comparisons will increasingly require a quantitative understanding of the scale of individual policies, as reflected in their budgets and the resources invested in them.

---

17. OECD (1999).

While it is difficult to directly accept uniform capacity reductions without coming to grips with these points, one can to some extent predict the existence of areas with too few and too many workers. This leads to the issue of how public employees should be reallocated.

Maeda Kentarō has argued that the relatively low number of public officials in Japan is related to limitations imposed on Japanese finance and fiscal policy by the Bretton Woods system.[18] Maeda first investigated when the number of Japanese public servants dipped below the number in other countries, and identified when that gap was widest. He then considered the policy issues confronted by countries implementing administrative reforms that halted increases in public-sector employees, and compared this with the case of Japan.

His analysis focused on how the increase in public servants came to a relatively early halt in Japan, whereas in postwar Europe it increased for an extended period. In postwar Japan, personnel expenditures for public servants were largely determined according to salary systems proposed by the National Personnel Authority. Therefore, salary increases in the public sector mirrored increases in the private sector. This created financial pressures that reduced the freedom of fiscal policy.

In April 1964 Japan came under Article 8 of the IMF, which forbade currency trading to improve a nation's international balance of payments, thereby making the yen a convertible currency. As a result, when balance-of-payment issues necessitated fiscal restraint, an increase in public sector salaries would decrease room for fiscal policy maneuvering and weaken its effects. This made it necessary to limit the number of public employees in order to retain methods for controlling the economy so as to maintain a given exchange rate. Maeda suggests that the 1969 Administrative Agency Staff Capacity Act, which established specific limits on the number of administrative positions, put the "finishing touches" on this shift.

Civil servants as experts

In the larger, more complex industrial societies of the twentieth century, it became increasingly difficult to provide politicians with the specialized technical information needed to addresses policy issues. According to common textbook theory, politicians set policy in the Diet, and the government implements those policies. However, in actuality it is difficult to monitor and control how policy is implemented. It is even difficult for politicians without specialized knowledge to identify policy issues, to the detriment of

18. Maeda (2014).

the policy-making process. In most cases today, the identification and resolution of policy issues is handled not within the Diet, but through discussions within the bureaucracy, which is today essentially responsible for policy-making. The system has been distorted so that policy responses to a given issue are designed by a group of specialists, presented to the Diet as a bill, and formally approved.

This distortion has increased the power of the bureaucracy and exacerbated inter-ministry budget battles. Furthermore, enacted and budgeted policy measures become a kind of vested Ministry interest, so the bureaucracy devotes enormous energy toward finding new policy issues that it can manipulate into further budget increases.

The largest fault with this practice is its inflexibility: policies that were necessary at one time are not reviewed when their need has passed, which prevents the reallocation of resources to other issues. Obsolete policies thus remain in place while new policies are continually budgeted, seriously inflating policy expenditures. Worker allocations are similarly unable to adapt to the times, which leads to worker overloads and shortages.

Such systems that rely heavily on bureaucratic policy-making readily induce lobbying and other forms of political pressure directed at ministries. This incentivizes activity not only by individuals seeking to benefit select groups within the populace, but also by politicians with influence over the divisions they lead, and by industry groups. While the extent of lobbying varies, it can occur in any liberal democracy. Politicians, industry actors, and the bureaucrats are bound together through mutual benefit. When such relationships are left in place, politics becomes a profit-seeking activity that does not heed expert opinion.

It has been argued that Japan will never be an expert-oriented society because the country lacks effective specialists. Without doubt, the human resource development systems employed by Japanese institutions of higher learning are behind the times when assessed from the perspective of social sciences policy research. This holds true not only in comparison with the West, but also with the countries of east and south-east Asia. This is important for several reasons.[19]

As globalization increases, one consequence of economic cooperation in the world market is a heightened need for Japanese experts to continually provide convincing narratives from outside the market. One feature of globalism in the future will be expansion of international economic competition beyond product and technology markets to an external "war of words."

19. Inoki (2001).

International competition between specialists became globalized long ago, before Japan sufficiently recognized its importance. The establishment of international standards by engineers is one example.

In the West as well as in several East Asian countries, institutions of higher learning foster professionals with advanced skills and gather them in think tanks that are independent of government. These think tanks collect data and run simulations to analyze various scenarios. From a national policy standpoint, it is extremely important to consider the policy impact of, for example, a transformation of the political economy of North Korea, or a drastic change in China's economy. Japan is behind the times in this aspect too. There are still too few staff in the Japanese bureaucracy with graduate-level training. While international institutions and research labs expect contributions from Japanese specialists, Japan has not yet established the domestic framework for supplying such personnel.

Allocation of human resources among divisions

A nation's human resources are allocated among its various political, financial, and governmental areas according to some principle. The process of hiring into industries and professions is of course not determined according to decisions made at a single point in time, but rather takes shape gradually through processes including decisions related to formal education. Even when an individual chooses a given profession, this choice cannot be considered final because the individual may later change jobs. However, even if non-economic factors such as prestige, occupation of parents, self-esteem, and personal preference help determine the flow of personnel to a given job type, one must consider the extent to which economic factors such as wages and working conditions come into play. As stated by Adam Smith in his theory of freedom in choice of occupation, there are important "compensating wage differentials" separate from the wage itself. For example, non-wage differentials between public and private employment might include working hours, holidays, or the ease of taking maternity leave.

In the case of government officials, there may be differences in the economic factors that motivate elite "fast-track" individuals versus those in the standard career track. There are also likely to be differences in the labor market for the central and regional governments. Furthermore, the situation changes according to whether potential workers more heavily weight salary or job security as "economic factors." When comparing salary and working conditions, too, individual conclusions might vary according to the career path they assume.

Presuming for now that economic factors significantly affect the demand for public employees, it would be natural to assume that formulas for determining salary must consider market supply and demand. This might also lead us to question the basis of formulas that simply track private sector rates. In the United States since 1962, the salaries of federal employees have been determined in relation to private-sector base salaries. Each year the U.S. Bureau of Labor Statistics surveys white-collar salaries at private companies, and a presidential commission makes recommendations that preserve a balance between public and private wages. However, this method has long been harshly criticized by those who argue that that the U.S. Office of Personnel Management should instead analyze data regarding job changes and civil service exam takers, and adjust wages based on the results (in other words, based on supply and demand).

Economic factors that impact the movement of workers into the public sector generally include higher private sector wages when the economy is performing well, resulting in a flow toward those jobs, and lower private wages when the economy performs poorly, which induces public job seeking. While there is little doubt that the high job security of public sector jobs is one of their most attractive features, salary is also an important factor motivating entrance into the public sector.

Among public officials, the competitiveness of the Section I, II, and III Recruitment Examinations is highly sensitive to public–private salary differentials.[20] This implies that economic factors are highly important, regardless of any sense of mission to serve the public. Among these, the competitiveness of the Section II and III exams is particularly sensitive. In other words, factors outside of salary differentials are important for entrance into type I positions, but less important for entry to Section II and III positions, suggesting economic reasons behind workers' decisions to take these jobs.

"Job security" can be defined as "employment that can be retained regardless of economic fluctuations." We can therefore argue that "involuntary turnover rate in the private sector" can be used as a substituting variable. Similarly, rational comparisons of lifetime wages are problematic in considerations of wage differences, so simple differences in public and private wages are insufficient. In actuality, as can be seen from our ability to interpret revolving-door assignments as a form of delayed compensation, a grasp of lifetime wages is an important point.

We should thus consider which aspects of motivation for public employment should be investigated in the future. One potential topic is a substitution relation in selection for regional public service. A supply-side substitution

---

20. Inoki and Yugami (2001).

relation likely exists among Section I, II, and III positions, and there is certainly one between national and regional positions. This point necessitates a slight expansion of the boundaries of the human resource pool. These are important topics if we wish to reassess the concept of public service, obtain a quantitative grasp of it, or create public service jobs.

Movement of personnel from central to local government

When considering the extent to which the bureaucracy changed in postwar Japan, we must keep in mind that ministerial reorganizations and changes in names do not necessarily spur rapid change. The dissolution and reconstruction of ministries following World War II tend to be viewed as marking a complete separation between Japan's prewar and postwar governments, but the same individuals remained within the bureaucracy, and in many cases old organizational practices left an indelible mark. While the prewar Department of the Interior may have been abolished, for instance, its human network lingered on in the Ministry of Home Affairs, the Ministry of Health and Welfare, the Ministry of Labour, the Ministry of Construction, the National Police Agency, etc. This remains an important point in discussions of regional government in Japan seventy years later.

The *Naisei kankei-sha meibo* (Roster of Internal Affairs Officials) published by the Institute of Local Finance presents interesting materials that show the human network between ministries in postwar Japan. Its 1993 edition lists not only all persons hired into the Department of the Interior between 1876 and 1947, but also all executive hires at the National Police Agency, the Ministry of Health and Welfare, the Ministry of Labour, the Ministry of Construction, and the Ministry of Home Affairs following dissolution of the Department of the Interior. These listings demonstrate that even destruction of a large government ministry by occupying forces was insufficient to overcome prewar ties between its executives.

Even today, executives and executive candidates are sent from the central government to key posts in regional governments. As described above, some eventually return to their ministry of origin, while others remain and advance to governor or vice governor posts in their new location.[21] While a system for electing governors has been in place since the end of World War II, many regions have yet to establish practices for fostering local personnel, and still rely on dispatches from the central government to fill these positions. This continued flow of human resources from the former Department of the Interior to various outlying regions is evidence that they face

---

21. Inoki (2001).

not only funding issues, but also an insufficient system for human resources development, both in governance and administration.

Home of a Manchurian settler. (Photo: Jiji Press)

CHAPTER 8

EMIGRATION AND IMMIGRATION

In previous chapters, I explored human resource development in post-World War II Japan from a variety of perspectives. Immigrants bring with them new knowledge and information, and mass migrations have a profound effect on the culture of labor and the lifestyles of the population at large. The early history of overseas studies was discussed in chapter 1, but that chapter did not consider modern-day labor force changes through the lens of international relocation of non-student Japanese or the arrival of foreigners in Japan. The population of Japan has started to shrink, prompting extensive discussions since the 1980s of whether foreign workers might provide one solution to the labor shortages that are expected to occur in the future. This chapter concludes the book with an investigation of the history of labor flows into and out of Japan.

1. Overseas immigration and Japan–US friction

The Japanese have been described as a fundamentally inward-facing people, perhaps because they live on islands in relative isolation and have a limited perspective on international affairs. This may be true of Japan's era of seclusion during the Edo period, but both before and after this era the Japanese were oriented much more toward the outside world, including during the Azuchi–Momoyama period (1568–1600) and in the more recent Meiji (1868–1912), Taishō (1912–1926), and prewar Shōwa (1926–1989) periods. Likewise, Japan has experienced periods of both outflow and inflow of human resources. Let us begin by examining the migration of Japanese workers to other countries during the Meiji period and later.[1]

The first significant outflow of workers from Japan in modern times took place in 1868, when 153 Japanese workers, called the *gannenmono*, left to work on Hawaiian sugar plantations. After that, the Meiji government implemented anti-emigration policies that limited expatriation to a handful of persons moving to Hawaii and North America. Emigration increased again significantly when the government reversed course and launched an emigration program in 1885. Between that year and 30 June 1894, when the *Miike Maru* docked at Honolulu with its final shipment of workers, 26 government-sponsored voyages carried approximately 35,000 Japanese to Hawaii.

Subsequently, private emigration activities took the place of government-

---

1. The following discussion draws from Inoki (1984) and Ministry of Foreign Affairs Consular and Migration Section (1971). For more extensive sources, see the Works Cited section in Inoki (1984).

Table 19. Overseas migration from 1885 to 1904

Year	Total	USA	Hawaii	Canada
1885	2,390	312	1,959	
1886	1,491	332	971	
1887	2,605	461	1,893	
1888	4,108	757	3,308	
1889	5,107	599	4,244	
1890	5,429	611	4,540	
1891	9,585	1,461	7,171	181
1892	6,268	2,344	2,413	112
1893	9,446	1,978	4,764	1,135
1894	8,093	1,497	4,036	779
1895	9,110	1,049	2,445	454
1896	19,353	1,764	9,486	549
1897	14,114	1,945	5,913	206
1898	20,763	2,936	12,952	1,039
1899	31,354	3,140	22,973	1,726
1900	16,758	7,585	1,529	2,710
1901	6,490	32	3,136	
1902	15,919	70	14,490	35
1903	14,055	318	9,091	178
1904	14,663	640	9,443	159
Total	217,101	29,831	126,757	9,263

Source: Japan International Cooperation Agency (1977, 1978).

run programs, with numerous emigration assistance companies increasing the number of persons moving overseas. Table 19 shows the number of Japanese emigrants to Hawaii and North America from 1885 to 1905, and Table 20 shows the destinations of Japanese emigrants by country from 1868 through 1945. The "List of People Going Overseas Using Emigration Companies," a document from the Diplomatic Record Office of the Japanese Ministry of Foreign Affairs, includes passport information that allows us to track emigrants by their prefecture of origin. This data shows notable concentrations of emigrants from Yamaguchi, Hiroshima, Kumamoto, and Okinawa prefectures.

Emigration companies were only permitted to operate in certain prefectures. Many specialized in emigration to Hawaii, while others like the Welfare Immigration Company of Wakayama focused on Canada, the United States, and Australia. Some of the contracts between these companies and emigrants have been preserved, and provide insight into the role of emigrant handlers. This became an increasingly promising business field, leading to an over-supply of these companies; there were at least forty at one point. This in turn led to fierce competition and corner-cutting, and thus to various misdeeds.

Table 20. Prewar (1868–1945) overseas migration by destination

Total	774,717
Breakdown (for countries and regions with over 10,000 migrants):	
Brazil	188,901
Peru	32,917
Malaysia and Singapore	11,842
Philippines and Guam	53,027
USA	107,253
Hawaii	231,206
Canada	35,522
Soviet Union	56,524

Source: Japan International Cooperation Agency (1977).

Anti-Japanese movements after the Russo-Japanese War

After the Russo-Japanese War, anti-Japanese sentiment and immigration restrictions increased markedly in some countries, including the United States, Canada, and Australia.

Japanese emigration to California presents an interesting example of the racial and economic strife that immigrants experienced. This is of particular interest because it illustrates how racial discrimination within a given country generally results from economic background factors.

Japan solidified its position in East Asia by holding back a Russian invasion in the Russo-Japanese War, and was supported in this war by sympathetic public opinion in the United States and mediation by U.S. President Theodore Roosevelt. However, American recognition of Japan's power had the side effect of fueling the wariness of the general public. This increased the antagonism toward Japanese immigrants that already existed in the U.S., particularly in California. The Chinese Exclusion Act had been passed in 1882, paving the way for similar measures to drive Japanese and Korean immigrants out of the United States.[2]

In 1905, the mayor of San Francisco and several labor unions formed the Japanese and Korean Exclusion League. The *San Francisco Chronicle* launched an anti-Japanese campaign around the same time, claiming that the end of the Russo-Japanese war would bring hundreds of thousands of Japanese veterans to the United States in search of jobs. Indeed, while no more than 10,000 Japanese relocated to the U.S. over the five years prior to 1907, the number jumped to over 30,000 annually. This exacerbated the problems surrounding Japanese immigration, prompting the Japanese and U.S. governments to form a "gentlemen's agreement" to establish limits. In March 1907, the California State Legislature passed a law forbidding land

2. Wakatsuki (1972); National Institute of Population and Social Security Research (1942).

ownership by Japanese persons.

The 1913 California Alien Land Law (the Webb–Haney Act) prohibited agricultural land ownership and leases exceeding three years by "aliens ineligible for citizenship," namely all Asians except for those from the Philippines. This law was further strengthened by the California Alien Land Law of 1920, which allowed confiscation of illegally owned land and forbade cropping contracts. While legally owned land was not confiscated, it could not be resold or bequeathed, meaning that it would eventually be lost. To avoid this, many first-generation Japanese transferred ownership to native-born children born with U.S. citizenship.[3]

The activities of labor unions in particular are responsible for this sad chapter in the history of Japan–U.S. relations. The Japanese were latecomers in terms of immigration to North America, and the inflow of low-cost, high-quality Japanese workers caused anxious white laborers to riot. Predominantly white labor unions responded with systematic activities aimed at Japanese exclusion. This eventually led to discrimination in society at large. To win over a voter base strongly opposed to Japanese laborers, San Francisco's municipal government made anti-Japanese pledges that led to further exclusion. Social sanctions outweighed any economic benefit of hiring Japanese workers or leasing land to them, so even individuals who ordinarily would have done so were now unwilling to break caste. This clearly illustrates the power of labor unions.

Rōdō undō nijū-nen (Twenty Years of Labor Movement)[4] — written in 1931 by Suzuki Bunji, one of the founders of the labor union movement in Japan — provides an interesting record of these times, particularly with regards to Japanese exclusion and the activities of the *Yūai-kai* (Friendly Society) labor union in Japan (mentioned in chapter 2, section 2). American educator Sidney Gulick investigated the roots of Japanese exclusion in the U.S. after having spent time in Japan, and found American labor unions to be predominantly to blame. As a result of discussions with California Federation of Labor leader Paul Schalenberg and American Federation of Labor president Samuel Gompers, Gulick came to believe that negotiations between Japanese labor representatives and U.S. labor unions could improve the situation to at least some extent. With the support of Soeda Juichi, Suzuki was encouraged to take advantage of this opportunity to visit the United States to observe its society and labor unions. Japan's Ministry of Foreign Affairs stood in his way, however, because officials there believed

---

3. Kaikoku Hyakunen Kinen Bunka Jigyōkai (1956).
4. Suzuki (1985, pp. 94–108).

the problem was due to racism rather than labor unions or economic issues.

After clearing a number of diplomatic hurdles, Suzuki finally arrived in the United States in June 1915, but his reception was chilly; with the exception of one or two labor leaders, most union members saw his activities as spying for Japan. Schalenberg stood firm against the pressure that surrounded him, insisting that this was an excellent opportunity for unions to present their arguments in favor of Japanese exclusion. He eventually cleared the way for Suzuki to attend California and U.S. labor conferences.

As this case demonstrates, failure to solve economic conflicts can lead to racial discrimination, sometimes disguised as "cultural friction." Furthermore, when economic behavior is politicized, political and economic behaviors become inextricably intertwined.

Immigration to South America and the Manchurian colonies

Exclusionary measures and immigration caps put a damper on Japanese emigration to North America and Australia, so the focus shifted to South American countries like Brazil and Peru. Immigrants to Brazil at the time were generally employed as *coloni*, agricultural laborers at coffee plantations living in shanties under harsh working conditions. This "employment" was so near to slave labor, in fact, that the Italian government forbade its citizens from migrating to Brazil. During this period nearly 200,000 Japanese immigrated, particularly to the state of São Paulo.

After the Mukden Incident in 1931, migration to Manchuria and China dramatically increased. The leadership of the Kwantung Army and the Ministry of Colonial Affairs promoted settlement in Manchuria and nearby areas in Mongolia, where agricultural migrants were called "settlers." In 1936, the cabinet of Hirota Kōki set a national goal of establishing one million Japanese households in Manchuria over twenty years, in part because Brazil and Peru had started to implement restrictions on Japanese migration to those countries. While the plans were never realized to that scale, by the end of World War II approximately 270,000 Japanese had migrated to Manchuria and Mongolia.

Increasing the Japanese population in those locations was considered important for political and military reasons, as a way of maintaining security and of preparing for war with the Soviet Union. The Great Depression impoverished many Japanese farming villages and as a result provided a constant flow of willing migrants. These were typically second or third sons, who were armed and relocated in groups. As Japan became increasingly mired in the Sino-Japanese War, however, the demand for military and civilian workers within Japan increased,[5] resulting in an insufficient supply of adult migrants. The *Manmō Kaitaku Seishōnen Giyūgun* (Manchurian Settlement Youth Volunteer Brigade) was established in response in 1937, and during the eight years between then and the end of World War II, approximately 87,000 young men aged fifteen to eighteen relocated through this program. While they nominally went on a volunteer basis, there are many reports of upper elementary school teachers pressing their students to join the program.[6]

Youth entering the program gathered at a training facility in present-day Mito city, Ibaraki prefecture, where they received several months of training under the agrarianist and educator Katō Kanji. Further training was provided after settlement parties relocated to Manchuria. When surveying the remains of a Hitachi mine near Mito, I had the opportunity to visit the Uchihara Local History and Youth Volunteer Brigade Museum, located on the old grounds of the training center. Among the items on display was a photograph of a Hitler Youth representative, who visited the facility in September 1938, just after its establishment, to observe how Japanese youth were being trained there — an interesting page from the history of the Anti-Comintern Pact. Records also indicate that a group of seven German observers arrived in November 1940.

The Kwantung Army retreated immediately after the Red Army invaded in August 1945, leaving Japanese settlements behind. Those who were unable to flee were forced to leave small children with Chinese families as stranded orphans.

Internment of Japanese

Anti-Japanese sentiment continued to grow in the United States during this period, culminating in Executive Order 9066 in January 1942, just one month after the Japanese attack on Pearl Harbor. Under this order, individuals of Japanese ancestry could be designated as security risks and forced to move from their homes to internment camps in California, Arizona, Idaho, Wyoming, Colorado, Utah, and Arkansas. Approximately 110,000 persons of Japanese descent were interred, 64% of whom were U.S. citizens.[7]

---

5. The Manchurian Settlement Peace Memorial Hall in Achi village, Nagano prefecture is a notable resource center for materials related to Manchurian colonization. While settlers originated from many parts of Japan, a particularly large number—around 33,000—came from Nagano prefecture, largely due to its limited arable land and economic distress caused by the decline of the sericulture industry. Another factor was the prefecture's active promotion of overseas migration, for example through the Shinano Overseas Association.
6. See Shiratori (1986, 1990) for detailed analyses of the Manchurian Settlement Youth Volunteer Brigade.
7. Kitano (1980); Inoki (1999).

At the time, small-scale entrepreneurship was the economic foundation for first-generation Japanese, with many working as domestic servants, launderers, antique dealers, shopkeepers, barbers, or restaurateurs. As was the case for many other ethnic minorities, the Japanese shared business contacts and set up mutual help organizations to provide financial support. These relationships of economic interdependence heightened unity within the Japanese community. This type of synergistic strengthening of regional and family bonds through help of those in need is by no means a rare occurrence. However, it can seem quite peculiar when viewed from the outside.

Those first-generation Japanese who attained economic success took on leadership roles in their communities. They built up the financial resources of their organizations through fund-raising, and worked to provide the Japanese community with social services such as English education and translation. Associations of persons originally from the same prefecture, called *kenjinkai*, were one type of community organization for Japanese living overseas. These associations supported Buddhist and Christian religious groups, youth associations, women's associations, and Japanese language schools.

The activities of these organizations contributed to the education of second-generation Japanese, who were born into U.S. citizenship and spoke English thanks to American schooling. Strong family ties and the support of informal networks for mutual aid and social services helped them gradually emerge into American society. Even so, second-generation Japanese faced extreme employment discrimination in the 1920s and 1930s. Many sociological studies have focused on the Japanese Americans of this era, and most of them describe widespread exclusion from good employment opportunities despite clearly demonstrated high IQ and moral standards, low crime rates, and exceptional academic ability.

The attack on Pearl Harbor was a drastic blow to Japanese living in America, heightening distrust directed toward them and, as mentioned above, leading to internment. The economic power of Japanese residents was already seen as a threat by mainstream society, and the media fanned the flames of anti-Japanese sentiment — flames that opportunistic politicians were happy to pour oil on. Because the U.S. was now at war with Japan, there was little motivation for other citizens to organize for the protection of Japanese-American civil rights.

Judging from photographic depictions, life in the internment camps was busier and more stressful than one might imagine.[8] Conflicts emerged between first- and second-generation Japanese and between detainees who strengthened their Japanese patriotism and those who expressed obsequiousness toward the U.S. government. Family relationships were disrupted and communities clashed over gambling.

One path out of the confines of the internment camp was military service. World War II was, from a U.S. perspective, a battle against European fascism, and joining that fight was a powerful way to demonstrate national loyalty. The 442nd Regimental Combat Team and the 100th Infantry Battalion were made up of 33,000 Japanese Americans from Hawaii and the mainland, who are the subjects of many famous stories. Six hundred of these soldiers were killed during the war and 9,000 were injured, amply demonstrating their strong devotion to the United States.[9]

2. Immigration and Emigration after World War II

Internment and withdrawal
As described in chapter 3, wars dislocate people of all ages and at all levels of society. Near the end of the World War II, there were increasingly many domestic mass evacuations in Japan. At the close of the war, there were approximately 3.5 million Japanese military personnel and 3 million non-military workers overseas. In addresses to the Imperial Army and Navy on 17 and 25 August 1945, the emperor issued an imperial rescript calling for an orderly demobilization to protect the "everlasting foundation of the nation." As a result, approximately 3.09 million out of 5.45 million army personnel and 450,000 out of 1.80 million navy personnel greeted the end of the war overseas, in places like Sakhalin and the Kuril islands, Korea, the Chinese mainland, southeast Asia, and various Pacific islands.[10] Extracting military personnel from regions under Chinese and Soviet control was exceedingly difficult. In addition to the 580,000 disarmed troops of the Kwantung Army and those in Northern Korea, Sakhalin, and the Kuril islands, who together made up the bulk of stranded soldiers, over 10,000

---

8. Conrat and Conrat (1972) provides many photographs and other records of these internment camps.
9. Watanabe (2003) and many others have described or dramatized the history of the 442nd Regimental Combat Team. One well-known member of the 442nd was Daniel Inouye, who was a student at the University of Hawaii when Pearl Harbor was attacked. He volunteered for the army and fought with the 442nd on the European front line. After the war, he served as a U.S. senator for close to fifty years.
10. Chapter 5 in Umemura et al. (1988) presents statistics related to numbers of Imperial Army and Navy personnel. He notes, however, that "starting around the turn of the twentieth century, the quality of Imperial Army statistics significantly worsened, and as the war escalated around 1935, statistics for both the army and navy became quite poor" (p. 42).

civilians were living in these regions at the end of the war. They included government officials and Concordia Association functionaries in Manchuria, and employees of national policy companies, colonial governing organizations, and newspapers.

The Soviet Union captured 472,000 Japanese in Siberia, 13,000 in Outer Mongolia, 65,000 in central Asia, and 25,000 in Europe and Russia, imprisoning them in approximately 1,200 POW camps, where they performed forced labor. Around 50,000 Japanese detainees were sent to help build the second Trans-Siberian railway. Detainee rosters are incomplete, making it difficult to ascertain exact figures, but by April 1950 around 530,000 of the prisoners had been returned to Japan. Those who were civilians were forced to abandon all possessions and assets before returning. Many others never made it home, dying due to illness or the extreme cold and harsh labor conditions in the POW camps.[11]

This withdrawal involved an unprecedented mass movement of Japanese people. The Japanese government implemented emergency measures, specifying the ports at Maizuru, Uraga, Kure, Shimonoseki, Hakata, Sasebo, Kagoshima, Yokohama, Senzaki, and Moji as repatriation sites in September 1945. In 1950 the port at Maizuru became the sole repatriation site, and it continued to play an important role in the Japanese withdrawal through September 1958, when the last boat arrived — the *Hakusan Maru*, which brought 472 returnees from Sakhalin and Kholmsk. Stragglers continued to be discovered until nearly thirty years after the war's end. Yokoi Shōichi was discovered in Guam in February 1972, and Onoda Hirō on Lubang Island in the Philippines in March 1974. Table 21 lists the number of repatriated military and civilian Japanese by region.

Overseas migration resumed after the War, with most settlers heading to Brazil and other countries in South, Central, and North America. For some time after the war, the food shortages and sudden increase in Japan's domestic population related to repatriation increased pressure for emigration. Governments in Central and South America accepted immigrants without regard to national origin, which temporarily boosted the numbers of Japanese moving overseas. As the domestic economy entered a period of rapid growth, however, it began to absorb more workers, thereby depressing emigration. Japan's own policies related to immigrants and foreign residents also encountered several issues after the Treaty of San Francisco came into force in 1952. Of particular concern were the repatriation of North Koreans, the granting of permanent residence to Koreans remaining in Japan,

---

11. Maizuru City (1995); Maizuru City History Compilation Committee (1975, 1988).

Table 21. Number of persons repatriated after World War II by region (1,000s of persons)

Soviet Union, Kuril Islands, Sakhalin	766
Manchuria (including Dalian)	1,271
China	1,540
North Korea, South Korea	920
Southeast Asia	712
Other (Taiwan, Pacific Islands, Oceania)	1,086
Total	6,295

Source: Ministry of Health and Welfare, Dept. of Social Assistance (1997).   (as of Jan. 1, 1996)

and the amendment of immigration policies to accommodate the inflow of Indochinese refugees. The Calcutta Agreement, signed between the Red Cross Societies of Japan and North Korea in 1959, resolved some of these issues by repatriating approximately 100,000 Koreans from Japan.[12]

Asian power in the United States

Over time, the social standing of Japanese in America gradually improved. Indeed, they eventually came to be viewed less as "Japanese Americans" than as "Asian Americans." The United States took in many Asian immigrants, particularly in the 1970s, when 360,000 persons arrived from the Philippines, 270,000 from South Korea, and 250,000 from China and Hong Kong. A further 450,000 immigrants came to the United States from southeast Asia between 1980 and 1985, including 170,000 from South Korea.

This sudden increase in "Asian power" has significantly impacted American society, and will continue to powerfully energize it in the future. Within this context, the issue of Japanese Americans residing in the U.S. has become relatively minor. While many Japanese visit the U.S. today, their stays are generally transient, with few remaining to become permanent residents. Still, the U.S. has a significant population of Japanese Americans, particularly in Hawaii and on the West Coast. Most are firmly established in the middle class, and many have reached the upper strata of society. This represents a significant change: while only 4% of young Japanese American men were engaged in specialist or management jobs in 1940, approximately 30% held these jobs in 1970. Many were doctors and engineers.[13]

The Asian presence in the United States is immediately evident when one visits the famous universities there; by the mid 1990s, 15–20% of students entering Massachusetts Institute of Technology and Harvard University

---

12. During this period North Korea developed an international image as a "paradise on earth," in large part because little accurate information about the country was available. As illustrated by the 1962 Japanese film *Foundry Town*, the mass media of the time was supportive of repatriation efforts.
13. Kitano (1980).

were Asian Americans, as were one in four new students at the University of California, Berkeley. These numbers demonstrate the birth of a "new Asia" in the United States at the end of the twentieth century.

Asian American immigrants have also impacted lifestyles in large cities. This is evidenced by the growing popularity of items such as futons, and the increasingly international eating habits of Americans. Today not only Chinese and Japanese restaurants are common, but also Thai, Vietnamese, and Korean restaurants that would have been highly unusual in the 1960s. Tofu, soy sauce, and Asian noodles are now available at most supermarkets. Considering that disparaging cultural foodstuffs is a common method of demonstrating bias, this internationalization of eating habits is highly significant.

Another change is that not only university students and faculty, but also the general American populace is now more interested in other countries, and the American narcissism that was so prevalent through the 1960s is weakening. Young people in particular increasingly realize that the United States is just one country among many, and a growing number are studying Asian languages. A U.S. Association of Departments of Foreign Languages study showed that while only 1,700 U.S. students studied Japanese at higher education institutions in 1960, that number had increased to 45,000 by 1990, the height of Japan's international economic performance.[14]

American society has changed greatly since World War II, and even since the 1960s, when America was at the height of its power. However, this change does not signify a permanent weakening of American power; there is a good chance that it will regain its former political and economic prowess, and Asian Americans will likely provide much of the driving force behind that recovery. The numbers given above regarding Asian participation in higher education support this.

Foreign workers in Japan in the 1990s

In the years leading up to the Russo-Japanese War, boats carrying Japanese immigrants were refused entry to Hawaii on a number of occasions, and the Chinatowns and Japantowns in some cities were burned to the ground in the name of pest control. Many on the U.S. mainland feared the "Yellow Peril," and as described above, some took part in anti-Japanese movements.

A century later, Japan is engaged in its own debate over how to deal with immigrant workers. People from poor countries often migrate to richer countries in search of work, and in the absence of strong restrictions on

---

14. Brod and Huber (1997).

immigration, any country will face issues related to these workers. The U.S. response to Japanese immigrants in the years following the Russo-Japanese War represents just one example of measures for restricting immigration. Even societies with modern economies often take an extremely strict and cautious attitude toward accepting foreign workers. Foreign manual laborers are the first to lose their jobs in periods of economic downturn, making unemployment problems all the more serious and complex. When offering aid to poorer countries, it is preferable from a long-term perspective to cooperate on human resource development within those countries, rather than accept their workers. There are many reasons for caution in these areas, such as the housing and educational challenges that immigration may bring, and the delay in industrial development that may result from reliance on cheap foreign labor.[15]

The common international preconception that Japan is highly exclusionary toward foreign workers is far removed from the actual state of affairs. Compared with other economically advanced countries, Japan is by no means a closed country. I would like to conclude this chapter with a brief discussion of this topic.

Japan's Immigration Control and Refugee Recognition Act has been revised several times since its initial enactment in 1951. Its 1990 revision was criticized as simply a clarification of how it should be implemented, without any increase in the number of foreign workers allowed into Japan or the categories of work for which they were eligible. However, while it is true that the revision did not end bans on entry into the country for the purposes of manual labor or work involving general skills, production, or clerical tasks, it represented a major change in that it disclosed the entry requirements and examination criteria for foreigners in the form of laws and ordinances. To my knowledge, no other country explicitly publicizes all standards for admittance. In this regard, Japanese immigration policy stands out as the most fair and transparent system in the world.

It is difficult to propose an index for openness within a given country. In many cases, it is also difficult to provide a simple determination of whether a given policy is discriminatory. What is clear, however, is that while both the United States and Japan have imposed an increasing number of restrictions on immigration, they have simultaneously increased transparency and fairness. Growing respect for equality and human rights has led to corresponding policy changes, the rules for which have been made clearer and

---

15. See Higuchi (1988) and Ōhashi (1995) for a theoretical consideration of related economic effects.

their application more consistent. Just as the American view of the Japanese is very different today than it was a century ago, Japanese perceptions of foreigners have greatly changed as well.

Ministry of Justice studies show an ever-increasing number of foreign laborers in Japan. At the end of 1992, there were approximately 90,000 foreign workers with technical expertise, 150,000 persons of Japanese descent from South American countries working in Japan temporarily, and around 300,000 foreigners working in Japan illegally.[16] In 1993, the government introduced a technical internship program that allowed foreign residents to learn while working. This greatly increased the number of foreign trainees in Japan, two-thirds of whom were Chinese, but also led to an increased number of illegal immigrants and workplace human rights violations. Immigration policy is closely linked to national sovereignty, making it a key element of preserving national interests. The Japan of today must find a way to mesh its national interests with the need for international cooperation and humanitarianism, particularly as relates to recognition of refugee status.

---

16. Mori (1988) uses immigration control and alien registration statistics to determine the number of illegal workers present in Japan.

CONCLUSION

The previous chapters have aimed to describe with as much specificity as possible the quantitative and qualitative changes in human resources that occurred in twentieth-century Japan. They have made clear that education does not take place solely at home and at school. In factories and offices, and even in government and military workplaces, we Japanese are provided with relatively broad opportunities for continued learning, and we improve ourselves through fierce competition to obtain living knowledge and skills. Some time ago, we noticed that true education takes place as part and parcel of our everyday working lives.

As noted in the introduction, human resource development in Japan can be summarized as a competitive system based on equal opportunities. Of course, I do not claim perfect fairness, nor a lack of forces that distort competition. Nevertheless, the principles of equal opportunity and fierce competition have clearly been widespread in Japan for a very long time.

Upward mobility through the competitive climbing of social ladders is not unique to modern Japan. Indeed, careerism is a core characteristic of modern democracies in any country. Humans in all places and eras have also taken an interest in scientific knowledge. However, Europe was the first region to tie science to industrial activity, forming a path for economic careerism. Japan followed a similar path, albeit in a later era and, due to cultural differences, in an altered form.

Japanese society has been characterized by relatively broad opportunities for participation in competition as well as freedom of ideas since very early times. Places without freedom of ideas cannot maintain healthy production activities. For example, Confucianism in Japan was never overwhelmingly dominated by a single school of thought, even during the Edo period. While the government imposed restrictions during certain periods, such as the time of the Kansei Edicts, many schools of thought existed even then, including Zhu Xi, Wang Yangming, and *kogaku* neo-Confucianism. This is quite a different situation from that which existed in countries like Korea. Particularly during the five centuries of the Joseon dynasty, Confucianism in Korea was strictly limited to the Zhu Xi school. Members of the *yangban* gentry competed for administrative posts as members of Confucian factions, and ideals of *li* enforced rigid social and familial status.

While not addressed in this book, the Edo-period introduction of Western thought into Japan via Nagasaki also had profound effects. Indeed, I have done my readers a disservice by failing to sufficiently emphasize the impacts of Western science, technology, and art on modern Japan. I learned much on this subject from my visits to the Tsuyama Archives of Western Learning in Tsuyama city, Okayama prefecture. The Udagawa and Mitsukuri clans and many other Western studies scholars hailed from the Mimasaka region, and in particular from Tsuyama. Notable Meiji-period scholars from this region include Dutch law scholar Tsuda Mamichi, French law scholar and compiler of civil law Mitsukuri Rinshō, and Kikuchi Dairoku, the first Japanese to graduate from the University of Cambridge. That so many luminaries came out of this region can only be the result of clans embracing the heritage and customs of Western learning.

Japan is characterized by its variety of competing ideological schools, notably with many scholars in the fields of empirical science distancing themselves from Confucian thought by the early eighteenth century. Criticism of the teachings of Zhu Xi, or at least critical reception of those teachings, indicate that freedom and competition of thought were to some extent established by that time.

Of course, the Japanese have not always enjoyed unfettered freedom of thought. There are many episodes in our history that we would prefer to forget, including the persecution of Christians during the Edo period, the suppression of free expression in the years leading to and during World War II, and the rise of Marxism in postwar academic circles. What we have seen, however, is that most Japanese have the vitality to overcome such episodes.

I would also like to note that while Japanese intellectuals have long been drawn to abstract and deductive theories, the people of Japan as a whole are quite practical. They have, for example, created many organizations focused on the worksite. This trend is particularly prominent in industry. The Japanese noticed early on that production skills are in essence comprised of indefinable knowledge. This keen realization is evidenced in the broad on-the-job training that workers at production sites undergo. As this book has shown, on-the-job training is the most effective method of skill acquisition in many situations, and in industry and other areas of practical application there exist certain skills and knowledge that can *only* be passed on through on-the-job training.

Even so, we cannot rely on realism alone. The bravery to recognize reality and the danger of losing sight of our ideals are two sides of the same coin. Over the past century, we Japanese have been forced to walk the tightrope of learning how to discern reality while keeping our eyes on distant goals. The question is whether we can maintain this tension as we progress into the future.

Difficult times call for a levelheaded stance that is neither optimistic nor pessimistic. In recent years, I have increasingly come to feel that *concours* presumes both cooperation and individual enjoyment of the results of competition, and also that educational settings demand cultivation of a common spirit that connects profits and public interest. There can be no competition without opponents, nor without a recognition of the public. What the future demands is not undue emphasis on egalitarianism, but rather the cultivation of workers who are capable of considering public–private balance both within the organization and in society.

Afterword to the first edition

Many books have discussed education in contemporary Japan. This is one such book, set apart by its focus on human resource development and allocation without limiting the discussion to systemic aspects of formal education and industrial training. In it, I have presented a historical overview of Japanese systems for human resource development.

Due to the limitations of space as well as of my own abilities, I have left many problems unaddressed. For example, I was unfortunately unable to touch upon the genesis of the "politician" or the cultural aspects of human resource development. Furthermore, even with regard to the topics covered in the book, I cannot be sure that I have accumulated sufficient research. I hope that I will be able to address these shortcomings in a longer work in the future.

Despite the brevity of the present volume, its completion has been possible only through the support of many individuals. I express my particular thanks to Koike Kazuo of Hosei University and my colleague Miyamoto Matao at Osaka University. My discussions with Sawai Minoru were highly inspiring. I also thank the excellent staff of Hinokuchi Studio for their help in preparing the manuscript for this book.

This book was scheduled to be completed in September of last year, and I apologize to all involved for the troubles I caused by its lateness. I would like to thank Kataya Katsumi and Kawahito Ken'ichi of the *Yomiuri Shimbun* newspaper for their hard work on historical fact-checking, creating the appendices, and proofreading. Any remaining errors are my own responsibility.

Inoki Takenori
March 1996

Afterword to the expanded edition

Human resource development requires a spirit of sustained accumulation. It must be based on public ideals and long-term perspectives that are not swayed by short-term profits or results. The Japanese workforce of today, however, is characterized by mobility and increased use of irregular employees, and current wage systems primarily reward short-term results. To my eyes, this indicates a trend toward myopic public policy.

Our schools and companies seem to be heading in a direction of negatively affecting on-site skill formation in the labor force, one of our sources of international competiveness. We seem to be ignoring the advantages of the systems we developed after World War II. Wage systems that are based on short-term profit–loss calculations and that emphasize results, current abilities, and immediate strategies lack consideration for the more far-sighted goal of fostering worker growth, and therefore weaken the human resources that form the core of our economy. Such systems risk leading Japan into economic decline.

Humanity faces many dangers, from environmental and energy issues to viruses and armed conflict. If Japan is to overcome these challenges, it must develop systems and workforces capable of addressing new problems that cannot be solved with knowledge attained through formal education alone. Japanese society has surmounted many difficulties in the seventy years since the end of World War II, and continuing to do so will be a prime concern in the future.

One of my goals in writing a book about the human resources development and selection systems of twentieth-century Japan was to reconfirm the characteristics of these systems, and to show how they provided a wellspring of economic bounty. Advancing our historical understanding of these topics requires careful confirmation of seemingly trivial matters. Equally important are the international comparisons that clarify which features of human resource development are unique to Japan. Scholarship requires an ascetic attitude toward digging up detailed source materials and reflecting on what they alone can tell us. It is also important for scholars to utilize existing knowledge and information when making predictions about the future.

When this book was first published in 1996 under the title *Gakkō to kōjō: Nihon no jinteki shigen* (Human Resource Development in Japan), volume seven in the *Yomiuri Shimbun* newspaper's *Nijū-seiki no nihon* (Japan in the Twentieth Century) series, it received both praise and criticism from interested colleagues and researchers. I thank Hirota Teruyuki of Nihon

University in particular for his comments regarding its shortcomings. I hoped at the time for the opportunity to provide an expanded and revised edition that would address some of these points.

In the winter of 2009, Nagata Shirō of Chikumashobo proposed a paper-back release of this work. While I appreciated the offer, the comments and criticisms I had previously received made me pause, because I was well aware that I did not have the mental energy at the time to undertake a large revision. In the end, while I was not able to fully rewrite the text, I decided to make a number of additions, fix some errors, and expand the footnotes and bibliography for the benefit of readers wishing to know more. Because this is a broad field that defies full review of all accumulated research, how-ever, my limited selection of resources may be somewhat biased.

During the spring 2013 academic semester, Prof. Kimura Mitsuhiko selected the original edition of this book as discussion material for a course at Aoyama Gakuin University's Graduate School of International Political Economics, giving me a welcome opportunity to reread it alongside the students in the course. I received invaluable comments not only from Prof. Kimura, but also from graduate students including Gotō Hideo, Ashizawa Shūji, and Mineta Naoko. Their reviews of the book were extremely useful as I made the additions and corrections for the paperback release.

I would also like to express my gratitude to Tamura Taichi of Ryutsu Keizai University for carefully reading the final drafts of this edition and providing constructive comments.

It has now been almost seven years since I received from Mr. Nagata the digital files he would eventually use to print the paperback edition. I experi-enced some illness during that time, but the primary reason for the delay in publishing was my own neglect. I do not have the words sufficient to express my gratitude for his consistently positive attitude, frank opinions, and perseverance.

Inoki Takenori
March 2016

Addendum: The "staff of Hinokuchi Studio" mentioned in the afterword to the first edition were my departed wife Yoshiko and our three daughters, Yuri, Yumi, and Yuki. I take this opportunity to mention them by name, in fond remembrance of that time twenty years ago.

WORKS CITED

Non-Japanese works

Ashenfelter, O., & Rouse, C. (1998). Income, Schooling and Ability: Evidence from a New Sample of Identical Twins. *Quarterly Journal of Economics, 113*(1), 253–284.

Ashenfelter, O., & Rouse, C. (2000). Schooling, Intelligence, and Income in America. In K. Arrow, S. Bowles, & S. Durlauf (Eds.), *Meritocracy and Economic Inequality*. Princeton: Princeton University Press.

Bälz, E. (1932). *Awakening Japan: The Diary of a German Doctor* (E. Paul, & C. Paul, Trans.). New York: Viking Press.

Bartel, A.P., & Lichtenberg, F.R. (1987). The Comparative Advantage of Educated Workers in Implementing New Technology. *Review of Economics and Statistics, 69*(1), 1–11.

Becker, G.S. (1993). *Human Capital: A Theoretical and Empirical Analysis, with Special Reference to Education*. Chicago: University of Chicago Press.

Borjas, G. (2007). *Labor Economics* (4th ed.). New York: McGraw-Hill/Irwin.

Bright, J.R. (1958). Does Automation Raise Skill Requirements? *Harvard Business Review, 36*(4), 85–98.

Brod, R., & Huber B.J. (1997). Foreign Language Enrollments in United States Institutions of Higher Education, Fall 1995. *ADFL Bulletin, 28*(2), 55-60.

Conrat, M., & Conrat, R. (1972). *Executive Order 9066: The Internment of 110,000 Japanese Americans*. Cambridge: The MIT Press.

Cunha, F., Heckman, J., Lochner, L., & Masterov, D.V. (2005). Interpreting the Evidence on Life Cycle Skill Formation. *NBER Working Paper, No. 113311*.

Dore, R. (1965). *Education in Tokugawa Japan*. Oakland: University of California Press.

Dore, R. (1976). *The Diploma Disease: Education, Qualification, and Development*. Sydney: Allen and Unwin.

Freeman, R.B., & Medoff, J.L. (1979) The Two Faces of Unionism. *Public Interest 57*, 69–93.

Fryer, R.G., & Levitt, S.D. (2004). Understanding the Black-White Test Score Gap in the First Two Years of School. *The Review of Economics and Statistics, 86*(2), 447–464.

Godo, Y., & Hayami, Y. (2002). Catching Up in Education in the Economic Catch-up of Japan with the United States, 1890-1990. *Economic Development and Cultural Change, 50*(4), 961-978.

Goldin, C., & Katz, L.F. (1998). The Origins of Technology-Skill Complementarity. *Quarterly Journal of Economics, 113*(3), 693-732.

Hayek, F. (1945). The Use of Knowledge in Society. *American Economic Review, 35*(4), 519–530.

Herrnstein, R.J., & Murray, C. (1994). *The Bell Curve*. New York: Free Press.

Hunter, J. (2003). *Women and the Labour Market in Japan's Industrializing Economy: The Textile Industry before the Pacific War*. Oxford: Routledge.

Inoki, T. (1988). Formes de Gestion du Personnel et Nouvelles Technologies. In M. Maurice et al. *Des Entreprises Francaises et Japonaises Face a la Mecatronique*, LEST–CNRS, France.

Inoki, T. (1991). Personnel Management under New Technology: Training, Wages and
    Workers' Mobility in France and Japan. *Osaka Economic Papers, 41*, 276–315.

Inoki, T. (1995). Japanese Bureaucrats at Retirement: The Mobility of Human Resources
    from Central Government to Public Corporations. In H. Kim (Ed.), *The Japanese
    Civil Services and Economic Development.* Wotton-under-Edge: Clarendon Press.

Inoki, T. (2001). Staff Loans and Transfers among Central and Local Governments in
    Japan. In M. Muramatsu, I. Farrukh, & I. Kume (Eds.) *Local Government Development
    in Post War Japan.* Oxford: Oxford University Press.

Kitano, H. (1980). Japanese. In S. Thernstrom (Ed.), *Harvard Encyclopedia of American
    Ethnic Groups.* Cambridge: Harvard University Press.

Knight, F.H. (1964) [1957], Risk, Uncertainly, and Profit. *Reprints of Economic Classics.*
    New York: A.M. Kelly.

Koike, K., & Inoki, T. (Eds.). (1991). *Skill Formation in Japan and Southeast Asia.*
    Tokyo: University of Tokyo Press.

Krämer, H. (2005). Just Who Reversed the Course? The Red Purge in Higher Education
    During the Occupation of Japan. *Social Science Japan Journal, 8*(1), 1–18.

Kuznets, S.S. (1968). *Toward a Theory of Economic Growth.* New York: W.W. Norton &
    Company.

Kuznets, S.S. (1971). *Economic Growth of Nations: Total Output and Production
    Structure.* Cambridge: Harvard University Press.

La Force, J.C. (1964). Royal Textile Factories in Spain, 1700–1800. *Journal of Economic
    History, 24*(3), 337–363.

Marshall, A. (1890). *Principles of Economics.* London: Macmillan and Co.

Mathias, P. (1979). *The Transformation of England.* London: Methuen.

Mosse, A., & Mosse, L. (1995). *Fast wie mein eigen Vaterland, Briefe aus Japan 1886–1889,
    Herausgegeben von Shirō Ishii, Ernst Lokowandt und Yūkichi Sakai.* Iudicium.

Murnane, R.J., & Levy, F. (1996). *Teaching the New Basic Skills.* Florence: Free Press.

Nelson, R.R., & Phelps, E. (1966). Investment in Humans, Technological Diffusion, and
    Economic Growth. *American Economic Review, 56*(1–2), 69–75.

OECD (1993). *Employment Outlook.* OECD.

OECD (1999). *La Mesure de L'emploi Public dans les Pays de L'OCDE: Sources, Méthodes et
    Résultats.* OCDE.

OERI Japan Study Team (1987). *Japanese Education Today.* United States Department of
    Education.

Polanyi, M. (1958). *Personal Knowledge: Towards a post-Critical Philosophy.*
    Chicago: University of Chicago Press.

Schultz, T.W. (1963). *The Economic Value of Education.* New York: Columbia University
    Press.

Schultz, T.W. (1975). The Value of Ability to Deal with Disequilibria. *Journal of Economic
    Literature, 13*(3), 827-846.

Schultz, T.W. (1981). *Investing in People: The Economics of Population Quality.*
    Oakland: University of California Press.

Scoville, W.C. (1951). Minority Migrations and the Diffusions of Technology.
    Journal of Economic History, 11(4), 347–360.

Smith, A. (1904). *An Inquiry into the Nature and Causes of the Wealth of Nations, 1*. London: Methuen.

Taylor, A.J.P. (1983). *A Personal History*. London: Hamilton.

Ueshima, Y., Funaba, T., & Inoki, T. (2006). New Technology and Demand for Educated Workers: The Experience of Japanese Manufacturing in the Era of High-Speed Growth. *Journal of the Japanese and International Economies, 20*(1), 50–76.

United States Education Mission to Japan (1979). *Report of the United States Education Mission to Japan*.

United States Strategic Bombing Survey (1946). *The Effects of Strategic Bombing on Japan's War Economy*. Overall Economic Effects Division.

Japanese works

Note: All Japanese books published in Tokyo unless otherwise noted.

Amano, I 天野郁夫 . (2005). *Gakureki no shakai-shi: Kyōiku to nihon no kindai* 学歴の社会史：教育と日本の近代 . Heibonsha.

Amano, I 天野郁夫 . (2013). *Kōtō kyōiku no jidai: Senkanki nihon no daigaku* 高等教育の時代：戦間期日本の大学 . Chuokoron-Shinsha.

Aruga, T 有賀貞 ., Ōshimo, S 大下尚一 ., Shimura, A 志邨晃佑 ., & Hirano, T 平野孝 . (Eds.) (1993). *Amerika-shi 2:1877–1992* アメリカ史 2: 1877–1992. Yamakawa Shuppansha.

Asahara, K 淺原健三 . (1930). *Yōkōro no hi wa kietari* 鎔鉱炉の火は消えたり . Shinkensha.

Association for the Preservation of the Shizutani School 特別史跡旧閑谷学校顕彰保存会 (2003). *Shizutani gakkō yukari no hitobito* 閑谷学校ゆかりの人々 . Okayama: Sanyo Shimbun.

Boyles, C.J. (1993). Josei no kumiai ishiki to kanyū kōdō 女性の組合意識と加入行動 . In T. Tachibanaki, & Association of Comprehensive Life Development Institute (Eds.) *Rōdō kumiai no keizai-gaku: Kitai to genjitsu* 労働組合の経済学：期待と現実 . Toyo Keizai.

Brunton, R.H. (1986). *Oyatoi gaijin no mita kindai nihon* お雇い外人の見た近代日本 . (S. Tokuriki, Trans.). Kodansha.

Central Occupational Placement Office 中央職業紹介事務局 (1924–1927). *Shokugyō betsu rōdō jijō* 職業別労働事情 .

Chimoto, A 千本暁子 . (1986). Meiji-ki ni okeru kōgyō-ka to zairai-teki koyō kankei no henka 明治期における工業化と在来的雇用関係の変化 . *Socio-Economic History* 社会経済史学 , *52*(1).

Chimoto, A 千本暁子 . (1989). Mitsui no shiyōnin saiyō hōhō no shiteki kōsatsu 三井の使用人採用方法の史的考察 . *The Social Sciences* 社会科学 , *42*.

Chimoto, A 千本暁子 . (1994). Howaitokarā no jinzai ikusei to gakkō kyōiku e no izon ホワイトカラーの人材育成と学校教育への依存 . *Hannan University Journal of Social Sciences* 阪南論集　社会科学編 , *29*(3).

Chimoto, A 千本暁子 . (1998a). Naibu rōdō shijyō no keisei to keishō: Mitsui ni okeru jinzai ikusei to chōki koyō 内部労働市場の形成と継承：三井における人材育成と長期雇用 . In H. Itami, T. Kagono, M. Miyamoto, & S. Yonekura (Eds.), *Nihonteki keiei no seisei to hatten* 日本的経営の生成と発展 . Yuhikaku.

Chimoto, A 千本暁子 . (1998b). Meiji-ki bōseki-gyō ni okeru tsūkin jokō kara kishuku jokō
     e no tenkan 明治期紡績業における通勤女工から寄宿女工への転換 .
     Hannan University Journal of Social Sciences 阪南論集 社会科学編 , *34*(2).

Chimoto, A 千本暁子 . (1999). Nijū-seiki shotō ni okeru bōseki-gyō no kishuku jokō to
     shataku seido no dōnyū 20 世紀初頭における紡績業の寄宿女工と社宅制度の導入 .
     Hannan University Journal of Social Sciences 阪南論集 社会科学編 , *34*(3).

Chūma, H 中馬宏之 . (1987). "Nihonteki" koyō kankō no keizai gōri-sei saikentō:
     1920-nendai no nichibei hikaku no shiten kara " 日本的 " 雇用慣行の経済合理性再検討 :
     1920 年代の日米比較の視点から . *The Economic Review*, *38*(4).

Chūma, H 中馬宏之 ., & Oishi, A 大石亜希子 . (1997). Danjo-kan chingin kakusa hassei
     yōin: Saikō 男女間賃金格差発生要因 : 再考 . In Study Group on Employment and Wages
     of Female Workers (Eds.) *Josei rōdō-sha no koyō to chingin ni kansuru chōsa kenkyū*
     女性労働者の雇用と賃金に関する調査研究 . 労働問題リサーチセンター .

Comenius, J.A. (1995). *Sekai zue* 世界図絵 (J. Inokuchi, Trans.). Heibonsha.

Council of the Labor Federation of Government Related Organizations
     政府関係特殊法人労働組合協議会 (1973–1992). *Seirō-kyō amakudari hakusho*
     政労協天下り白書 .

Doshisha Sanmyaku Editorial Board 同志社山脈編集委員会 (2003). *Dōshisha sanmyaku:*
     113-nin no purofīru 同志社山脈 : 113 人のプロフィール . Koyo Shobo.

Endo, K 遠藤公嗣 . (1995). *Densan-gata chingin taikei ni okeru nōryoku-kyū to jinji satei*
     電産型賃金体系における能力給と人事査定 . *The Journal of Ohara Institute for Social*
     Research 大原社会問題研究所雑誌 , 1995(4).

Executive Committee for the 330th anniversary of the Shizutani School, Shizutani
     School Archives Catalog Subcommittee 閑谷学校創学 330 年記念事業実行委員会閑谷
     学校資料館図録部会 (Eds.) (2000). *Shizutani gakkō shiryōkan zuroku* 閑谷学校資料館図録 .
     Bizen: Association for the Preservation of the Shizutani School.

Film Art フィルムアート社 (Eds.) (1982). *Ozu yasujirō o yomu: Furuki mono no utsukushī*
     fukken 小津安二郎を読む : 古きものの美しい復権 . Film Art.

Friendly Society Labor Department 協調会労働課 . (Eds.) (1932). *Taishokukin seido no*
     genjō 退職金制度の現状 .

Fujimura, H 藤村博之 . (1989). Seiseki satei no kokusai hikaku 成績査定の国際比較 .
     Monthly journal of the Japan Institute of Labour 日本労働協会雑誌 , *362*(11).

Fujimura, K 藤村欣市朗 . (1992). *Takahashi korekiyo to kokusai kin'yū* 高橋是清と国際金融 .
     Fukutake Shoten.

Fukuda, M 福田眞人 . (2008). *Kitasato shibasaburō: Netsu to makoto ga areba* 北里柴三郎 :
     熱と誠があれば . Kyoto: Minerva Shobo.

Fukuzawa, Y 福沢諭吉 . (1981). Onna daigaku hyōron 女大学評論 , vol. 9. In M. Tomita, &
     S. Tsuchihashi (Eds.) *Fukuzawa yukichi senshū* 福沢諭吉選集 . Iwanami Shoten.

Fukuzawa, Y 福沢諭吉 . (1991). Kyōto gakkō no ki 京都学校の記 . In M. Yamazumi (Ed.),
     Fukuzawa yukichi kyōiku ronshū 福沢諭吉教育論集 . Iwanami Shoten.

Gōdo, Y 神門善久 . (2003). Kyōiku to keizai-teki kyatchiappu: Nichi-kan-bei no chōki
     hikaku 教育と経済的キャッチアップ : 日韓米の長期比較 . In K. Ōtsuka, & T. Kurosaki
     (Eds.), *Kyōiku to keizai hatten: Tojōkoku ni okeru hinkon sakugen ni mukete*
     教育と経済発展 : 途上国における貧困削減に向けて . Toyo Keizai.

Hara, A 原朗 . (Ed.) (1995). *Nihon no senji keizai: keikaku to shijyō* 日本の戦時経済：計画と市場 . University of Tokyo Press.

Hara, K 原覚天 . (1984). *Gendai ajia kenkyū seiritsu shiron; Mantetsu chōsabu, tōa kenkyūjo, IPR no kenkyū* 現代アジア研究成立史論：満鉄調査部・東亜研究所・IPR の研究 . Keiso Shobo.

Hashimoto, J 橋本寿朗 . (2000). *Gendainihon keizai-shi* 現代日本経済史 . Iwanami Shoten.

Hashimoto, T 橋本哲哉 . (1997). *Entotsu otoko: Tanabe kiyoshi shōron* 煙突男：田辺潔小論 . *Bulletin of the Kanazawa University College of Economics* 金沢大学経済学部論集, *17*(2).

Hata, I 秦郁彦 . (1981). *Senzen-ki nihon kanryō-sei no seido soshiki jinji* 戦前期日本官僚制の制度・組織・人事 . University of Tokyo Press.

Hazama, H 間宏 . (1963). *Ōtomēshon to rōmu kanri* オートメーションと労務管理 . *The Monthly journal of the Japan Institute of Labour* 日本労働協会雑誌, *52*.

Hazama, H 間宏 . (Ed.) (1993). *Nihon rōmu kanri-shi shiryōshū, issue 3, vol. 6: Minarai-kō mondai* 日本労務管理史資料集, 第 3 期第 6 巻：見習工問題 . Gozando Books.

Hepburn, J.C. (1978). *Hebon no tegami* ヘボンの手紙 . (M. Takaya, Trans.). Yokohama: Yurindo.

Higuchi, Y 樋口美雄 . (1988). Gaikokujin rōdō-sha mondai no keizai-gaku-teki sokumen: Kokunai rōdō shijyō e no eikyō 外国人労働者問題の経済学的側面：国内労働市場への影響 . *The Monthly journal of the Japan Institute of Labour* 日本労働協会雑誌, *348*(8).

Hirose, M 広瀬正雄 . (1973). *Hirose tansō tehodoki* 廣瀬淡窓手ほどき . Oita: Hirose Shiryokan.

Hirota, T 広田照幸 . (1987). Kindai nihon ni okeru rikugun shōkō no rikurūto 近代日本における陸軍将校のリクルート . *Journal of Educational Sociology* 教育社会学研究, *42*.

Hirota, T 広田照幸 . (1989). Shinro to shite no gunjin 進路としての軍人 . *Journal of the Nanzan Academic Society: Humanities, Social Sciences* アカデミア 人文・社会科学編, *50*.

Hirota, T 広田照幸 . (1997). *Rikugun shōkō no kyōiku shakai-shi: Risshinshusse to tennōsei* 陸軍将校の教育社会史：立身出世と天皇制 . Yokohama: Seori Shobo.

Hisamoto, N 久本憲夫 . (1986). Nishi-doitsu no shokugyō kunren 西ドイツの職業訓練 . In K. Koike (Ed.), *Gendai no jinzaikeisei: Nōryoku kaihatsu o saguru* 現代の人材形成：能力開発をさぐる . Kyoto: Minerva Shobo.

Horikoshi, J 堀越二郎 ., & Okumiya, M 奥宮正武 . (1992). *Zerosen* 零戦 . Asahi Sonorama.

Hosoi, W 細井和喜蔵 . (1980). *Jokō aishi* 女工哀史 . Iwanami Shoten.

Hyodō, T 兵藤釗 . (1997). *Rōdō no sengo-shi* 労働の戦後史 . University of Tokyo Press.

Iijima, M 飯島幡司 . (1949). *Nihon bōseki-shi* 日本紡績史 . Osaka: Sogensha.

Imada, S 今田幸子 ., & Hirata, S 平田周一 . (1995). *Howaitokarā no shōshin kōzō* ホワイトカラーの昇進構造 . Japan Institute for Labour Policy and Training.

Inatsugu, H 稲継裕昭 . (1996). *Nihon no kanryō jinji shisutemu* 日本の官僚人事システム . Toyo Keizai.

Inatsugu, H 稲継裕昭 . (2005). *Kōmuin kyūyo josetsu: Kyūyo taikei no rekishi-teki hensen* 公務員給与序説：給与体系の歴史的変遷 . Yuhikaku.

Inoki, T 猪木武徳 . (1984). Meijichū oyobi kōki no hawai hokubei ijū 明治中及び後期のハワイ北米移住 . *Osaka Economic Papers* 大阪大学経済学, *39*(2-3).

Inoki, T 猪木武徳 . (1991). Nihon no rōshi kankei ni okeru marukishizumu no eikyō 日本の労使関係におけるマルキシズムの影響 . *Bunka Kaigi* 文化会議 , *259*. Nihon Bunka Kaigi.

Inoki, T 猪木武徳 . (1993). Jinteki shigen kara mita sengo nihon no kanryō soshiki to tokushu hōjin 人的資源から見た戦後日本の官僚組織と特殊法人 . *Journal of Modern Japanese Studies* 年報日本近代日本研究 , *15*. Yamakawa Shuppansha.

Inoki, T 猪木武徳 . (1995). To no jinji kanri shisutemu no ichi-sokumen: Kikai no byōdō to kyōsō 都の人事管理システムの一側面：機会の平等と競争 . In T. Mikuriya (Ed.), *Tochō no shikumi: Shirīzu tōkyō o kangaeru 3* 都庁のしくみ , シリーズ東京を考える 3. Toshi Shuppan.

Inoki, T 猪木武徳 . (1998). Kinzoku nensū to ginō 勤続年数と技能 . In H. Itami, T. Kagono, M. Miyamoto, & S. Yonekura (Eds.) *Nihon-teki keiei no seisei to hatten* 日本的経営の生成と発展 . Yuhikaku.

Inoki, T 猪木武徳 . (1999). Amerika no naka no nihon to ajia アメリカの中の日本とアジア . In Y. Ishii, & M. Yamauchi (Eds.), *Nihonjin to tabunkashugi* 日本人と多文化主義 . Yamakawa Shuppansha.

Inoki, T 猪木武徳 . (2001). *Jiyū to chitsujo* 自由と秩序 . Chuokoron-Shinsha.

Inoki, T 猪木武徳 ., & Yugami, K 勇上和史 . (2001). Kokka kōmuin e no nyūshoku kōdō no keizai bunseki 国家公務員への入職行動の経済分析 . In T. Inoki, & F. Ōtake (Eds.), *Koyō seisaku no keizai bunseki* 雇用政策の経済分析 . University of Tokyo Press.

Inoki, T 猪木武徳 . (2002a). Howaitokarā moderu no riron-teki fukumi: Hito soshiki kankyō no fukakujitsusei o chūshin ni ホワイトカラー・モデルの理論的含み：人・組織・環境の不確実性を中心に . In K. Koike, & T. Inoki (Eds.), *Howaitokarā no jinzaikeisei: Nichi-bei-ei-doku no hikaku* ホワイトカラーの人材形成：日米英独の比較 . Toyo Keizai.

Inoki, T 猪木武徳 . (2002b). Keizaigaku-teki shiza kara ronten o seiri suru 経済学的視座から論点を整理する . *Journal of Japanese Labor Research* 日本労働研究雑誌 509.

Inoki, T 猪木武徳 . (2004). Shokugyō gunjin no sengo: Rikushi dōkisei-kai kaiin meibo o yomu 職業軍人の戦後：陸士同期生会会員名簿を読む . *Papers of the Institute of Statistical Research* 統計研究会報告論文 *(3 Sept 2004)*. Kansai Labor Research Institute.

Inoki, T 猪木武徳 . (2006). Ōhara magosaburō: Kitai no shakai jigyō-ka 大原孫三郎：稀代の社会事業家 . In Nihon Keizai Shimbun (Ed.) *Keiei ni taigi ari: Nihon o tsukutta kigyōka-tachi* 経営に大義あり：日本を創った企業家たち . Nihon Keizai Shimbun.

Inoki, T 猪木武徳 . (2008). Jinteki shigen-ron kara mita kindai keizai seichō: Rōdō keizai-gaku to kaihatsu keizai-gaku kara no chiken 人的資源論から見た近代経済成長：労働経済学と開発経済学からの知見 . *Socio-Economic History* 社会経済史学 , *73*(6).

Inoki, T 猪木武徳 . (2009). *Rōdō-ryoku no kōzō to sokutei, oyobi nenkō chingin-ron* 労働力の構造と測定 , および年功賃金論 . *The Soka economic studies quarterly* 創価経済論集 , *38*(1).

Inose, N 猪瀬直樹 . (1994). *Shōka tanjō: Furusato o tsukutta otoko* 唱歌誕生：ふるさとを創った男 . Bungeishunju.

Inoue, T 井上徹英 . (1991). *Shimada saburō to kindai nihon: Kokō no jiyū shugi-sha* 島田三郎と近代日本：孤高の自由主義者 . Akashi Shoten.

Ishida, M 石田光男 . (1990). *Chingin no shakai kagaku: Nihon to Igirisu* 賃金の社会科学：日本とイギリス . Chuokeizai-sha.

Ishikawa, K 石川謙 . (1957). *Kinsei no gakkō* 近世の学校 . Koryosha.

Ishikawa, K 石川謙 . (1972). *Nihon shomin kyōiku-shi* 日本庶民教育史 . Tamagawa University Press.

Ishikawa, M 石川松太郎 . (Ed.) (1977). *Onna daigaku-shū* 女大学集 . Heibonsha.

Ishikawa, M 石川松太郎 . (1978). *Hankō to terakoya* 藩校と寺子屋 . Kyoikusha.

Ishizaki, T 石崎唯雄 . (1957). Nippon-keizai to koyō no shiteki hensen 日本経済と雇用の史的変遷 . In Shōwa Dōjin-kai (Eds.) *Wagakuni kanzen koyō no igi to taisaku* 我国完全雇用の意義と対策 . Shōwa Dōjin-kai.

Ishizuki, M 石附實 . (1972). *Kindai-nihon no kaigai ryūgaku-shi* 近代日本の海外留学史 . Kyoto: Minerva Shobo.

Iwai, H 岩井八郎 . (2014). *Senji keizai no isan kasetsu no kentō: SSM chōsa no sai bunseki* 戦時経済の遺産 仮説の検討：SSM調査の再分析 . *Kyoto University Research Information Repository* 京都大学大学院教育学研究科紀要 , *60*, 25-43.

Japan Institute for Labour Policy and Training 日本労働研究機構 (Ed.) (1995). Howaitokarā no jinji kanri ホワイトカラーの人事管理 . *Research Reports* 調査研究報告書 , *68*.

Japan International Cooperation Agency 国際協力事業団 (1977, 1978). Kaigai ijū tōkei 海外移住統計 . *Reports, 435, 494*.

Japan Society for the Preservation of Naval History 海軍歴史保存会 . (1995). Shōkan rireki 将官履歴 , *9*. In *Nippon kaigun-shi* 日本海軍史 . Japan Society for the Preservation of Naval History.

Kabuto, K 加太邦憲 . (1982). *Ji-reki fu* 自歴譜 . Iwanami Shoten.

Kagoshima Chamber of Commerce 鹿児島商工会議所 . (Ed.) (2005). *Kagoshima kentei: Kagoshima kankō bunka kentei kōshiki gaidobukku* かごしま検定：鹿児島観光文化検定公式ガイドブック . Kagoshima: Nanpō Shinsha.

Kaikoku Hyaku-nen Kinen Bunka Jigyōkai 開国百年記念文化事業会 . (Eds.) (1956). *Sōsetsu gaikō* 総説・外交 , vol. 1 In H.Kamikawa (Ed.) (1980) *Nichibei bunka kōshō-shi* 日米文化交渉史 . Hara Shobo.

Kaneda, R 兼田麗子 . (2012). *Ōhara magosaburō: Zen'i to senryaku no kenkyūsha* 大原孫三郎：善意と戦略の研究者 . Chuokoron-Shinsha.

Kaneko, R 金子良事 . (2014). Kōjō iinkai kara sangyōhōkokukai e: Kigyō betsu kumiai seisei no ronri 工場委員会から産業報国会へ：企業別組合生成の論理 . *Journal of the Ohara Institute for Social Research* 大原社会問題研究所雑誌 , *664*.

Kanō, M 加納正巳 . (2005). Tanaka fujimaro 田中不二麻呂 In T. Itō, & Y. Suetake (Eds.), *Kingendai nihon jinbutsu shiryō jōhō jiten 2* 近現代日本人物史料情報辞典 2. Yoshikawa Kōbunkan.

Kansai Economic Research Center 関西経済研究センター . (1984). *Tokushima-ken ni okeru shokugyō kunren no jittai to tenbō ni kansuru chōsa hōkoku-sho* 徳島県における職業訓練の実態と展望に関する調査報告書 .

Karasawa, T 唐沢富太郎 . (1974). *Kōshinsei: Bakumatsu ishin-ki no erīto* 貢進生：幕末維新期のエリート . Gyosei.

Kasai, S 笠井助治 . (1960). *Kinsei hankō no sōgōteki kenkyū* 近世藩校の綜合的研究 . Yoshikawa Kōbunkan.

Katayama, M 片山杜秀 . (2012). *Mikan no fashizumu: Motazaru kuni nihon no unmei* 未完のファシズム：持たざる国日本の運命 . Shinchosha.

Katō, K 加藤亀太郎 . (1991). *Iraka no yume: Aru kawara-shoku no waza to kokoro kenchiku shokunin no sekai* 甍の夢：或る瓦職の技と心 建築職人の世界 . Kenchiku Shiryō Kenkyūsha.

Kawai, M 川井充 . (2005). Jūgyōin no rieki to kabushiki rieki wa ryōritsu shi uru ka?: Kanebō ni okeru mutō sanji no kigyō tōchi 従業員の利益と株式利益は両立しうるか？： 鐘紡における武藤山治の企業統治 . *Japan Business History Review* 経営史学 , *40*(2).

Kikkawa, E 吉川英史 . (1965). *Nihon ongaku no rekishi* 日本音楽の歴史 . Osaka: Sogensha.

Kino, K 木野主計 . (1995). *Inoue kowashi kenkyū* 井上毅研究 . Yagi Shoten.

Kishimoto, H 岸本英夫 ., & Kaigo, T 海後宗臣 . (Eds.) (1980). *Shūkyō kyōiku* 宗教教育 , vol. 3. In *Nichibei bunka kōshō-shi* 日米文化交渉史 . Hara Shobo.

Kitajima, M 北島正元 . (1962). *Edo shōgyō to isedana: Momen don'ya hasegawa ke no keiei o chūshin to shite* 江戸商業と伊勢店：木綿問屋長谷川家の経営を中心として . Yoshikawa Kōbunkan.

Kiyokawa, Y 清川雪彦 . (1995). *Nihon no keizai hatten to gijutsu fukyū* 日本の経済発展と 技術普及 . Toyo Keizai.

Kiyokawa, Y 清川雪彦 . (2009). *Kindai seishi gijutsu to ajia: Gijutsu dōnyū no hikaku keizai-shi* 近代製糸技術とアジア：技術導入の比較経済史 . Nagoya: University of Nagoya Press.

Kobayashi, H 小林英夫 . (2005). *Mantetsu chōsabu: Ganso shinkutanku no tanjō to hōkai* 満鉄調査部：元祖シンクタンクの誕生と崩壊 . Heibonsha.

Koike, K 小池和男 . (1966). *Chingin: Sono riron to genjō bunseki* 賃金：その理論と現状分析 . Diamond.

Koike, K 小池和男 . (1976). Senji keizai no isan 戦時経済の遺産 . In T. Iida, et al. (Eds.) *Gendai nihon keizai-shi* 現代日本経済史 . Chikumashobo.

Koike, K 小池和男 . (1977). *Shokuba no rōdō kumiai to sanka: Rōshi kankei no nichibeihikaku* 職場の労働組合と参加：労使関係の日米比較 . Toyo Keizai.

Koike, K 小池和男 . (1981). *Nihon no jukuren: Sugureta jinzaikeisei shisutemu* 日本の熟練： すぐれた人材形成システム . Yuhikaku.

Koike, K 小池和男 ., & Tomita, Y 冨田安信 . (Eds.) (1988). *Shokuba no kyariaūman* 職場のキャリアウーマン . Toyo Keizai.

Koike, K 小池和男 . (Ed.) (1991). *Daisotsu howaitokarā no jinzai kaihatsu* 大卒ホワイトカラーの人材開発 . Toyo Keizai.

Koike, K 小池和男 . (1993). *Amerika no howaitokarā: Nichibei dochiraga yori jitsuryoku shugi ka* アメリカのホワイトカラー：日米どちらがより実力主義か . Toyo Keizai.

Koike, K 小池和男 ., & Inoki, T 猪木武徳 . (Eds.) (2002). *Howaitokarā no jinzai keisei: Nichi-bei-ei-doku no hikaku* ホワイトカラーの人材形成：日米英独の比較 . Toyo Keizai.

Koike, K 小池和男 . (2005). *Shigoto no keizai-gaku* 仕事の経済学 . Toyo Keizai.

Kōno, H 河野仁 . (1989). Kindainihon ni okeru gunji erīto no senbatsu 近代日本における軍 事エリートの選抜 . *Journal of Educational Sociology* 教育社会学研究 , *45*.

Kumagai, T 熊谷光久 . (1994). *Nippongun no jinteki seido to mondaiten no kenkyū* 日本軍の 人的制度と問題点の研究 . Kokushokankokai.

Kumamoto, K 隈元謙次郎 . (1976). *Oyatoi gaikokujin 16: Bijutsu* お雇い外国人 16: 美術 . Kajima Institute Publishing.

Kurosaki, T 黒崎卓 . (2003a). Nōgyō hi nōgyō no seisansei to kyōiku 農業・非農業の生産性と教育 . In K. Ōtsuka, & T. Kurosaki (Eds.), *Kyōiku to keizai hatten: Tojōkoku ni okeru hinkon sakugen ni mukete* 教育と経済発展：途上国における貧困削減に 向けて . Toyo Keizai.

Kurosaki, T 黒崎卓 . (2003b). Hinkon no dōgakuteki henka to kyōiku 貧困の動学的変化と教育 . In K. Ōtsuka, & T. Kurosaki (Eds.), *Kyōiku to keizai hatten: Tojōkoku ni okeru hinkon sakugen ni mukete* 教育と経済発展：途上国における貧困削減に向けて . Toyo Keizai.

Kyoto Municipal Museum of School History 京都市学校歴史博物館 . (Eds.) (1998). *Kyō no gakkō rekishi tanbō: Wagakuni no kindai kyōiku no sakigake* 京の学校・歴史探訪：我が国の近代教育の魁 . Kyoto: Kyoto City Social Education Promotion Foundation.

Kyoto Prefectural Tango Regional Museum 京都府立丹後郷土資料館 . (Eds.) (1975). *Tenkyō gijuku: Tango no jiyū minken undō 1875–1884* 天橋義塾：丹後の自由民権運動 1875–1884 特別陳列 . Kyoto: Kyoto Prefectural Tango Regional Museum.

Maeda, K 前田健太郎 . (2014). *Shimin o yatowanai kokka: Nihon ga kōmuin no sukunai kuni e to itatta michi* 市民を雇わない国家：日本が公務員の少ない国へと至った道 . University of Tokyo Press.

Maizuru City 舞鶴市 (Eds.) (1995). *Hikiagekō: Maizuru no kiroku* 引揚港：舞鶴の記録 . City of Maizuru.

Maizuru City History Compilation Committee 舞鶴市史編さん委員会 (Eds.) (1975). *Maizuru-shi-shi: Kakusetsu-hen* 舞鶴市史 各説編 . City of Maizuru.

Maizuru City History Compilation Committee 舞鶴市史編さん委員会 (Eds.) (1982). *Maizuru-shi-shi: Tsūshi-hen* 舞鶴市史 通史編 . City of Maizuru.

Maizuru City History Compilation Committee 舞鶴市史編さん委員会 (Eds.) (1988). *Maizuru-shi-shi: Gendai-hen* 舞鶴市史 現代編 . City of Maizuru.

Management and Coordination Agency 総務庁 (各年版). *Kagaku gijutsu kenkyū chōsa* 科学技術研究調査 .

Matsuda, Y 松田芳郎 ., Arita, T 有田富美子 ., & Kimura, K 木村健二 . (1990). *Meiji-ki kōjō tōkei chōsa no fukugen shūkei II: Meiji 35-nen "kōjō tsūran" fukugen shūkei-hyō* 明治期工場統計調査の復元集計 II: 明治 35 年 " 工場通覧 " 復元集計表 . Hitotsubashi University Institute of Economic Research Japan Economic Statistics Information Center.

Matsuda, R 松田良一 . (1993). *Kindainihon shokugyō jiten* 近代日本職業事典 . Kashiwashobo.

Matsushige, H 松繁寿和 . (Ed.) (2004). *Daigaku kyōiku kōka no jisshō bunseki: Aru kokuritsu daigaku sotsugyōsei-tachi no sonogo* 大学教育効果の実証分析：ある国立大学卒業生たちのその後 . Nippon Hyoron Sha.

Matsushima, S 松島静雄 . (1962). *Gijutsu kakushin ni yoru rōdō oyobi rōmu kanri no hensen* 技術革新による労働及び労務管理の変遷 . Diamond.

Meiji Culture Study Group 明治文化研究会 (1928). *Meiji bunka zenshū* 明治文化全集 , vol. 16. Nippon Hyoron Sha.

Meiji Documents Publishing Committee (1966) 明治文献資料刊行会 . *Meiji zenki sangyō hattatsu-shi shiryō* 明治前期産業発達史資料 , supplement 8, nos. 3–5.

Ministry of Agriculture and Commerce 農商務省 (1902). *Kōjō tsūran* 工場通覧 .

Ministry of Agriculture and Commerce, Department of Commerce and Industry 農商務省商工局 (1998). *Shokkō Jijō* 職工事情 *1–3*. Iwanami Shoten.

Ministry of Agriculture and Commerce, Department of Mines 農商務省鉱山局 (Eds.) (1907). *Meiji sanjū-kyū-nen honpō kōgyō no sūsei* 明治三十九年 本邦鑛業ノ趨勢 .

Ministry of Education 文部省 (1955–2000). *Monbu kagaku tōkei yōran* 文部科学統計要覧 .

Ministry of Education 文部省 (1956). *Sangyō kyōiku shichijū-nen-shi* 産業教育七十年史 . Working Group on Employment Issues.

Ministry of Education 文部省 (1972). *Gakusei hyaku-nen-shi* 学制百年史 . Gyosei.

Ministry of Education 文部省 (1992). *Gakusei hyaku-nijū-nen-shi* 学制百二十年史 . Gyosei.

Ministry of Education 文部省 (1993–1994). *Monbu tōkei yōran* 文部統計要覧 .

Ministry of Education 文部省 (1994), *Gakkō kihon chōsa hōkoku-sho* 学校基本調査報告書 .

Ministry of Education, Research Office of the Bureau of Practical Education 文部省実業学務室調査室 (1930). Kaisha kōjō jūgyōin gakureki chōsa hōkoku 会社工場従業員学歴調査報告 . In H. Hazama (Ed.), (1987) *Nihon rōmu kanri-shi shiryōshū, issue 1, vol. 9: Kigyō to gakureki* 日本労務管理史資料集 , 第 1 期第 9 巻：企業と学歴 . Gozando Books.

Ministry of Foreign Affairs, Consular and Migration Section 外務省領事移住部 . (Eds.) (1971). *Waga kokumin no kaigai hatten: Ijū hyaku-nen no ayumi* わが国民の海外発展：移住百年の歩み .

Ministry of Health and Welfare 厚生省 (1945). *Daitōa-sensō-ka ni okeru kinrō jōkyō* 大東亜戦争下における勤労状況 .

Ministry of Health and Welfare, Dept. of Social Assistance 厚生省援護局 (1997). *Engo gojū-nen-shi* 援護 50 年史 . Gyosei.

Ministry of Labour 労働省 (1982). *Rōdō hakusho: Shōwa 57-nenban* 労働白書：昭和 57 年版 .

Ministry of Labour 労働省 (1992, 1994). *Chingin kōzō kihon tōkei chōsa* 賃金構造基本統計調査 .

Ministry of Labour, Secretariat for Policy Research 労働大臣官房政策調査部 (Eds.) (1995). *Nihonteki koyō seido no genjō to tenbō* 日本的雇用制度の現状と展望 .

Mitani, N 三谷直紀 . (1997). *Kigyō-nai chingin kōzō to rōdō shijyō* 企業内賃金構造と労働市場 . Keiso Shobo.

Mitani, N 三谷直紀 . (2003). Rōdō: Ginō keisei to rōdō-ryoku haibun 労働：技能形成と労働力配分. In T. Tachibanaki (Ed.), *Sengonihon keizai o kenshō suru* 戦後日本経済を検証する . University of Tokyo Press.

Miyake, K 三宅宏司 . (1993). *Osaka hōhei kōshō no kenkyū* 大阪砲兵工廠の研究 . Kyoto: Shibunkaku.

Miyata, S 宮田親平 . (1983). *Kagaku-sha-tachi no jiyūna rakuen: Eikō no rikagaku kenkyūsho* 科学者たちの自由な楽園：栄光の理化学研究所 . Bungeishunju.

Miyoshi, N 三好信浩 . (1983). *Meiji no enjinia kyōiku: Nihon to igirisu no chigai* 明治のエンジニア教育：日本とイギリスのちがい . Chuokoron-Shinsha.

Mizutani, M 水谷三公 . (1999). *Kanryō no fūbō* 官僚の風貌 . Chuokoron-Shinsha.

Momose, T 百瀬孝 . (1990). *Jiten: Shōwa senzenki no nihon: Seido to jittai* 事典：昭和戦前期の日本：制度と実態 . Yoshikawa Kōbunkan.

Mori, H 森博美 . (1988). Shutsunyūkoku kanri tōkei ni yoru fuhō zanryū gaikokujin-sū no suikei 出入国管理統計による「不法」残留外国人数の推計 . *Report of the Hosei University Japanese Statistics Laboratory* 研究所報 , 15.

Morimoto, T 森本武利 . (Ed.) (2011). *Kyōto ryōbyōin: Oyatoi ishi shoibe: Tainichi shokan kara* 京都療病院：お雇い医師ショイベ：滞日書簡から . (K. Sakai, Trans.). Kyoto: Shibunkaku.

Muramatsu, K 村松久良光 . (1984). Rishoku kōdō to rōdō kumiai: taishutsu-hatsugen apurōchi 離職行動と労働組合：退出 - 発言アプローチ . In K. Koike (Ed.), *Gendai no shitsugyō* 現代の失業 . Dobunkan.

Muramatsu, K 村松久良光 . (1987). Nōryoku-kyū seido ni kansuru nichi-bei-ei hikaku 能力給制度に関する日米英比較 . *Monthly journal of the Japan Institute of Labour* 日本労働協会雑誌, *29*(11).

Muramatsu, M 村松岐夫 . (1981). *Sengonihon no kanryō-sei* 戦後日本の官僚制 . Toyo Keizai.

Naitō, H 内藤初穂 . (1999). *Gunkan sōchō hiraga yuzuru* 軍艦総長・平賀譲 . Chuokoron-Shinsha.

Nakagawa, Y 中川靖造 . (2010). *Kaigun gijutsu kenkyūsho: Erekutoronikusu ōkoku no senkusha-tachi* 海軍技術研究所：エレクトロニクス王国の先駆者たち . Kojinsha.

Nakai, N 中井信彦 . (1966). Mitsui-ke no keiei: Shiyōnin seido to sono un'ei 三井家の経営：使用人制度とその運営 . *Socio-Economic History* 社会経済史学 , *31*(6).

Nakajima, T 中嶋哲夫 ., Umezaki, O 梅﨑修 ., Igawa, S 井川静恵 ., Kakizawa, H 柿澤寿信 ., & Matsushige, H 松繁寿和 . (Eds.) (2013). *Jinji no tōkei bunseki: Jinji maikurodēta o mochiita jinzai manejimento no kenshō* 人事の統計分析：人事マイクロデータを用いた人材マネジメントの検証 . Kyoto: Minerva Shobo.

Nakamura, K 中村圭介 . (1996). *Nihon no shokuba to seisan shisutemu* 日本の職場と生産システム . University of Tokyo Press.

Nakamura, M 中村恵 . (1994). Josei kanrishoku no ikusei to sōgō-shoku 女子管理職の育成と総合職 . *The Japanese Journal of Labour Studies* 日本労働協会雑誌 , *415*(9).

Nakamura, T 中村隆英 . (1993). *Shōwa-shi I, II* 昭和史 I, II. Toyo Keizai.

Naramoto, T 奈良本辰也 . (Ed.) (1969). *Nihon no shijuku* 日本の私塾 . Kyoto: Tankosha.

National Institute for Educational Policy Research 国立教育研究所 (1974). Gakkō kyōiku 3 学校教育 3, vol. 5. In *Nihon kindai kyōiku hyaku-nen-shi* 日本近代教育百年史 .

National Institute of Population and Social Security Research 厚生省人口問題研究所 (1942). *Hōjin kaigai hatten shiryaku* 邦人海外発展史略 .

National Personnel Authority 人事院 (1963–1991). *Eiri kigyō e no shūshoku no shōnin ni kansuru nenji hōkoku-sho* 営利企業への就職の承認に関する年次報告書 .

National Personnel Authority 人事院 (1975). *Kokka kōmuin-hō enkaku-shi (kijutsu-hen)* 国家公務員法沿革史 (記述編).

Nippon Institute for Research Advancement 総合研究開発機構 (1994). Kigyō no kokusai-ka ni tomonau koyō oyobi jinji seido no henkaku ni kansuru kenkyū: Howaitokarā no shogū ni kansuru jirei chōsa. 企業の国際化に伴う雇用及び人事制度の変革に関する研究：ホワイトカラーの処遇に関する事例調査 .

Nishimura, M 西村美香 . (1999). *Nihon no kōmuin kyūyo seisaku* 日本の公務員給与政策 . University of Tokyo Press.

Nishinarita, Y 西成田豊 . (1988). *Kindainihon rōshi kankei-shi no kenkyū* 近代日本労資関係史の研究 . University of Tokyo Press.

Nishinarita, Y 西成田豊 . (1997). *Zainichi chōsenjin no sekai to teikoku kokka* 在日朝鮮人の世界と帝国国家 . University of Tokyo Press.

Nitta, M 仁田道夫 . (1988). *Nihon no rōdō-sha sanka* 日本の労働者参加 . University of Tokyo Press.

Noda Soy Sauce Company 野田醬油株式会社 (Eds.) (1940). *Noda shōyu kabushikigaisha nijū-nen-shi* 野田醬油株式会社二十年史 . Chiba: Noda Soy Sauce Company.

Nomura, K 野村光一 . (1971). *Oyatoi gaikokujin 10: Ongaku* お雇い外国人 10: 音楽 . Kajima Kenkyusho Shuppankai.

Nomura, R 野邑理栄子 . (2006). *Rikugun yōnen gakkō taisei no kenkyū: Erīto yōsei to gunji kyōiku seiji* 陸軍幼年学校体制の研究：エリート養成と軍事・教育・政治 . Yoshikawa Kōbunkan.

Odaka. K 尾高煌之助 . (1984). *Rōdō shijyō bunseki: Nijūkōzō no nipponteki tenkai* 労働市場分析：二重構造の日本的展開 . Iwanami Shoten.

Odaka. K 尾高煌之助 . (1993a). *Shokunin no sekai kōjō no sekai* 職人の世界・工場の世界 . NTT Publishing.

Odaka. K 尾高煌之助 . (1993b). *Kigyō-nai kyōiku no jidai* 企業内教育の時代 . Iwanami Shoten.

Ogata, H 尾形裕康 . (1980). *Nihon kyōiku tsūshi kenkyū* 日本教育通史研究 . Waseda University Press.

Ogawara, M 小川原正道 . (2013). *Meiji no seijika to shinkō: Kurisuchan minken-ka no shōzō* 明治の政治家と信仰：クリスチャン民権家の肖像 . Yoshikawa Kōbunkan.

Ōhama, T 大浜徹也 ., & Ozawa, I 小沢郁郎 . (Eds.) (1995). *Kaiteiban teikoku rikukaigun jiten* 改訂版 帝国陸海軍事典 . Dōseisha.

Ohara Institute for Social Research 大原社会問題研究所 . (Eds.) (1921). *Nihon rōdō nenkan* 日本労働年鑑 .

Ohara Magosaburo Biography Publishing Committee 大原孫三郎傳刊行会 . (Eds.) (1983). *Ōhara magosaburō-den* 大原孫三郎傳 . Chuokoron Jigyo Shuppan.

Ōhashi, I 大橋勇雄 . (1995). Rōdō shijyō no kōzō to gaikokujinrōdōsha no ryūnyū 労働市場の構造と外国人労働者の流入 In T. Inoki, & Y. Higuchi (Eds.), *Nihon no koyō shisutemu to rōdō shijyō* 日本の雇用システムと労働市場 . Nihon Keizai Shimbun.

Okabe, Y 岡部幸徳 . (2001). Meiji-ki bōseki-gyō ni okeru rōdō jōken to mutō sanji ni tsuite no ichikōsatsu: Kanebō ni okeru rōdō jōken to mutō sanji no oitachi o tōshite 明治期紡績業における労働条件と武藤山治についての一考察：鐘紡における労働条件と武藤山治の生い立ちを通して . *The review of Graduate School of Business and Management* 研究年報 , 5, 19-41. Kanagawa Univesity.

Okazaki, T 岡崎哲二 ., Sugayama, S 菅山真次 ., Nishizawa, T 西沢保 ., & Yonekura, S 米倉誠一郎 . (1996). *Sengo nihon keizai to keizai dōyūkai* 戦後日本経済と経済同友会 . Iwanami Shoten.

Ōkita, T 大喜多甫文 . (narr.) (2005-2006). *Matsuzaka shōnin no subete* 松坂商人のすべて , 1-3. Matsusaka: Ise-no-kuni Matsuzaka Juraku.

Orii, H 折井日向 . (1961). Gijutsu kakushin to rōmu kanri 技術革新と労務管理 . *The Monthly journal of the Japan Institute of Labour* 日本労働協会雑誌 , 31, 21-24.

Osaka Municipal Central Job Placement Office 大阪市立中央職業紹介所 . (1927). Kinzoku jōkyō ni kansuru chōsa 勤続状況に関する調査 . In H. Hazama (Ed.), *Nihon rōmu kanri-shi shiryōshū* 日本労務管理史資料集 . Gozando Books.

Ōshima, M 大島正健 . (1993). *Kurāku sensei to sono deshi-tachi* クラーク先生とその弟子たち . Kyobunkan.

Ōtake, F 大竹文雄 . (1995). *Satei to kinzoku nensū ga shōkaku ni ataeru eikyō: Erebētā hoshu sābisu kaisha no kēsu* 査定と勤続年数が昇格に与える影響：エレベーター保守サービス会社のケース . *The Economic Review* 経済研究 , 46(3).

Ōtsuka, K 大塚啓二郎 ., & Sonobe, T 園部哲史 . (2003). Kyōiku no yakuwari: Sangyō hatten no shiten kara 教育の役割：産業発展の視点から . In K. Ōtsuka, & T. Kurosaki (Eds.), *Kyōiku to keizai hatten* 教育と経済発展 . Toyo Keizai.

256 WORKS CITED

Ozawa, S 小沢三郎 . (2004). *Uchimura kanzō fukei jiken* 内村鑑三不敬事件 . Shinkyo Publishing.

Saitō, O 斎藤修 . (1987). *Shōka no sekai uradana no sekai: Edo to ōsaka no hikaku toshi-shi* 商家の世界・裏店の世界：江戸と大阪の比較都市史 . Libroport.

Saitō, O 斎藤修 . (1996). Rōdō 労働 . In S. Nishikawa, K. Odaka, & O. Saitō (Eds.), *Nihon keizai no 200-nen* 日本経済の 200 年 . Nippon Hyoron Sha.

Saitō, S 齊藤憲 . (1987). *Shinkō kontsuerun riken no kenkyū: Ōkouchi masatoshi to riken sangyō-dan* 新興コンツェルン理研の研究：大河内正敏と理研産業団 . Jichosha.

Saitō, S 齊藤憲 .(2009). *Ōkouchi masatoshi: Kagaku gijutsu ni shōgai o kaketa otoko* 大河内正敏：科学・技術に生涯をかけた男 . Nihon Keizai Hyoronsha.

Sakai, S 酒井三郎 . (1992). *Shōwa kenkyūkai: Aru chishikijin shūdan no kiseki* 昭和研究会：ある知識人集団の軌跡 . Chuokoron-Shinsha.

Sakane, Y 坂根嘉弘 . (Ed.) (2010–2014). *Gunkō toshi-shi kenkyū I, II, III* 軍港都市史研究 , I, II, III. Osaka: Seibundo Publishing.

Sanematsu, Y 実松譲 . (1993). *Kaigun daigaku kyōiku: Senryaku senjutsu dōjō no kōzai* 海軍大学教育—戦略・戦術道場の功罪 . Kojinsha.

Sasaki, N 佐々木信夫 . (1991). *Tochō: Mō hitotsu no seifu* 都庁：もうひとつの政府 . Iwanami Shoten.

Sawai, M 沢井実 . (1996). Meiji-ki ōsaka no kikai kōgyō: Meiji-ki ni okeru sangyō hatten to chiiki keizai 明治期大阪の機械工業：明治期における産業発展と地域経済 . In M. Miyamoto,. *Heisei 7-nendo kagaku kenkyū-hi seika hōkoku-sho.* 平成 7 年度科学研究費成果報告書 .

Sawai, M 沢井実 . (2012a). *Kindainihon no kenkyū kaihatsu taisei* 近代日本の研究開発体制 . Nagoya: University of Nagoya Press.

Sawai, M 沢井実 . (2012b). *Kindai ōsaka no kōgyō kyōiku* 近代大阪の工業教育 . Osaka: Osaka University Press.

Sawai, M 沢井実 . (2015). *Teikoku nihon no gijutsu-sha-tachi* 帝国日本の技術者たち . Yoshikawa Kōbunkan.

Shiba, R 司馬遼太郎 . (1978). *Saka no ue no kumo* 坂の上の雲 . Bungeishunju.

Shinjinbutsu Oraisha Military History Archives 新人物往来社戦史室 (Eds.) (1996). *Kaigun etajima kyōiku* 海軍江田島教育 . Shinjinbutsu Oraisha.

Shirai, T 白井泰四郎 . (1976). Kinrō hōshi 勤労奉仕 . In H. Arisawa (Ed.), *Shōwa keizai-shi* 昭和経済史 . Nihon Keizai Shimbun.

Shirai, T 白井泰四郎 . (1992). *Gendai nihon no rōmu kanri* 現代日本の労務管理 . Toyo Keizai.

Shiratori, M 白取道博 . (1986). Manshū imin seisaku to manmō kaitaku seishōnen giyūgun 満州移民政策と満蒙開拓青少年義勇軍 . *Bulletin of the Faculty of Education, Hokkaido University* 北海道大學教育學部紀要 , *47.*

Shiratori, M 白取道博 . (1990). Manmō kaitaku seishōnen giyūgun no hen'yō (1938–1941): Kyōdobutai hensei dōnyū no igi 満蒙開拓青少年義勇軍の変容 (1938–1941 年)：郷土部隊編成導入の意義 . *Bulletin of the Faculty of Education, Hokkaido University* 北海道大學教育學部紀要 , *54.*

Sugayama, S 菅山真次 . (2000). Chūsotsu-sha kara kōsotsu-sha e: Danshi gakusotsu rōdō shijyō no seido-ka to sono kiketsu 中卒者から高卒者へ：男子学卒労働市場の制度化とその

帰結 . In T. Kariya, S. Sugayama, & H. Ishida (Eds.), *Gakkō shokuan to rōdō shijyō: Sengo shinki gakusotsu shijyō no seido-ka katei* 学校・職安と労働市場：戦後新規学卒市場の制度化過程 . University of Tokyo Press.

Sumiya M 隅谷三喜男 . (Ed.) (1970). Shokkō oyobi kōfu chōsa 職工および鉱夫調査 , *3.* In *Seikatsu koten sōsho* 生活古典叢書 . Koseikan.

Suzuki, B 鈴木文治 . (1985). *Rōdō undō nijū-nen (gendaibun-yaku)* 労働運動二十年（現代文訳）. (F. Suzuki, Trans.). Suzuki Bunji Labor Movement 20 Year Publication Committee.

Suzuki, F 鈴木不二一 . (1994). Howaitokarā no teigi to ichizuke ホワイトカラーの定義と位置付け . *Reports of the Japanese Electrical Electronic & Information Union* 電機連合 , 調査時報 , *270.*

Tachibanaki, T 橘木俊詔 . (Ed.) (1992). *Satei shōshin chingin kettei* 査定・昇進・賃金決定 . Yuhikaku.

Takagi, S 高木惣吉 (1995). *Jiden-teki nippon kaigun shimatsu-ki: Teikoku kaigun no uchi ni himeraretaru eikō to higeki no jijō* 自伝的日本海軍始末記：帝国海軍の内に秘められたる栄光と悲劇の事情 . Kojinsha.

Takahashi, H 高橋英夫 . (1984). *Idai-naru kurayami* 偉大なる暗闇 . Shinchosha.

Takahashi, Y 高橋裕子 . (2002). *Tsuda umeko no shakai-shi* 津田梅子の社会史 . Tamagawa University Press.

Takeuchi, Y 竹内洋 . (1991). *Risshin kugaku shusse: Jukensei no shakai-shi* 立身・苦学・出世：受験生の社会史 . Kodansha.

Takeuchi, Y 竹内洋 . (1995). *Nihon no meritokurashī: Kōzō to shinsei* 日本のメリトクラシー：構造と心性 . University of Tokyo Press.

Takeuchi, Y 竹内洋 . (1997). *Risshin-shusse shugi: Kindai nihon no roman to yokubō* 立身出世主義：近代日本のロマンと欲望 . NHK Publishing.

Takeuchi, Y 竹内洋 . (2005). *Risshin-shusse shugi: Kindai nihon no roman to yokubō zōho-ban* 立身出世主義：近代日本のロマンと欲望 . Kyoto: Sekaishisosha.

Takeuchi, Y 竹内洋 . (2011). *Gakurekikizoku no eikō to zasetsu* 学歴貴族の栄光と挫折 . Kodansha.

Takii, K 瀧井敬子 ., & Hirataka, N 平高典子 . (2012). *Kōda nobu no taiō nikki* 幸田延の滞欧日記 . Tokyo University of the Arts Press.

Tayama, K 田山花袋 . (1907). *Inaka kyōshi* 田舎教師 .

Tōjō, Y 東條由紀彦 . (1995). Rōmu dōin 労務動員 . In A. Hara (Ed.), *Nihon no senji keizai: Keikaku to shijyō* 日本の戦時経済：計画と市場 . University of Tokyo Press.

Tokyo Human Resource System Institute 東京都人事制度研究会 (Eds.) (1993). *Chihōkōkyō dantai ni okeru jissen-teki jinjikōka* 地方公共団体における実践的人事考課 . Tosei Shimpo Press.

Tokyo Metropolitan Government Personnel Commission 東京都人事委員会 (1992). Jinji iinkai kaihō. *Bulletin of the Tokyo Metropolitan Government Personnel Commission* 人事委員会会報 , *62.*

Tomioka City Board of Education 富岡市教育委員会 (2010). *Tomioka seishijō no oyatoi gaikokujin ni kansuru chōsa hōkoku: Tokuni shuchō pōru buryuna no jiseki ni shiten o atete: Chūkan hōkoku* 富岡製糸場のお雇い外国人に関する調査報告：特に首長ポール・ブリュナの事績に視点を当てて：中間報告 .

Tomita, H 富田仁 ., & Nishibori, A 西堀昭 . (1983). *Yokosuka seitetsusho no hitobito: Hanahiraku Furansu bunka* 横須賀製鉄所の人びと：花ひらくフランス文化 . Yurindo.

Tomita, Y 冨田安信 . (1993). Rishoku-ritsu to rōdō kumiai no hatsugen kōka 離職率と労働組合の発言効果 In T. Tachibanaki, & Association of Comprehensive Life Development Institute (Eds.) *Rōdō kumiai no keizai-gaku: Kitai to genjitsu* 労働組合の経済学：期待と現実 . Toyo Keizai.

Toyama, M 外山操 ., & Morimatsu, T 森松俊夫 . (Eds.) (1987). *Teikoku rikugun hensei sōran* 帝国陸軍編制総覧 . Fuyo Shobo.

Umemura, M 梅村又次 . (1964). *Sengo nihon no rōdō-ryoku: Sokutei to hendō* 戦後日本の労働力：測定と変動 . Iwanami Shoten.

Umemura, M 梅村又次 . (1967). Nenkō chingin ni tsuite 年功賃金について . *The Economic Review* 経済研究 , *18*(3). Iwanami Shoten.

Umemura, M 梅村又次 . (1971). Nenrei-shotoku purofiru no kokusai hikaku 年齢＝所得プロフィルの国際比較 . *The Economic Review* 経済研究 , *22*(3).

Umemura, M 梅村又次 . et al. (1988). Rōdō-ryoku 労働力 , *2*. In *Chōki keizai tōkei* 長期経済統計 . Toyo Keizai.

Umetani, N 梅溪昇 . (1965). *Oyatoi gaikokujin* お雇い外国人 . Nihon Keizai Shimbun.

Umetani, N 梅溪昇 . (1971). *Oyatoi gaikokujin 11: Seiji, hōsei* お雇い外国人 11: 政治・法制 . Kajima Kenkyūsho Shuppankai.

Umetani, N 梅溪昇 . (1996). *Ogata kōan to teki juku* 緒方洪庵と適塾 . Osaka: Osaka University Press.

Umetani, N 梅溪昇 . (2000). *Kyōiku chokugo seiritsu-shi: Tennōsei kokka-kan no seiritsu* 教育勅語成立史：天皇制国家観の成立 . Seishi Shuppan.

Umetani, N 梅溪昇 . (2007). *Oyatoi gaikokujin: Meiji nihon no wakiyaku-tachi* お雇い外国人：明治日本の脇役たち . Kodansha.

Umihara, T 海原徹 . (1996). *Nippon-shi shōhyakka: Gakkō* 日本史小百科・学校 . Tokyodo Shuppan.

Uno, R 宇野利右衛門 . (Ed.) (1920). *Shokkō eizoku-saku ronshū* 職工永続策論集 . Kogyo Kyoikukai Shuppan.

Verback, G.F. (1978). *Furubekki shokan-shū* フルベッキ書簡集 . (M. Takaya, Trans.). Shinkyo Publishing.

Wakabayashi, Y 若林幸男 . (2007). *Mitsui bussan jinji seisaku-shi 1876-1931: Jōhō kōtsū kyōiku infura to shokuin soshiki* 三井物産人事政策史 1876-1931 年：情報交通教育インフラと職員組織 . Kyoto: Minerva Shobo.

Wakatsuki, Y 若槻泰雄 . (1972). *Hainichi no rekishi: Amerika ni okeru nihonjin imin* 排日の歴史：アメリカにおける日本人移民 . Chuokoron-Shinsha.

Wakisaka, A 脇坂明 . (1993). *Shokuba ruikei to josei no kyaria keisei* 職場類型と女性のキャリア形成 . Ochanomizu Shobo.

Wakita, O 脇田修 ., & Kishida, T 岸田知子 . (1997). *Kaitokudō to sono hitobito* 懐徳堂とその人びと . Osaka: Osaka University Press.

Watanabe, Masakiyo 渡辺正清 (2003). *Gō fō burōku: Nikkeinisei heishi-tachi no senjō* ゴー・フォー・ブローク：日系二世兵士たちの戦場 . Kojinsha.

Watanabe, Minoru 渡辺実 (1977-1978). *Kindainihon kaigai ryūgakusei-shi* 近代日本海外留学生史 . Kodansha.

Yamada, G 山田豪一 . (1977). *Mantetsu chōsabu: Eikō to zasetsu no yon-jū-nen* 満鉄調査部：栄光と挫折の四十年 . Nihon Keizai Shimbun.

Yamada, N 山田直匡 . (1968). *Oyatoi gaikokujin 4: Kōtsū* お雇い外国人 4: 交通 . Kajima Kenkyūsho Shuppankai.

Yamagata Prefectural Museum 山形県立博物館 (1998). *Hankō: Bushi no gakkō Edo no gakumon* 藩校：武士の学校・江戸の学問 . Exhibition catalog.

Yamaguchi, M 山口宗之 . (2000). *Rikugun to kaigun: Rikukaigun shōkō-shi no kenkyū* 陸軍と海軍：陸海軍将校史の研究 . Osaka: Seibundo Publishing.

Yamamoto, K 山本潔 . (1994). *Nihon ni okeru shokuba no gijutsu rōdō-shi: 1854–1990* 日本における職場の技術・労働史：1854 年 –1990 年 . University of Tokyo Press.

Yamazaki, S 山崎志郎 . (1995). Senji kōgyō dōin taisei 戦時工業動員体制 . In A. Hara (Ed.), *Nihon no senji keizai: Keikaku to shijyō* 日本の戦時経済：計画と市場 . University of Tokyo Press.

Yano, M 矢野眞和 . (2007). *Kōtō kyōiku no keizai bunseki to seisaku* 高等教育の経済分析と政策 . Tamagawa University Press.

Yashiro, A 八代充史 . (1995). *Dai kigyō howaitokarā no kyaria: Idō to shōshin no jisshō bunseki* 大企業ホワイトカラーのキャリア：異動と昇進の実証分析 . Japan Institute for Labour Policy and Training.

Yasuoka, S 安岡重明 . (1968). Mitsui-ke bekke no sōzoku keitai 三井家別家の相続形態 . *The Social Sciences, 3*(2–3).

Yasuoka, S 安岡重明 . (1984). *Zaibatsu no kaken to kazoku no kaken: Tokuni zaisan kanri ni tsuite* 財閥の家憲と華族の家憲：とくに財産管理について . Kyoto: Doshisha University Press.

Yasuoka, S 安岡重明 . (1998). *Kinsei shōka no keiei rinen seido koyō* 近世商家の経営理念・制度・雇用 . Kyoto: Koyo Shobo.

Yokosuka Naval Arsenal 横須賀海軍工廠 (Eds.) (1983). *Yokosuka kaigun kōshō-shi 1, 2* 横須賀海軍工廠史 1, 2. Hara Shobo.

Yokoyama, G 横山源之助 . (1899). *Nihon no kasō shakai* 日本之下層社会 . Kyobunkan.

Yoshiie, S 吉家定夫 . (1998). *Nippon-koku gakkan deibiddo marē: Sono shōgai to gyōseki* 日本国学監デイビッド マレー：その生涯と業績 . Tamagawa University Press.

Yoshimura, A 吉村昭 . (1968). *Zeroshiki sentōki* 零式戦闘機 . Shinchosha.

APPENDIX

School Systems in Japan

Source: Ministry of Education (1992).

1900

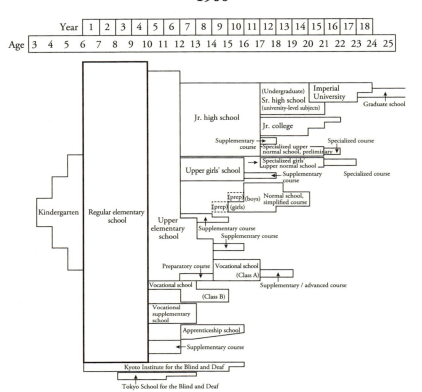